Researching Disability Sport

Marking a new direction for disability sport scholarship, this book explores cutting-edge issues and engages creatively with contemporary approaches to research in this important emerging discipline.

Featuring contributions from leading and up-and-coming scholars around the world, the book's wide-ranging chapters offer novel perspectives on the relationship between theory, method, and empiricism in disability sport research and highlight how researchers can be both innovative and informed when entering the field. It also explores methodological considerations when conducting disability sport research, including social, cultural, and political reflections of the research process from disabled and non-disabled academics. This much-needed resource supports disability sport scholars in developing a conceptual grounding in the subject and establishes a space for intersectional accounts of sport and physical activity which challenge homogenous understandings of disability.

This book is essential reading for any student or researcher working in disability sport, adapted physical activity, or adapted physical education, and a valuable reference for anybody with an interest in the sociology of sport, disability studies, cultural studies, the body, or research methodology.

Ben Powis is a Course Leader in the Faculty of Sport, Health and Social Sciences at Solent University, UK. His current research interests lie in the sociology of disability sport, the embodied experiences of visually impaired people in sport and physical activity, and investigating the significance of sensuous sporting experiences.

James Brighton is a Senior Lecturer in the Sociology of Sport and Exercise at Canterbury Christ Church University, UK. His theoretical and empirical research interests lie in disability studies, the sociology of the body and the social and cultural analyses of sport and fitness. Methodologically, he is interested in interpretive forms of qualitative inquiry including ethnography, life history, and narrative analyses.

P. David Howe is a social anthropologist and holds the Dr. Frank J. Hayden Endowed Chair in Sport and Social Impact in the School of Kinesiology at Western University, Canada. His ethnographic research focuses on unpacking the embodied sociocultural milieu surrounding inclusive physical activity and disability sport. He is also editor of the Routledge book series *Disability, Sport and Physical Activity Cultures*.

Disability Sport and Physical Activity Cultures
Series Editor:
P. David Howe
Western University, Canada

The *Disability, Sport and Physical Activity Cultures* series provides an outlet for high-quality books concerned with the politics and policy of sport broadly defined. It gives shape to and showcases the burgeoning academic field of 'Disability Sport Studies and Adapted Physical Activity'. Books within the series engage critically with the nature of sport and physical activity and the socio-cultural significance that this has on people with disabilities. A particular aim of the series is to encourage critical reflection on the cultural politics, governance, management, and philosophy of disability sport and physical activity cultures.

Available in this series:

Leveraging Disability Sport Events
Impacts, Promises, and Possibilities
Laura Misener, Gayle McPherson, David McGillivray and David Legg

Embodiment, Identity and Disability Sport
An Ethnography of Elite Visually Impaired Athletes
Ben Powis

Reflexivity and Change in Adaptive Physical Activity
Overcoming Hubris
Edited by Donna Goodwin and Maureen Connolly

Researching Disability Sport
Theory, Method, Practice
Edited by Ben Powis, James Brighton and P. David Howe

For more information about this series, please visit: https://www.routledge.com/Disability-Sport-and-Physical-Activity-Cultures/book-series/RDSPC

Researching Disability Sport

Theory, Method, Practice

Edited by Ben Powis,
James Brighton and P. David Howe

LONDON AND NEW YORK

First published 2023
by Routledge
4 Park Square, Milton Park, Abingdon, Oxon OX14 4RN

and by Routledge
605 Third Avenue, New York, NY 10158

*Routledge is an imprint of the Taylor & Francis Group,
an informa business*

© 2023 selection and editorial matter, Ben Powis, James Brighton and P. David Howe; individual chapters, the contributors

The right of Ben Powis, James Brighton and P. David Howe to be identified as the authors of the editorial material, and of the authors for their individual chapters, has been asserted in accordance with sections 77 and 78 of the Copyright, Designs and Patents Act 1988.

All rights reserved. No part of this book may be reprinted or reutilised in any form or by any electronic, mechanical, or other means, now known or hereafter invented, including photocopying and recording, or in any information storage or retrieval system, without permission in writing from the publishers.

Trademark notice: Product or corporate names may be trademarks or registered trademarks, and are used only for identification and explanation without intent to infringe.

British Library Cataloguing-in-Publication Data
A catalogue record for this book is available from the British Library

Library of Congress Cataloging-in-Publication Data
Names: Powis, Ben, editor. | Brighton, James (Lecturer in
   Sociology of Sport) editor. | Howe, P. David, 1966-editor.
Title: Researching disability sport : theory, method, practice /
   edited by Ben Powis, James Brighton and P. David Howe.
Description: 1 Edition. | New York, NY : Routledge, 2023. |
   Series: Disability sport and physical activity cultures |
   Includes bibliographical references and index.
Identifiers: LCCN 2022030270 (print) | LCCN 2022030271
   (ebook) | ISBN 9780367721565 (hardback) | ISBN
   9780367721589 (paperback) | ISBN 9781003153696 (ebook)
Subjects: LCSH: Sports for people with disabilities.
Classification: LCC GV709.3 .R47 2023 (print) | LCC GV709.3
   (ebook) | DDC 796.04/56--dc23/eng/20220630
LC record available at https://lccn.loc.gov/2022030270
LC ebook record available at https://lccn.loc.gov/2022030271

ISBN: 978-0-367-72156-5 (hbk)
ISBN: 978-0-367-72158-9 (pbk)
ISBN: 978-1-003-15369-6 (ebk)

DOI: 10.4324/9781003153696

Typeset in Goudy
by SPi Technologies India Pvt Ltd (Straive)

Contents

List of Contributors   vii
Acknowledgements   x

1 Researching Disability Sport: An Introduction   1
BEN POWIS, JAMES BRIGHTON AND P. DAVID HOWE

PART I
Foundations for Disability Sport Scholarship   11

2 Theorising Disability Sport   13
JAMES BRIGHTON, P. DAVID HOWE AND BEN POWIS

3 Cultural Politics, Disability Sport and Physical Activity Research   41
P. DAVID HOWE

4 What Are We Doing Here? Confessional Tales of Non-Disabled Researchers in Disability Sport   55
JESS MACBETH AND BEN POWIS

5 Barriers to Disability Sport Research and the Global South: A Personal View   70
LESLIE SWARTZ

PART II
Disability, Sport and Intersectionality   83

6 Disabled Female Sporting Bodies: Reflections on (In)Visibility of disAbility in Sport   85
KAREN P. DEPAUW

vi Contents

7 Playing, Passing, and Pageantry: A Collaborative Autoethnography on Sport, Disability, Sexuality, and Belonging 100
STEPHANIE WHEELER AND DANIELLE PEERS

8 Race, Disability and Sport: The Experience of Black Deaf Individuals 114
THOMAS IRISH, KATRINA MCDONALD AND FRANCESCA CAVALLERIO

9 Disability and Ageing: Dads, Sons, Sport and Impairment 126
JAMES BRIGHTON

PART III
From Theory to Practice: Contemporary Issues in Disability Sport 141

10 Seeing without Sight: The Athlete/Guide Partnership in Disability Sport 143
ANDREA BUNDON AND STACI MANNELLA

11 Confronting Ableism from within: Reflections on Anti-Ableism Research in Disability Sport 157
CARLA FILOMENA SILVA

12 Exercise, Rehabilitation and Posthuman Disability Studies: Four Responses 171
JAVIER MONFORTE, BARBARA E. GIBSON, BRETT SMITH AND DAN GOODLEY

13 Para-Sport Activism in South Korea 185
INHYANG CHOI, DAMIAN HASLETT AND BRETT SMITH

14 Conclusion: The Future of Disability Sport Research 198
P. DAVID HOWE, BEN POWIS AND JAMES BRIGHTON

Index 202

Contributors

Andrea Bundon is an Assistant Professor in the School of Kinesiology and a Principal Investigator at the International Collaboration on Repair Discoveries (ICORD) at the University of British Columbia (Canada). Her research explores the intersections of sport and disability and frequently draws on digital qualitative methodologies. Her interest in the Paralympics stems from her own experiences racing as a guide for Nordic skiers with visual impairments at the 2010 and 2014 Paralympic Games.

Francesca Cavallerio is a Senior Lecturer in Sport and Exercise Psychology in the School of Psychology and Sport Science, Anglia Ruskin University, UK. Her research uses qualitative methodologies to explore the psychosocial aspects affecting youth elite athletes' wellbeing and overall development during and following their sport career. She is also interested in the areas of diversity and inclusion in coaching, and high-performance gymnasts' experiences of the gymnastics culture.

Inhyang Choi (Alice) is a researcher in the Department of Sport and Exercise Sciences at Durham University, UK. Her research interests lie in the social and cultural analysis of sport, activism and critical disability studies. Methodologically, she is interested in interpretive qualitative research including art-based research, thematic, and narrative inquiry.

Karen P. DePauw, emerita Vice President and Dean for Graduate Education and tenured Professor of Sociology and Human Nutrition, Foods & Exercise at Virginia Tech, USA. DePauw is a leader in global higher education especially graduate education and an internationally recognized scholar of adapted physical activity and disability sport. Her scholarship focuses on inclusion, ableism, and the social construction of body, ability and disability.

Barbara E. Gibson is a Professor in the Department of Physical Therapy at the University of Toronto, Canada, and Senior Scientist in the Bloorview Research Institute. Her research examines the intersections of social, cultural, and institutional practices in producing health, inclusion/exclusion, and identity with disabled children and young people. She holds the Bloorview Kids Foundation Chair in Childhood Disability Studies.

Dan Goodley is Professor of Disability Studies and Education and co-director of iHuman at the University of Sheffield, UK. His work engages with the dual processes of disablism (the exclusion of people with impairments) and ableism (the idealisation of abled bodies and minds).

Damian Haslett is a Postdoctoral Research Associate at Loughborough University London, UK. Damian's research focuses on disability, sport and social activism. One example of this focus is his research on Para athletes as 'activists' that has been published in several edited books and academic journals including Psychology of Sport & Exercise, Sociology of Sport Journal and The Routledge Handbook of Disability Activism.

Thomas Irish graduated with a BSc and an MSc degree from Anglia Ruskin University, UK. He has worked with UK Deaf Sport and is a blogger, sharing his experiences as a deaf person. He is passionate about using qualitative methodologies to explore the experiences of deaf people participating in sports in the UK. He is interested in the areas of disability, race, deafness, and intersectionality in sport.

Jess Macbeth is a Senior Lecturer in Sport Studies in the School of Sport & Health Sciences, University of Central Lancashire, UK. Jess' research focuses on sport and physical activity in the lives of marginalised groups, with a particular interest in the impact of disability and gender. Her main research interest lies in the lived experiences of visually impaired athletes, on which she has published widely.

Staci Mannella is a doctoral student in the department of Counseling Psychology, Social Psychology, and Counseling at Ball State University (USA). Her research explores the intersections of high-performance disability sport cultures, experiences of impairments, and athlete mental health. This work has been inspired by her own experiences as a 2x visually impaired Paralympic alpine skier (Sochi 2014; PyeongChang 2018).

Katrina McDonald is a Senior Lecturer in Sport Coaching and PE at Anglia Ruskin University in Cambridge, UK. Her research interests are focused in and around the coaching domain and with qualitative research methods.

Javier Monforte is a postdoctoral research associate in the Department of Sport and Exercise Sciences at Durham University, UK. His qualitative research focuses on disability and physical activity. Currently, his work revolves around a co-produced project called Moving Social Work. Javier is a member of the ECR committee at the International Society of Qualitative Research in Sport and Exercise.

Danielle Peers (they/them) is a Canada Research Chair (Tier II) in Disability and Movement Cultures, and an Associate Professor in the Faculty of Kinesiology, Sport, and Recreation at the University of Alberta. Peers uses disability justice approaches to study how movement cultures (including art, recreation, and sport) can be used to transmit and transform a community's values, politics, and (in)equities. Danielle's work draws from their experiences as a Paralympic athlete, coach, dancer, and filmmaker.

Carla Filomena Silva is a social scientist of movement cultures and health in the Schools of Health Studies and Kinesiology at Western University, Canada. Carla's research focuses on key cultural aspects of disability sport as a marginal field, such as the role of media representations in social understandings of disability, and the ideologies and practices of disability sporting communities. Theoretically, she is driven by the potential offered by the intersection of different academic fields such as disability studies, political philosophy, sociology, and anthropology, to explore the empowerment potential of movement cultures.

Brett Smith is a Professor of Disability and Physical Activity in the Department of Sport and Exercise Sciences at Durham University, UK. His research is underpinned by ideas from psychology, sociology, public health, and critical disability studies. He is President of the International Society of Qualitative Research in Sport and Exercise. He also is the Chair of the Disability and Physical Activity Expert Working Group for the Chief Medical Officers' (CMOs) Disability and Physical Activity Guidelines.

Leslie Swartz is a clinical psychologist and professor of psychology at Stellenbosch University, South Africa. He holds a PhD in psychology from University of Cape Town and a PhD in English from Stellenbosch University. He is currently Editor-in-Chief of South African Journal of Science. He has published widely on disability rights and access in Africa.

Stephanie Wheeler (she/her) is the Head Coach for women's wheelchair basketball at the University of Illinois at Urbana-Champaign. Wheeler uses her coaching practice as a social justice project to disrupt sexism, homophobia, and ableism in disability sport in order to create safe spaces of belonging. Stephanie is also a doctoral candidate in Cultural Kinesiology at Illinois, studying sport at the intersections of disability, gender, sexuality, and gender identity. Stephanie's coaching and academic work is informed from her experiences as a Paralympic athlete and coach.

Acknowledgements

We thank Simon Whitmore, Rebecca Connor, and the rest of the production team at Taylor & Francis for their patience, understanding, and endeavour in the creation of *Researching Disability Sport*.

Ben would like to thank his co-editors for their friendship and collegiality throughout this process. He is also grateful for the support of his colleagues at Solent University. In particular, thanks to Kola Adeosun, Philippa Velija, Brian McDonough, and Rory Magrath for their enduring interest and enthusiasm during the book's development. Finally, and most importantly, thanks to Ellie and Ernie. Ellie, I couldn't have done it without you. Ernie, my beautiful son, I dedicate this book to you.

James would like to express his thanks to Ben and David for their help, insight, and patience and to all of the scholars that kindly agreed to contribute their valuable work to this collection. As always, my dearest thanks go to all of my family for their unequivocal love and support throughout the dark times as well as the good. Without you all, nothing would be possible.

David enjoyed the camaraderie of Ben and James as the project developed during tough times through the COVID-19 pandemic. Thank you for pushing me intellectually and creatively. Working with great people is always a pleasure! To disability activists who inspire me to attempt to make a difference on a daily basis. Finally, to my small but perfectly formed family for their love and support shown in diverse manners throughout this project, I am eternally grateful.

Chapter 1

Researching Disability Sport
An Introduction

Ben Powis, James Brighton and P. David Howe

From the wards of Stoke Mandeville Hospital to the global spectacle of the Paralympic Games, the story of contemporary disability sport is well documented (Legg and Steadward, 2011; Peers, 2012; Brittain, 2018). Its transformation from rehabilitation to elite competition has fundamentally altered conceptions of sport and physical activity for disabled people and, pointedly, the types of bodies and impairments that are most valued. Through increasing financial investment and ever-closer ties to mainstream sporting organisations, this evolution continues to advance at speed. Because of – and in response to – this contemporary landscape, disability sport is now established as a legitimate area of investigation for social scientists. Consequently, this has led to the inclusion of disability sport studies across multidisciplinary degree programmes and a rise in academic materials to cater for this growing audience. However, these works are often under theorised and overly descriptive with harsh ableist undertones. Disability is predominantly treated as a homogenous construct with authors failing to adequately acknowledge how experiences of oppression can intersect (e.g., race, ethnicity, gender, sexuality, age and class). Furthermore, despite a handful of offerings, empirical research in this field continues to attend to athletes with more 'normative' impairments and addresses Paralympic or elite sport – in preference to recreational or non-elite competition – while claiming to be representative of disability sporting culture.

Significantly, these shortcomings are indicative of a collective failure to engage with innovative theoretical and methodological frameworks and to acknowledge that being disabled is a social experience rather than a destination. As a critical remedy to the above critiques, we present *Researching Disability Sport*. Through this book, we have endeavoured to create a platform for scholars to debate cutting-edge issues and creatively engage with contemporary approaches in this emerging discipline. We capture the disability sporting *state-of-the-art* and foreground an intersectional understanding of embodied difference where those who are being researched take centre stage. This book's wide-ranging chapters also seek to translate theoretically and methodologically robust research into useful practice. The 'positive' rhetoric, which has enveloped much of the research published in the last twenty years, has had minimal impact on those who experience disability in sport and physical activity contexts. The time for simple description and representational research should be behind us; this edited collection marks the beginning of new direction for disability sport scholarship.

The *Researching Disability Sport* Manifesto

Like many creative projects, this book began life as a series of scribbles on a restaurant napkin. During the 2019 North American Society for the Sociology of Sport (NASSS) conference in Virginia Beach, over a smoothie at the Green Cat Juice Bar, Ben and James finally acted upon their endless conversations about disability sport research and began to sketch ideas for an edited collection. As well as discussing the book's contents and potential contributors, they established a manifesto for this project. Looking back at that napkin now (which we still have), we have stayed true to our vision. Our central intention of writing this book was to create a valuable resource that captures contemporary disability sport research *and* progresses future scholarship for students as well as established scholars. To achieve this, we wanted to curate an edited collection with the following in mind. Firstly, to engage with contemporary theoretical debates that support disability sport scholars in developing a conceptual grounding. Secondly, to draw together methodological considerations when conducting disability sport research, including the social, cultural and political reflections of the research process from disabled and non-disabled academics. Thirdly, to establish a space for intersectional accounts of disability sport that challenge homogenous understandings of disability as a fixed, unitary, singular category. And finally, to provide rich and innovative examples of how theory and methodology can be employed when exploring contemporary issues within the field.

In our manifesto, we were adamant that we did not wish to repeat what had already been covered in previous disability sport publications. Instead, this book bridges the gap between disability studies and sport studies by offering a novel understanding of the relationship between theory, method and empiricism in disability sport research. As you will discover, we paint a varied picture of disability sport beyond just the Paralympic games or 'Para-sport', including examinations of grassroots and recreational level athletes. Equally, we have brought together an eclectic mix of contributing authors. This includes disabled and non-disabled academics and, particularly for those chapters in which we address intersectionality, authors with lived experiences of intersecting identities. Furthermore, we have provided opportunities for early career researchers with fresh and exciting ideas – alongside more established scholars – to contribute to this edited collection.

At the heart of our *Researching Disability Sport* manifesto, from the restaurant napkin to the book in front of you now, is *you*, the Reader. We have worked closely with our contributors to curate an edited collection that speaks directly and accessibly to its audience. For students and researchers alike, this book demonstrates what we believe high-quality, innovative and informed disability sport research looks like and it is our hope that a new generation of scholars will draw inspiration from our contributors' work. If you are dipping your toes into disability sport research for the first time, this book is organised into three parts to help guide you through the field: *Foundations for Disability Sport Scholarship, Disability, Sport and Intersectionality*, and *From Theory to Practice: Contemporary Issues in Disability Sport*. At the end of this introduction, we will discuss these parts in more detail and provide a synopsis of the book's chapters, but first we consider a complex issue which, in our opinion, is insufficiently debated in the context of disability sport: language and terminology.

Person-First or Identity-First?

At this juncture, we believe it is important to explain our use of language and terminology in the book. Instead of enforcing linguistic rules, authors have been given the freedom to write about disability in their preferred vocabulary. As you flick through each chapter, you will read *disabled people, people with disabilities, people who experience disability, non-disabled people, able-bodied people* – but does this matter? Well, yes and no. Arguing over semantics is what academics do best and such debates may only serve to distract from the issues at hand (Shakespeare, 2013). However, the power of language (and those who use it) should not be minimised, particularly when conceptualising disability: choice of terminology is often rooted in individuals' lived experiences and/or their theoretical and political standpoint. It is when these linguistic differences become exclusionary (both in day-to-day life and academia) that open and honest discussion is needed. While our short dialogue will give insights into our preferred vocabulary, we recommend Danielle Peers and colleagues' (2014) engaging discussion of rethinking disability language in sport and physical activity research for further context.

As acknowledged above, we question the value of mandatory disability terminology, especially when it creates barriers to engagement. Whether it is ill-informed journal reviewers, conference organisers or institutional review boards, there is a pressure upon academics to conform or risk the dreaded rejection letter. Frustratingly, these constraints often do not account for disciplinary or regional differences. By designating what language is and is not inclusive, disability sport research only becomes more exclusive. However, we are not suggesting that anything goes; as Peers et al. (2014) argue, academics are accountable for their choice of terminology. It must be consistent with their theoretical and methodological framework and authentically represent their participants.

For researchers, particularly those new to the field, the pressure of saying the 'right' thing is inescapable and often presented as a moral decision. As an example, here is a message that Ben received from a colleague about a student's ethics application – which has been shared with their permission:

> Hey, quick question about the ethics you're a part of. In America, we were grilled very early that person first language was really important - Mike, who is in a wheelchair vs. Wheelchair Mike. There are plenty of examples we use

all the time where the disability is the signifier, not the human being. Is that not cared about here in England? Because I heard it used incorrectly ... and it bothered me. In reference to the ethics, **** uses disabled adult males and I'm wondering if my comments would be out of line.

In response, Ben briefly summed up the person-first/identity-first debate and explained his position, which he will also outline in this chapter. Ben ended the message saying, "It's a complex debate. I would use 'disabled person', but others would argue against it. As long as **** is being consistent in his usage, I am happy with either". This brief exchange demonstrates the value of open and honest discussion. Despite their deep-rooted viewpoint, which may have led to the student being rebuked, the colleague was willing to ask questions and learn about alternative perspectives. The purpose of the conversation was not to change their use of person-first language, but to discuss *why* we employ our preferred vocabulary.

During the editing process, we were also having very similar conversations in our meetings. When writing the proposal and initial chapters, it was clear that the three of us used different terminology and there was often a back-and-forth in both the comments section and our regular video calls. This space for debate is something we want to capture here. For Ben, he uses *disabled person* and *non-disabled person*. His position is drawn from the British disability studies movement and recognises that disability is a central facet of identity that should not be othered when defining personhood. Ben's use of non-disabled person, which is also consistent with the British approach, is a political choice that intends to disrupt the notion of able-bodiedness. In Ben's opinion, this "theoretically inconsistent and politically problematic" (Peers et al., 2014: 278) term serves to maintain a binary understanding of disability and reinforces the idea of the normate body. For James, his preferred term is *disabled person* as this reflects that disability is a social product rather than an individual characteristic. This is also how physically disabled participants predominantly refer to themselves in his empirical research, which is based in the United Kingdom. Like Shildrick (2020), James recognises that the choice of terminology should be culturally appropriate and considerate of individuals' self-definition. For David, the politics around language has always fascinated him – particular around the word disability. Being born with cerebral palsy (hemiplegia) his lifeworld has been a constant battleground of daily reminders that he is seen as 'less than' within society – in spite of the other privileges associated with his identity. Because of the ableist ideology that surrounds the philosophically driven socio-cultural understanding of disability, David prefers the expression *people who experience disability* to best capture his current thinking on the topic.

Notably, in the context of disability sport research, you will also encounter authors who do not use *disability* at all. Terms such as *para-athlete*, *parasport* and *adapted sport* are frequently preferred to the 'd-word' or used interchangeably. Considering our discussion above and the ever-increasing influence of the Paralympic Movement, this is understandable. However, the erasure of the disability in disability sport has unintended consequences (Powis, 2020). Arguably, without reference to disability, the elite *para* prefix fails to represent those who participate in grassroots and recreational disability sport as well as those whose bodies rule them as unclassifiable for parasport. It may also discourage disabled athletes – whether at an elite level or not – from identifying as disabled. The use of *para* in place of *disabled* may bypass the person-first/identity-first debate, but it also reinforces the disconnect between disability studies and disability sport research.

As evident throughout this discussion, context is all-important. We have cited disciplinary and regional differences, yet of equal significance is how research participants identity themselves. What language and terminology do they use? Is it impairment-specific? Or sport-specific? For example, athletes may use their sporting class or classification as identifiers rather than engage with disability-centred language (Peers et al., 2014; Powis, 2020; Powis and Macbeth, 2020). If participants identify in ways that contradict your chosen vocabulary, it is your responsibility to critically reflect upon this divergence and seek to justify your standpoint. Remember, you are accountable for the language and terminology you employ – but do not let this be a barrier to your involvement in disability sport research. Instead, be considered and consistent in your use of vocabulary and remain actively engaged in these on-going debates.

Overview of the Book

To begin the first part of the book – *Foundations for Disability Sport Scholarship* – we (Brighton, Howe and Powis) present an extended chapter that maps the theorisation of disability sport. We highlight the theoretical deprivation in the contemporary field and reflect upon the lack of guidance when using disability theory in sport and physical activity research. Fittingly, the remainder of the chapter is just that: a comprehensive and engaging theoretical overview, which includes I) the foundations of the disability studies movement and the emergence of critical disability studies; II) models of disability; III) sociocultural approaches; IV) disability and the body. As established above, this chapter is organised to support disability sport scholars in developing a conceptual grounding in the subject and showcase the exciting array of theoretical approaches at our disposal.

In Chapter 3, P. David Howe critiques the relationship between cultural politics and disability sport research. As a former Paralympic athlete and outspoken advocate for the needs of people who experience disability to have political voice that can be manifest in distinctive embodied forms, Howe considers the role of explicit advocacy through scholarship. He also provides insights into the politics of the Paralympic movement, including his wide-ranging experiences as an elected representative on the IPC Athletics committee. Drawing upon a range of seminal disability studies texts and the work of Michel Foucault, Howe reflects upon the importance of conducting research that challenges those in positions of power and robustly unpacks the rhetoric of disability sporting and physical activity cultures.

Jess Macbeth and Ben Powis' Chapter 4 provides confessional tales of their experiences as non-disabled researchers in disability sport contexts. In asking themselves "what are we doing here?", the authors draw upon debates that have underpinned the field of disability studies for over a quarter of a century and discuss the limited engagement with such questions in disability sport. Macbeth and Powis spotlight three pertinent aspects of the research process – positionality, asking about impairment and giving back – and, in doing so, offer critical reflections that challenge an impairment-based, insider-outsider binary. While focusing upon their experiences as non-disabled researchers, they encourage all researchers to purposefully reflect upon issues of status in the field and consider how this informs the ways in which we conduct research.

Leslie Swartz then concludes Part I by offering fascinating insights into the barriers to disability sport research in the Global South. In Chapter 5, he discusses the realities of disability inclusion in the majority world through the three Ts – transport, toilets and time – and passionately argues for the importance of understanding local cultural contexts. At the intersection of race and disability, Swartz uses the concept of the spectacle to explain how elite disability sport serves to reproduces colonial and ableist tropes and questions its role in meaningful social change. He urges researchers to look beyond the Global North-dominated landscape and work with grassroots organisations to develop robust approaches to evaluating disability sport interventions. In conclusion, Swartz calls us to think globally, work locally and be prepared to get our hands dirty.

To begin the second part of the book – *Disability, Sport and Intersectionality* – Karen De Pauw's Chapter 6 explores constructs of the disabled female sporting body. Revisiting her seminal 1997 work *(In)Visibility of disAbility in sport*, she uses the framework of marginality to critically reflect upon the intersectional experiences of disabled women in sport and argues for a paradigm shift in how such experiences are researched. De Pauw posits a cultural–feminist approach to disability sport research that bridges the gap between disability studies and the sociology of sport. In rethinking disability sport research, she implores researchers to question underlying assumptions of the body, disability, gender and sport and engage with emancipatory and participatory approaches that amplify the voices of those who are marginalised.

In Chapter 7, Stephanie Wheeler and Danielle Peers push theoretical and methodological boundaries in their collaborative autoethnography on sport, disability, sexuality and belonging. The chapter, which echoes De Pauw's arguments in Chapter 6, provides a critical lens to conceptualise intersectional experiences in and out of sport. From the monkey bars to the basketball court, Wheeler and Peers' rich and evocative storied conversation seeks to disrupt dominant discourses of disability, queerness and parasport and create new and contested ways of thinking. They also speak directly to practitioners and coaches and call for sporting spaces that are inclusive and view athletes' worth beyond their performance on the field of play. If the microaggressions of sport can be countered with microaffirmations, the authors argue that disability sport can be somewhere that all bodies belong.

Continuing the use of innovative methodology, Thomas Irish, Katrina McDonald and Francesca Cavallerio use creative nonfiction (CNF) in Chapter 8 to explore the challenges found at the intersection of disability, race and sport. Drawing upon interview data with Black Deaf individuals involved in sport, the authors discuss the collaborative process of developing CNF and exhibit why this methodological approach is such an effective way to authentically represent intersectional experiences. Through *Kyra's story*, Irish, McDonald and Cavallerio provide novel insights into how racism and ableism are experienced in the context of sport. The authors also discuss essentialised identities, passing and the potential freedom that sport can offer. This chapter, which is the first to explicitly analyse race and disability in sport, demonstrates the urgent need for further research at this intersection.

In Chapter 9, James Brighton draws Part II to a close by providing a powerful and insightful chapter that explores disability, ageing, family and sport. At the heart of Brighton's chapter is his relationship with his Dad and their shared yet distinct embodied relationship with sport and physical activity. Using life history interviews and a plurality of autoethnographic methodologies, including collaborative autoethnography, the author presents a series of storied extracts that delve into their experiences of impairment, ageing and shared human existence. Through each constructed story, Brighton demonstrates the salience of this creative approach, particularly when capturing the intersectionality of disability experience. The novel focus of this chapter presents themes of ableism, masculinity and embodiment in affecting and poignant ways and, as readers, we are encouraged to rethink our understanding of these concepts.

To begin the third and final part of book – *From Theory to Practice: Contemporary Issues in Disability Sport* – Andrea Bundon and Staci Mannella's Chapter 10 examines the significance of athlete-guide partnerships in disability sport. As a sighted guide in Nordic skiing and as a visually impaired (VI) athlete in alpine skiing respectively, the authors provide fascinating *Para'llel* autoethnographic accounts of competing at the Paralympic Games. Their separate yet parallel experiences of parasport successfully capture the unique partnership between VI athletes and their sighted guides and interrogate the disabled and non-disabled binaries that continue to be (re)produced in sport contexts. Bundon and Mannella also raise pertinent issues relating to disabled athletes' agency both in sport and non-sporting environments.

In Chapter 11, Carla Filomena Silva explores the possibilities and challenges of employing an anti-ableist lens in disability sport research. Engaging with seminal disability studies literature, she artfully unpacks the concept of ableism and examines the covert ways in which this system of oppression operates. Drawing upon rich ethnographic insights, Silva then turns her attention to sporting cultures and examines how sport serves as a powerful agent for ableism. She reflects on her wide-ranging sporting experiences, including as a physical education teacher, a sitting volleyball player and disability sport researcher, to analyse how ableist rhetoric pervaded these interactions. The chapter ends with a rallying call for a robust anti-ableist agenda whereby researchers challenge the grand narratives of ableism and advocate for sporting cultures that respect different forms of embodiment.

Taking a detour from sport, Javier Monforte, Barbara E Gibson, Dan Goodley and Brett Smith's Chapter 12 considers how posthuman disability studies (PDS) can be employed to theorise experiences of exercise-based rehabilitation. Firstly, Monforte critiques the notion of *exercise-is-restitution* and envisions a posthumanist rehabilitation that moves beyond the classic conception of the human and ableist framing of current rehabilitative practices. Secondly, Goodley highlights critical disability studies' uneasy relationship with exercise and rehabilitation and discusses the way in which PDS can illuminate issues of power, autonomy and the diversity of human and non-human interrelationships. Thirdly, Gibson explores how a posthuman appreciation of disability, which focuses upon bodily potentials rather than deficits, can reframe exercise-based rehabilitation as pleasure. Finally, Smith presents 'A *letter to my younger self*', a creative non-fiction based upon interviews with people who have acquired spinal cord injuries. The authors' four responses, which engage with PDS in diverse ways, demonstrate the significance of theory in understanding contemporary practice.

In Chapter 13, the final chapter of Part III, Inhyang Choi, Damian Haslett and Brett Smith discuss disability activism and the Paralympic movement in South Korea. Employing a Confucian approach, the authors establish a cross-cultural understanding of para-sport activism that engages with East Asian and Western philosophy. Drawing upon empirical research with South Korean para-athletes and disabled non-athletes, Choi, Haslett and Smith highlight important similarities and differences in para-sport activism across these cultural contexts, including hierarchical relationships, public attitudes and political autonomy. They also analyse the role of governing bodies in promoting disability activism. This chapter impressively exhibits how theory can be applied innovatively in disability sport research and reinforces the need for further work in non-Western contexts.

To conclude, we (Howe, Powis and Brighton) consider the future of disability sport research. Building upon our manifesto and the book's key themes, we pointedly ask, "Who represents the field?" and reflect upon how we believe the field needs to change moving forward. This discussion of representation includes the need for more disabled scholars, more globally and ethnically diverse voices and the translation of non-English scholarship. As well as representation, we reinforce our plea for theoretically and methodologically robust research and highlight the multifaceted ways in which this book has showcased the high-quality scholarship that is required to advance the field. Finally, we end with a call for action that we hope will embolden a new generation of disability sport researchers.

References

Brittain, I. (2018) 'Key points in the history and development of the paralympic games' in I. Brittain and A. Beacom (Eds). *The Palgrave Handbook of Paralympic Studies*. London: Palgrave Macmillian. (pp. 125–149).

Legg, D. and Steadward, R. (2011) 'The Paralympic games and 60 years of change (1948–2008): unification and restructuring from a disability and medical model to sport-based competition', *Sport in Society*, 14(9), 1099–1115, doi:10.1080/17430437.2011.614767.

Peers, D. (2012) 'Patients, athletes, freaks: Paralympism and the reproduction of disability', *Journal of Sport and Social Issues*, 36(3), 295–316, 10.1177/0193723512442201.

Peers, D., Spencer-Cavaliere, N. and Eales, L. (2014) 'Say what you mean: Rethinking disability language in adapted physical activity quarterly', *Adapted Physical Activity Quarterly*, 31(3), 265–282, doi:10.1123/apaq.2013-0091.

Powis, B. (2020) *Embodiment, Identity and Disability Sport: An Ethnography of Elite Visually Impaired Athletes*. London: Routledge, doi:10.4324/9780429317675.

Powis, B. and Macbeth, J.L. (2020) '"We know who is a cheat and who is not. But what can you do?": Athletes' perspectives on classification in visually impaired sport', *International Review for the Sociology of Sport*, 55(5), 588–602, doi:10.1177/1012690218825209

Shakespeare, T. (2013) *Disability Rights and Wrongs Revisited*. London: Routledge.

Shildrick, M. (2020) 'Critical disability studies: Re-thinking the conventions for the age of postmodernity' in N. Watson and S. Vehmas (Eds). *The Routledge Handbook of Disability Studies*. (pp. 32–44). London: Routledge

Part I

Foundations for Disability Sport Scholarship

Chapter 2

Theorising Disability Sport

James Brighton, P. David Howe and Ben Powis

Introduction

Social scientific research into disability sport has experienced a surge in momentum over the last decade. However, in spite of this growth, with a few notable exceptions there remains a lack of conceptual grounding and theoretical *imagination* through which these explorations are made. Accordingly, there has been a call for social scientists of sport to engage with the field of disability studies in order to conceptualise the experiences of disabled athletes and the sociocultural contexts in which they participate. However, due to philosophical debates at the heart of the disability movement which traditionally have focused upon structural barriers rather than individual experience, there remained few empirical investigations into the distinctive experiences of disabled athletes. Moola and Norman (2012) have previously underlined the failure of these disciplines to marry. For them, this separation created an epistemological gap that left the exploration of disabled athletes under represented, under theorised and under examined:

> Disability studies' failure to investigate the sporting lives of people with disabilities – and sport sociology's under theorisation of how the social institution of sport contributes toward the marginalisation and oppression of disabled athletes – has made for much intellectual and theoretical impoverishment. The failure of these two theoretical paradigms to wed means that the intellectual terrain of disability sport is yet uncharted and a sociological understanding of the sporting lives of disabled athletes beyond our intellectual grasp.
>
> (Moola & Norman, 2012: 285)

Since this plea to develop the conceptual frameworks used in social scientifically informed disability sport research, a small number of scholars have demonstrated a commitment to bridging this research lacuna with robust engagement into the socio-cultural experiences of disabled athletes (e.g. Peers, 2012a; Sparkes et al., 2014, 2017a, 2017b; Howe & Silva, 2017; Apelmo, 2018; Powis, 2020). These accounts have offered rich and evocative examples of the value of theoretical analyses in exposing the structural positioning of disabled sports participation as

DOI: 10.4324/9781003153696-3

'problematic' and in interpreting understandings of the experiences of disabled athletes themselves. Consequently, scholars have increasingly reinforced the *moral and intellectual responsibility* of engaging in understandings of disability as well as the sporting contexts in which disability is performed and produced (e.g. Smith & Perrier, 2014; Smith & Bundon, 2018; Brighton et al., 2021).

Engaging and using theory in disability sport research is not however straightforward. This is no more evident than in the reviews that each of us undertake for papers submitted to academic journals in which authors continually fail to adequately conceptualise or contextualise disability. Various reasons might contribute to this theoretical deprivation. *Firstly*, there is a need to develop an appreciation of the foundations of the disability studies movement. This is important in order to understand the academic, political and activist underpinnings of disability studies and to develop ideological stances when engaging in the key debates at play – which are inevitably complex, sensitive and divided. *Secondly*, given that disability cannot be explained by a single overarching, grand theoretical narrative, gaining an understanding of the breadth of approaches that have been forwarded is required in order to make critical and ideologically informed choices of what theory to use (Sparkes & Smith, 2014; Powis, 2020). *Thirdly*, disability studies is still a rapidly evolving and diversifying interdisciplinary field and keeping abreast with current theoretical progressions is challenging. *Finally*, many social scientists of sport will have entered into disability sport from a variety of alternative fields (e.g. sport science, sports psychology, sports coaching, sports management) and jumping into disability studies literature can cause anxiety and apprehension. In short, for social scientists of sport, engaging in disability studies can be daunting. This situation is further exacerbated given that there are virtually no in-depth sport specific conceptual overviews to draw on in developing understandings of disability and a lack of structured guidance on *how* disability theory can be used in sport-based research (Powis, 2020; Brighton et al., 2021).

Accordingly, in this chapter we begin by revisiting the foundations of the disability studies movement and explore why this historical background is important in contemporary disability sport research. In doing so, we outline forms of knowledge that have informed understandings of disability (moral and medical perspectives) and the 'models' (social and minority) that marked the inauguration of disability studies as a distinct field of intellectual politics. From this point of departure, we provide a tour of the significant theoretical architecture that is available for social scientists of sport to use in their research into disability. To contextualise this theory, we reference theoretical approaches powerfully employed in previous empirical disability sport research and provide readers with examples of real-life applications of how theory can be used in their own investigations. Additionally, we present some theoretical approaches which to date have not been widely used, but we believe hold value in progressing analyses of disability in sport. Lastly, we set the scene for what it is to follow in this collection, providing a conceptual underpinning through which readers can resonate with the approaches used by authors in subsequent chapters. Before we do so however, we must first locate the field in which disability research has emerged – which came to be known as 'Disability Studies' – and discuss the subsequent emergence of 'Critical Disability Studies' as distinct shifts in thinking about disability.

Disability Studies and/or Critical Disability Studies?

Disability studies has a relatively brief history as a distinguishable field of academic study (Goodley, 2014; Shakespeare, 2014). Central to this formal identification was the repositioning of disability as an individualised moral or medical 'problem' that should be overcome to a social and culturally constructed phenomenon which should be stoically challenged. This radical and transformative re-evaluation of disability has largely been accredited to the Union of the Physically Impaired Against Segregation (UPIAS), a group of activists established in 1976 in the United Kingdom (UK), who drew on sociological theory to highlight complex forms of social oppression disabled people encountered (Barnes, 2020). Importantly, in centring on the *material* and *structural* barriers encountered by disabled people, this movement drew heavily on materialist sociological thought aligned with neo-Marxist and Gramscian thinking and provided a counter hegemonic critique of the negative positioning of disabled people within the contemporary dynamics of capitalism (e.g. Thomas, 2007). Over time, helped by the pioneering work of a nucleus of core scholars including Barnes (1990) and Oliver (1990), this mode of thinking became known as the 'social model' of disability and was, and still is, crucial in exposing the alternative forms of structural oppression disabled people encounter in the world and the restrictions placed on their lives.

Meanwhile, at around the same time as the formation of the UPIAS, there was a growing movement in North America – *the minority group model* - which aligned the marginalised experiences of disabled people with other racial, ethnic and minority groups and civil right movements. Underpinned by offering a challenge to American neo-liberal politics which aggressively promoted individuality and achievement (Davis, 2002; Mitchell & Snyder, 2020), the minority model sought to challenge *ableism* or discrimination in favour of the able-bodied norm (Campbell, 2009, 2013). It promotes the construction of positive minority identities, denoted by person-first language in order to recognise this (i.e. people with disabilities), and appreciates that disabled people experience cultural as well as material restriction in their lives (McRuer, 2002). Significantly, this approach advocates that the oppression, prejudice and discrimination encountered by people with disabilities are best addressed through civil rights legislations, guaranteeing individual rights. As Shakespeare (2006: 25) outlines, although it does not go as far as redefining disability as social oppression as is the case under the British social model, its "overarching orientation is social and cultural, not medical or individualist" (Shakespeare, 2006: 25) and is therefore liberated from endless conceptual debates emanating from the social model.

Together with the UK social model, the minority model marked the 'birth' of disability studies (Goodley, 2017) which at its core aims to contest essentialised norms that position disabled people as "less than human, abnormal, deviant, deficient and broken" (Goodley,2020: 12) and challenge the ignorance, stigma, prejudice, and material discrimination disabled people encounter. Since these beginnings, exploring the phenomena of disability evolved to include a broad span of scholarship from the academic fields of sociology, gender studies, postcolonialism, queer theory, critical psychology, psychoanalysis, cultural studies, law and education in theorising and accounting for experiences of disability. For some, this theoretical and disciplinary eclecticism presented a distinct shift away from the predominantly structural materialist foundations of the social model and so should be more adequately termed 'critical disability studies' (CDS) (e.g. Goodley, 2014). As Vehmas and Watson (2014) highlight, whereas disability studies and the social model challenged individualised understandings of disability that dominated medical sociology, CDS challenges the materialist arguments central to disability studies through deconstructing, destabilising and unsettling ideologies and assumptions of disability and innovatively challenging categories that construct the 'problem' of disability.

According to Shildrick (2020: 32), CDS offers a necessary progression from the central arguments of the social model by adding theoretical impetus and "taking it in innovative directions that challenge not only existing *doxa* about the nature of disability, but questions of embodiment, identity and agency as they affect all living beings" (emphasis in original). This includes recognition of the intersectionality of disability alongside other important and politicised dimensions of identity, such as gender, sexuality, race, and class. Feminist scholars in particular have challenged the traditional version of the social model for marginalising the lived experiences of disabled women (e.g. Morris, 1991; Wendell, 1996a; Apelmo, 2017). As encapsulated by Smith and Perrier (2014: 97) the CDS discipline is committed to exposing injustice through challenging dogmatic theoretical approaches, engaging with thinking from multiple academic disciplines, emphasising community, social change, and well-being, moving "beyond thinking *about* disabled people to thinking *with* disabled people" (italics in original) and including culture, the body, impairment and narrative approaches in exploring the experiences of disabled people. For others however, CDS simply presents a maturing of the discipline of disability studies and, if distinguishable at all, offers a dangerous movement away from political and activist arguments that actually make a material difference to improving disabled people's lives (e.g. Barnes & Mercer, 2003; Meekosha & Shuttleworth, 2009). Additional critiques of CDS have extended to challenging unnecessary and superfluous theorisation, outlining difficulties in applying theory to praxis, diminishing the emphasis on collective struggle, risking the promotion of hidden ethical agendas, and focusing on a normative approach to revealing 'difference' – all of which serve to take away from emancipating and empowering disabled people (e.g. Vehmas & Watson, 2014).

In this volume, there are scholars who use terms for our research field as either disability studies or CDS. From our perspective either is fine, but we would argue that those who advocate for CDS may wish to reconsider the adjective critical as a distinguishing factor because, from its outset, materialist disability studies have always been critical. Perhaps we could suggest 'Neo' disability studies as a more appropriate marker of distinction. It is important to raise these arguments so that researchers of disability sport do not enter blindly into the political and activist landscapes that lay at the foundations of the discipline. Furthermore, in reinforcing these ideological underpinnings, it helps researchers locate where their research sits, allowing justifications for philosophical and theoretical approaches undertaken. In other words, theoretical choices made by researchers in disability sport can be taken freely but should be employed within the context of the ideological foundations of the disability studies movement. In doing so, researchers themselves are necessarily required to employ an openly ideological position. That is, the theoretical choices we take should be substantiated in relation to benefitting the lives of disabled participants we engage with. As Goodley (2021: 18) emphasises, the study of disability, including in sport, is inherently political because "it denotes inequality alongside human difference". As will be revealed in later chapters, contributors to this volume demonstrate a breadth of theoretical approaches in their conceptual and empirical work with disabled people in sport, each of which have political messages. As researchers of disability sport therefore, it is our moral responsibility to both understand and make ideologically informed political choices on what theories to make use of. This can now be explored in the following sections which seek to provide a repertoire of theoretical approaches that may be employed in research into disability sport.

Models of Disability

A 'models' approach to disability was central to the formulation of the disability studies discipline. Although now commonly referred to as 'models', they can be more accurately defined as assemblages of intellectual thoughts that help us make sense of the phenomena of disability (Bickenbach, 2020). Disability models have provided crucial conceptual and transformational lenses which not only challenge the ways in which we understand the concept but have also been foundational in implementing potentially inclusive policies and practices within a number of fields, including sport. In spite of the widespread critique of the models presented below, the very existence of models of disability has sparked intellectual debate that has helped us trouble the assumptions that inform understandings of disability. Accordingly, we begin by offering a brief summary of these models and subsequently discuss the importance of their implementation in disability sport research.

The Medical Model

As Barnes (2020: 14) reminds us, until relatively recently, disability was seen "almost exclusively" as an individualised medical problem or a personal tragedy in Western culture. Modernistic rationalities have for a long time dominated the fields of science, medicine and rehabilitation. In these fields, prejudicial understandings of disabled people became accepted rhetoric, systemically disavowing them from economic, social and cultural life (Barnes, 2020). In doing so, impairment was positioned as a biological abnormality and marker of difference that required fixing through medical, rehabilitative and aesthetic intervention in order to return the individual to the 'norm'. Disability was therefore constructed as an identity category that was a binary opposite to 'normal' people, with disabled people deemed inferior and victims of circumstance (Oliver, 1990). Consequently, in essentialising impairment as something that needs to be fixed and overcome, the identity of disability was designated as deviant or 'spoiled' (Goffman, 1963). This binary between the able and disabled leads to the development of dominant stereotypes of disability which affect every day social interactions. It also informs social policy, and shapes perceptions and practices amongst health professionals, governments and sport administrators. Whilst the importance of appropriate medical, rehabilitative and educational interventions is not undermined, ways of thinking informed by the medical model limit disabled people's opportunities for agency and empowerment. The medical model therefore ultimately acts as a hegemonic device, pathologising disabled people's lives, restricting material, perceptual and structural change resulting in them being subjugated, separated, and Othered. In response to these individual, pathologised tragic ways of understanding disability, the 'social' and 'minority' models of disability emerged which explicitly sought to illuminate the assumptions of the medical model by repositioning disability as a product of society, culture and the environment that surrounds it.

The Social Model

At the heart of the social model was the splitting of impairment and disability. Here, impairment was defined as *biological* (i.e. part of the body that was missing or deemed dysfunctional), and disability defined as a *social construction* (i.e. the prejudice and discrimination imposed on disabled people by a predominantly able-bodied society) (see Oliver, 1990). This distinction allowed emphasis to be placed on the material and structural barriers disabled people face in society and highlighted how impairment only becomes salient in specific settings (Oliver, 1992, 1996; Barnes & Mercer, 1996). As Barnes (2020: 20) asserts "impairment may be a human constant but 'disability' need not and should not be". Rather than disability being seen as an individual medical dysfunction that needs to be cured or fixed, the social model 'flipped' the argument, asserting that disability is constructed by society and that "disabled people are disabled not by their impairments but by society's inability to accommodate and include people with impairments" (Goodley, 2020: 12). In doing so, the social model can be conceptualised both as an exploratory device that aids our understanding of disability, and a counter-hegemonic device that radically challenges the medical model in influencing politics, policy and practice.

Undoubtedly then, the social model was integral in raising adverse perceptions and politicising disability through addressing structural inequality and providing a powerful set of tools for disability advocacy and ethically informed research. As an academic debate however, it has been subjected to a number of critiques. These centre around the controversial splitting of impairment and disability. Whilst this allowed attention to be turned away from a personal tragedy model to public problems of disablism, many scholars have highlighted how impairment should not be ignored as it forms the very essence of experience (e.g. Shakespeare, 2014). By suggesting that "disability is wholly and exclusively social" and "disablement is nothing to do with the body" (Oliver, 1996: 41–42) however, the social model excludes impairment and is therefore unable to adequately account for the embodied, emotive, psychological dynamics of experience (e.g. Shakespeare & Watson, 1997, 2001; Thomas, 2002, 2007).

In separating impairment from disability, the social model also disregards how pain, inability and tiredness are disabling in their own right (Morris, 1992; French, 1993) and gives insufficient attention to the ways in which alternative and multiple forms of impairment(s) come to be associated with different manifestations of disablism. This includes not adequately accounting for experiences of disablism enmeshed with other socially differentiating identities such as gender, race, sexuality and class. Feminist scholars for example have eloquently argued that by ignoring lived experience, the unique social and embodied realities of disabled women are marginalised (e.g. Morris, 1991). Under the social model, therefore, disability is situated as a universal, fixed, trans-historical social phenomenon that homogenises experience and ideologically privileges some disabled identities over others. Importantly, as Shakespeare (2006: 35) recognises, what actually counts as impairment is itself a social judgement, in that the definition and meaning of impairment "depend on the expectations and arrangements in a particular society". For him, impairment is "always already social, while disability is almost always intertwined with impairment effects. Impairment is only ever experienced in a social context" (ibid). In response to critiques, fierce rebuttal is offered by staunch social modellists who remain resolute that interpretative accounts of impairment and individual struggle are antithetical to collective effort (e.g. Barnes, 2020). Other advocates of the social model suggest impairment should be acknowledged more as an embodied experience shaped by culture rather than being essentialised and reduced to a biological entity (Abberley, 1996). More recently, many scholars (e.g. Goodley, 2014; Shildrick, 2020) have posited that theorising disability through the social model alone is not able to provide an explanation for *all* disabled people's exclusion or experiences of impairment. As Goodley (2017: 35) states, "A social model can only explain so much before we need to return to the experiential realities of 'impairment' as object(s) independent of knowledge".

In addition to the critiques emerging from the splitting of impairment and disability, the social model has been also been accused of: i) creating idealistic assumptions that social and environmental change and 'barrier-free utopia" is possible, positively impacting all disabled people's lives (Shakespeare, 2014), ii) being untransferable when conducting empirical research with disabled people (Shakespeare, 2014), and iii) not accounting for global understandings beyond British politics and manifestations of structural oppression (Goodley, 2011). In spite of these critiques, the social model remains at the very heart of the disability studies movement because it is the first attempt to politicise disability. However, not all activists and scholars are in agreement as to its utility. This is summarised by Shakespeare and Watson (2010: 57) who identify how allegiance to the social model acts like a 'litmus test' when making political and moral choices on what theoretical approaches to adopt – either align to this model and join the collective effort against structural oppression or be seen as not representing disabled people. The social model ultimately represents the disability community and much of the marginalisation and oppression felt by its membership. This is why contemporary national and international policies and laws use its rhetoric and advocate its importance. However, the material collective stance of the social model clouds the diversity of experience as understood by disabled people. As a result, there has been much academic interest in what other conceptual approaches might be employed to develop our understandings of disability.

Social Relational Model

Seeking to further develop the social model, Thomas (1999, 2004, 2007) championed a 'social relational model' (SRM) within which disability arises from the interactions between those embodying a privileged and powerful 'non-impaired' social status and those who are deemed insignificant and problematised due to having a physical and/or cognitive impairment. Analyses of these relationships provide insight into how people designated as having impairments are constrained and controlled in their interactions with those people designated as non-impaired. In doing so, the SRM is inclusive of both how impairment has direct and immediate effects on disabled people's experience (e.g. pain, functionality, physical weakness), known as *impairment effects*, and the effects of disabling and discriminatory conditions (e.g. structures, attitudes, perceptions) that impede engagement in everyday activities and participation in social life, known as the *psycho-emotional* dimensions of disability. Thomas (2007) points out that whilst "social barriers 'out there' certainly place limits on what disabled people can do" it is psycho-emotional disablism which "places limits on who they can be by shaping individuals 'inner worlds', sense of 'self' and social behaviours" (p.72). Through exploring these forms of social oppression, the SRM helps develop understandings of disablism by placing importance on the interplay between the individual and the social and cultural fashioning of experience. It allows for the more sophisticated exposure of socially and culturally constructed forms of oppression at different times, in different places, for different people (Goodley, 2013).

Models Approaches and Sport

Taking a models approach has advanced understandings of disability and helped develop critique in social science informed sport research. Historically, perceptions of disability and sport were underpinned by the medical model. Throughout time, sport has been seen as an exclusive preserve for the white, middle and upper-class, protestant, heterosexual, able-bodied male "majority" within capitalist society (DePauw, Bonace & Karwas, 1991). These beliefs served to exorcise disabled people from active participation and contribute to the very idea of elite sport for disabled people as anathema (Brittain, 2004) through positioning disabled people as biologically 'imperfect' within the 'perfecting' structures of sport (see DePauw & Gavron, 2005). In spite of the growing acceptance of disability sport, or more specifically parasport in the public consciousness of contemporary society, sport remains a prism through which medicalised views of disability and ableism persist. For example, disabled sporting bodies are exposed to the medical gaze through being inspected, assessed, quantified and surveilled in generating complex classification systems (Wheeler, 2004; Jones & Howe, 2005; Pickering Francis, 2005; Howe & Jones, 2006; Van Hilvoorde & Landeweerd, 2008) and subjected to supercripdom in which athletic achievements are belittled and instead positioned as evidence of 'overcoming' of the tragedy of impairment (Hardin & Hardin, 2004; Howe, 2011; Silva & Howe, 2012). Resultantly, disabled athletes continue to be subjected to economic, psychological, and cultural barriers affecting sports participation, restricting opportunity for agency (DePauw & Gavron, 2005; Thomas & Smith, 2009). Within high performance sport, the medical model promises utility precisely because the body remains constant in definitions of ability. However, as Townsend et al. (2016) argue, medicalised knowledge should be challenged in its application amongst sports coaches and practitioners when accounting for the individual needs of disabled athletes, providing specialist equipment and coaching strategies, and constructing classificatory competition. This involves coaches being knowledgeable about manifestations of ableism, being self-reflexive, developing innovative practices and being reciprocal in co-constructing knowledge. For example, in the field of strength and conditioning (S&C), Brighton (2018) outlines the negative consequences of the unquestioned perpetuation of the medical model through S&C coaches' non-reflexive practices, in which the wishes of athletes themselves were disregarded.

Whilst not denying the value of appropriate medical and rehabilitative intervention, the social model promises a more empowering approach to exploring the barriers and forms of social oppression encountered by disabled athletes (e.g. Brittain, 2004; Macbeth, 2009). However, there are well-established difficulties in applying this emancipatory model to empirical research (see Stone & Priestley, 1996; Mercer, 2002; Macbeth & Powis, this volume). Furthermore, although the social model remains a dominant idea in much disability sport research (Bundon & Hurd Clarke, 2015), it is often employed tokenistically (Powis, 2020). More encouragingly, the SRM has recently been employed effectively in disability sport research. For example, Haslett et al. (2017) utilise the SRM in interpreting the psychological experiences of participation amongst wheelchair rugby players and how their lives are shaped by individual, societal and cultural assumptions about physical disability and sport. Alternatively, Allan et al. (2020) use the SRM to highlight how interactions with coaches influenced disabled athletes' positive and negative experiences, making important pedagogical and practical recommendations for coaches working in disability sport. This research offers essential insight into the value of the SRM, but there remains a need to 'move beyond' just a models approach (Brighton et al., 2021) and be more open to the wealth of theories currently available from disability studies and the broader social sciences to progress understandings of disability inclusive of the social, cultural and psychological and the biological reality of the body (Goodley, 2013). A selection of these approaches and empirical applications in disability sport research will now be addressed in the sections below.

Sociocultural Approaches

Poststructural Approaches

Similarly to research emerging in the sociology of sport at the turn of the millennium, many scholars in disability studies shifted their attention to the linguistic analysis of disability. Presenting a move away from the materialist-economic origins of the social model, poststructural approaches to disability interrogate language, culture and the formation of dominant discourses in the construction of negative, medical and tragic understandings of disability. Dominant disability discourses, which have become essentialised or normalised as given 'truths' regulating and restricting disabled people in able-bodied 'normative' society, are deconstructed and challenged in order to revel disabling perceptions and practices (see the work of Corker & Shakespeare, 2002; Garland-Thomson, 1997, 2002, 2005; Tremain, 2002, 2005; Goodley, 2011, 2014; Mitchell & Snyder, 1997). Poststructural approaches therefore replace "truth with discourse and scrutinises the latter" (Goodley, 2011: 14) in questioning knowledge that has been regarded as 'natural'. In doing so, disabled people are not conceived as autonomous creators of themselves or their social worlds but constituted in and through specific social and cultural arrangements determining "which subjects appear, where and in what capacity" (Corker & Shakespeare, 2002: 3). Poststrucuturalist thinking in disability studies, led by the authors mentioned above, has been heavily influenced by foundational thinking of Foucault, Butler, Deleuze and Derrida[1]. Due to space restraints, we cannot cover all of these theorists. However, in order to give a flavour of how these works can challenge cultural construction and representation of disability, we shall address the influence of Derrida and Foucault here.

A body of Derrida's work questioned how we understand the world in binary opposites, thus giving precedence to one group over the other. As Corker (1999: 638) asserts, this serves to "deceive us into valuing one side of the dichotomy more than the other" and so we should be encouraged to deconstruct meaning as a way of breaking free from such oppositional thinking. For Corker, this involves examining how the biological (impairment) provides foundation for the social (oppression). Under such lenses, normativism and disability appear antagonistic. However, Derrida would argue that disability and impairment are central to each other's very construction, thus opposing social model thinking in which disability is conceptualised as a collective experience of oppression. As Corker and Shakespeare (2002: 7) distinguish: "…'normativism' needs 'disability' for its own definition: a person without an impairment can define him/herself as 'normal' only in opposition to that which he/she is not – a person with impairment".

Developing a social space in which identities could be constructed and liberated from constrains placed on disabled/non-disabled identities offers a way to challenge such binary positioning. This involves, for example, deconstructing the discourses through which disabled people learn to establish cultural competence by adhering to the functionalist sick role set by normative society (Thomas, 2007) or deconstructing the medical voices that regulate disabled people into patienthood in rehabilitation (e.g. Frank, 2000). Taking this into consideration, Derridean concepts can be employed in deconstructing the medical, rehabilitative and educational discourses which inform what sport disabled people choose to take part in and how participation is regulated and if 'inclusive' sporting spaces really offer potential to destabilise dualistic positioning of sporting bodies or if they are reproductive of disabled/non-disabled binaries. Alternatively, Derridean lenses might be employed in analysing dominant media texts that culturally position disabled athletes as inferior in comparison to able bodied athletes like Cockain (2020) has in deconstructing UK Channel 4's 2012 and 2016 Paralympic advertisements in which the Paralympians were labelled 'superhumans'. Although such campaigns might provide an example of what Frank (2000: 360) deems a "provisional reversal of this normal priority", caution should be taken in such analyses where meaning is subject to slippage and multiple re-readings in which the status quo is preserved once more.

Despite the potential for Derridean conceptualisation, disability sport research has utilised Foucault's works more often in revealing the discursive oppression faced by disabled athletes (e.g. Ashton-Shaeffer et al., 2001; Howe, 2008; Peers, 2012a, 2012b). These works employed Foucauldian genealogical methodologies to analyse contemporary power/knowledge structures, revealing how discourse and language shape social institutions and regulate individual attitudes and behaviours. In doing so, these scholars illuminated discursive normalising forces (termed the tools of 'governmentality') in problematising essentialist epistemologies, challenging the naturalness of a multitude of social issues and the disciplinary forces present in sustaining them. Of the 'toolkit' of conceptual ideas that Foucault forwarded, disability studies scholars have found particular value in analysing the forces of external surveillance that render disabled bodies (panopticonism) as docile. Also of importance is how discourses have become absorbed and infiltrated into the body (biopower) as well as the dynamics of internal surveillance and action (technologies of self) (e.g. see Tremain, 2002, 2005, 2006). Such analyses have helped reveal how people designated as 'disabled' and 'impaired' are understood, the social oppression and subjugation they experience, the disabling practices present in a multitude of contexts, and how disabled people come to normalise themselves as inferior. Significantly, elucidating ableism in these ways allows for making parallels with other oppressed groups in society in relation to gender, sexuality, race and ethnicity (Goodley, 2011).

For example, the power of Foucauldian theorisation is evocatively employed in Peers' work into the discursive construction of elite disabled sporting identities. Conceptualising that "both disability and impairment are produced and continually reproduced through enactments of power within specific power relationships" (2012a: 299), they employ a Foucauldian discourse analysis of historical Paralympic texts to illuminate how dominant discourses of disability and sport have (in)formed Paralympism and contest the seemingly straightforward and linear progression from rehabilitation to empowerment in elite sport. Rather, Peers demonstrates how these shifts are:

> ...alternatively characterized by the adoption, adaptation, and inter-weaving of a series of discourses that were previously embedded within sport, rehabilitation, and the freak show: discourses that have served to produce disabling practices, to reproduce (and produce new) disabled, able-bodied, and expert subjects, and to perpetuate the ability of Paralympic experts to limit the possible field of actions of those experiencing disability... Paralympic discourses and practices, in contrast to the claim of empowerment, are implicated in the perpetuation of the practices and unequal power relationships in and through which disability is experienced and sustained.
>
> (pp. 310–311)

Building on this work, Peers (2012b) utilises Foucauldian conceptualisation of the confessional, the examination and the panopticon to interrogate the construction and lived experience of their own Paralympic identity auto-ethnographically. Intertwining personal stories of their life, disablement and sporting career alongside media representations, they initially identify how they created themselves though the transparency of external surveillance. However, subsequently in their role as a critical researcher they were able to deconstruct "de-naturalise and to de-compose the dominant stories and practices of disability" (p.175) re-imagining possibilities of narrating and doing disability differently. Peers' work offers early examples of the potency of theoretical and methodological eclecticism in disability sport research, which sadly has not been adopted more extensively.

Reflecting a cultural turn, poststructuralism therefore provides an example of moving disability theory beyond materialist origins, challenging "the (over) reliance on crude dichotomies (social model versus medical model, impairment versus disability, disability studies versus medical sociology) and the neglect of culture and identity for issues of enquiry" (Shakespeare, 2014: 48). As Meekosha and Shuttleworth (2009: 50) highlight, such developments are pivotal in promoting not only the struggle for social, economic and political justice, but also the "psychological, cultural, discursive and carnal" essence of disability. Through revealing alternative forms of ableism in these ways, poststructural approaches can connect disability studies with social and minority models and transformative feminist, queer and critical race movements (Goodley, 2017). Recently, poststructural approaches have experienced a change of direction, moving "to interrogate the work done by disability to culture and the work done by culture to disability" (Goodley, 2017: 15). Accordingly, further research is required into the impact of disability sport and physical activity practices on culture. In particular, we suggest focus should be given to the gendered, sexed, classed and racial identities of disabled people that participate in sport and physical activity to challenge not only the multiple expressions of ableism that arise from embodying alternative identities but also how embodying a disabled identity can challenge the forms of oppression experienced by other minority groups. This could include research with disabled people who do not associate with being disabled or 'normal' and who instead create positive and proud disabled identities through sport that challenge the hegemony of normativism in their everyday lives (Corker & Shakespeare, 2002; McRuer, 2006).

In spite of the value of poststructural analyses, important critiques have been raised. Barnes (2020: 25), for example, returns to the key point that whilst poststructural approaches reinforce "the importance of the cultural in the process of disablement, they downplay the material reality of disabled people's lives" and fail to offer insight into how problem of institutional disablism might be resolved at a political level. Similarly, Shakespeare (2014: 52) argues that poststructuralists "generally seem much more interested in texts and discourses than in the ordinary lives of disabled people" spending less attention on addressing material conditions such as poverty, unemployment, and a lack of sports facilities and funding. Another key critique of poststructural theorisation is that it is discursively essentialist, thereby not adequately accounting for the living, breathing, sensing, sentient, emotional, visceral experiences of disability. This is addressed in more detail in the section on 'Disability and the Body' below, but first we turn attention to how the final sociocultural approach of this section can help us develop theoretically informed scholarship on disability sport and physical activity.

Practice Theory

The approach to understanding the social world posited by Pierre Bourdieu is commonly referred to as practice theory and has been used across the humanities and social sciences. Bourdieu (1977) argued that his theory of practice articulated that culture is neither simply a product of underlying structures nor the product of individual or collection of agency but rather is developed actively by cultural actors in relation to and structured by historical events. In this regard, he criticised his contemporaries' accounts of social practice by arguing that most social scientists do not forget objectivist grand theories of society, such as Marxism, but they must also avoid the unreflective use of the subjectivism of phenomenology and existentialism.

One of the reasons that Bourdieu's work has been adopted so readily in the social science of sport is that he is the only major social theorist to write directly on sport (Bourdieu, 1977). To understand Bourdieu's work there are three interrelated concepts (habitus, field and capital) that he highlights as central to the analysis of socio-cultural contexts in the study of the practice of daily life. For Bourdieu, these concepts and the struggles between them occur at micro, meso and macro levels (Kitchin & Howe, 2013) and shape what members of groups see as the world around them. To get a more detailed understanding we suggest exploring one of the many volumes that unpacks his concepts (for example Grenfell, 2014) before reading his original work.

Habitus is broadly related to an acquired character or nature that Bourdieu refers to as dispositions. This is a sense of an individual or social groups' place in the world that is embodied. The concept of habitus in Bourdieu's practice theory can also refer to social structures that constrain an individual and help them learn socially appropriate practice. For Bourdieu, the conceptualisation of field should be seen as the space in which social interactions takes place. These fields make up a society and can be autonomous or can exist in relation to one another. Because they are autonomous, they have their own structure and logic which are organised around different types of capital where struggles ensue between individuals and groups to gain or sustain an advantageous position in the field. It is import here to note that Bourdieu's use of capital is distinct. It does not simply mean money as it does in a traditional Marxist sense, it adds the idea that capital can also be cultural and symbolic as ways through which power and class positions are distinct. Capital, for Bourdieu, is a good with social value. In the context of disability sport, for example, an athletes' prowess to move their wheelchair around the athletics track in the fashion of a champion can, in the professional world of parasport, turn this cultural capital into financial reward. The importance of symbolic capital is evident in research in disability sport that articulates high profile athletes as supercrips (Howe, 2011; Silva & Howe, 2012) as well as at a macro level how the field of Paralympic studies may be articulated (Purdue & Howe, 2015).

Disability and the Body

Early disability studies scholarship avoided discussions of the body because they "tug – somewhat disconcertingly – at the key conceptual distinction which was at the heart of the transformation of disability discourse" (Hughes & Paterson, 1997: 325), that is, the splitting of impairment (biological) and disability (social). Increasingly however, disability scholars have explored how the body and bodily experience is integral in theorising the lives of disabled people and how revealing the rich carnality of lived experience can offer important critique of social and structural oppression. Of the approaches taken to bringing the body back in to disability studies, we address here i) phenomenological approaches, ii) narrative, iii) sensual, and iv) posthumanist perspectives and discuss the value each might hold in social research into disability sport.

Phenomenological Approaches

Phenomenological analyses of disability provide a response to both the biological determinism of the medical model and the discursive essentialism of poststructuralism. Of the multiple strands of phenomenology, Merleau-Ponty's (1945/2012) existential approach of being in the world as an 'embodied consciousness' have proved useful in transcending the Cartesian mind/body dualism and welcoming the materiality of the disabled body back into analysis. Central to these understandings are that we not only have a body, but we *are* our bodies. That is, our bodies are conceived of not merely as objects but as the loci through which we generate our subjective experiences and perspectives of the world. Accordingly, under phenomenological lenses, primacy is afforded to embodied or lived experience of impairment in the context in which it takes place. This allows for the development of a philosophical framework of studying disability that does not ignore the biological body – offering a stark contrast to disembodied notions of disability portrayed in the social model or poststructuralism.

Hughes and Paterson's (1997) work on the sociology of impairment was foundational in demonstrating the value of applying phenomenology to conceptualising and researching disability. In stressing that "the (impaired) body is not just experienced: It is also the very basis of experience" (p.335), they recognise the centrality of impairment on experiences of disability. This allowed for the corporeality, subjectivity and emotionality experienced by disabled people to be acknowledged. It also offered ways of problematising the impairment-as-biological distinction by re-claiming lost corporeal space by positioning body and consciousness and nature and culture as inseparable. Through this lens, impairment can be positioned as both physical (e.g. pain) and social (e.g. social barriers and perceptions an individual with impairment encounters) and should therefore be analysed as both an intracorporeal (self-perception) and an intercorporeal (perception of the other) phenomenon.

The sociology of impairment therefore adds "sentience and sensibility to notions of oppression and exclusion" (Paterson & Hughes, 1999: 335) and has become widely employed in empirical research into disability (e.g. Monden et al., 2014) helping to progress conceptualisation. For example, it underpins the SRM's concept of psycho-emotional effects of impairment by recognising the psycho-emotional dimensions of life necessitates embracing the materiality of the body and the lived, emotional, psychological experiences of disability. Recently, however, calls have been made for the further conceptual development of the sociology of impairment by highlighting the multiple forms of power simultaneously operating on the body as a result of multiple and intersecting embodiments of identity (e.g. race, class, sex, gender, age) (see Sherry, 2016).

Although the value of phenomenological approaches have been well debated in CDS (e.g. Diedrich, 2001; Papadimitriou, 2001; Abrams, 2016), in the same way as 'phenomenological' sociology of sport research (e.g. Allen-Collinson & Evans, 2019), few empirical accounts offer rigorous theoretical and methodological phenomenological frameworks. Perhaps due to its overt focus upon the essences of experience, without developing critical understandings of disability and politics (Goodley, 2011), this may not be surprising. Phenomenologically informed analyses of impairment are therefore often incorporated into broader theoretical frameworks in which they offer rich depiction of the corporeality and embodiedness of disabled peoples experience and how this helps reveal alternative forms of structural oppression.

For example, Apelmo (2012, 2017, 2018) explores the embodied experiences of young disabled women's participation in sport. She uses Merleau-Ponty's (1945/2012: 151) notion of the unity of the body to reveal how the shared experiences of joyousness, praise, invincibility, pride and happiness are felt during strength training and boxing amongst her participants. In doing so, they were able to transcend individual body parts and conscious bodily movement (which is often embedded in disability discourses, such as rehabilitation, where one is required to work on a specific body part) by not just having their bodies but becoming their bodies and transgressing gendered and ableist norms. Also employing phenomenologically informed approaches, Apelmo (2012, 2017) and other authors (e.g. Sparkes, Brighton & Inckle, 2017a; Monforte, Smith & Pérez-Samaniego, 2021) discuss how transcendence can be facilitated through amalgamation of technology with the impaired body. Here, it has been debated as to whether technology, through practice and routine over time, can be incorporated into one's 'natural' body, self, consciousness, and identity in a hybridised fashion at the agency of the owner. In becoming sedimented or embodied, new forms of what Merleau-Ponty (1945/2012) terms a habitual bodies, or the body that we become accustomed to, emerge.

Narrative

Narrative approaches to social research focus on in depth stories and how they are told and lived as cultural and personal models for arranging experience (Riessman, 2008). Storylines and the biographical particulars of the way people live are scrutinised in order to help reveal the complexity of human meaning and subjectivity (Chase, 2005; Smith & Sparkes, 2009a, 2009b). This involves analysing both the mechanics, or the hows, and the content, or the whats and whys, and how they arrange personal experience (Gubrium & Holstein, 2009). Offering a shift away from interactionism to a focus on the self and the body through which the meaning is revealed, narrative has courted criticism from some disability studies scholars for what they perceive as an "individualising" approach, diverting attention away from collective struggle (e.g. Finkelstein, 1996).

Smith and Sparkes (2008b) argue however, exploring narratives of disability and disablement offers much strength in disability studies including: "i) providing empirically grounded, thick, description of the rich sentience of embodied human experience; ii) enriching understandings of the self and identity over time; iii) taking into account the everydayness of embodied experience in helping to reveal difference; iv) enhancing our understandings of culture and language through speaking through an individual's story; v) acknowledging the temporality of our bodies and lives and the fluidity of identity construction, and; vi) allowing for explorations of agency and structure rather than limiting people as "passive recipients of an embodied behaviour and storyline" (Smith & Sparkes, 2008b: 18).

Rather than detract from the collective effort in challenging ableism therefore, narrative approaches, when politically motivated, offer precious ways of contributing to disability politics and activism through critiquing the influence of culture, power and discourse on the repertoire of storylines available for disabled people to live their lives. Importantly, narrative has emancipatory power. Storylines may be reflected on, reimagined and reconstructed at both the personal and the cultural level, empowering disabled people by resisting "dichotomous nature of modernist understandings of identity" (Butryn & Massuci, 2003: 126) and offering new ways of being.

Narrative research has proven instrumental in exploring the experiences of bodily loss and bodily contingency and illuminating how individuals undertake processes of narrative reconstruction having acquired disability (e.g. Yoshida, 1993). In particular, Arthur Frank's (1995) three dominant narrative types in response to illness within Western cultures have been utilised to good effect in disability research: i) 'restitution' in which emphasis and hope is placed on restoring the body; ii) 'chaos' in which life is never going to get better; and, iii) 'quest' in which the contingency of the body is accepted and suffering is used in travelling on new personal journeys. Sparkes and Smith (2002, 2003, 2005, 2011, 2012) and Smith and Sparkes (2002, 2004, 2005, 2008a, 2011) for example, vividly draw on these ideal storylines in their narrative research with men who have experienced spinal cord injury (SCI) and become disabled through playing the sport of Rugby Union to reveal how dominant narratives can be enabling or constraining. Frank's seminal work has also been employed effectively by Perrier, Smith, and Latimer-Cheung (2013) in their exploration of narratives of leisure time amongst individuals with spinal cord injury and by Brighton (2021) in his empirical derivation of the experiences of post-traumatic growth in disability sport following SCI.

Further examples of research incorporating narrative frameworks have highlighted its importance in investigating the storied dynamics between disability, sport, and health (Smith, 2013), disabled athletes' construction of activist identities (e.g. Smith, Bundon & Best, 2016), and the role of sport in recovery and growth following permanent acquired disability (Day & Wadey, 2016). Narrative has also proved fruitful in analysing autoethnographic accounts of disability and sport. For example, Lindemann (2010) interchangeably reflects on ethnographic findings of wheelchair rugby with his self-narrative of his relationship with his father to illuminate how disabled men literally and figuratively struggle to bring their bodies under control in achieving coherence between body and self and in (re)aligning with dominant narratives of masculinity and heteronormativity. More recently, Lumsdaine and Lord (2021) employ Franks narrative typologies to examine the sporting autoethnographic storylines told and lived by a young female disabled athlete with cerebral palsy and how they help her "make sense of who she was, who she is and who she can be" (p.1).

Such empirical investigations demonstrate the value of narrative approaches in revealing the storied, sentient, visceral experiences of disabled athletes. They also provide contextualised accounts of the oppressive cultural discourses in sport influencing the creation of what selves disabled athletes construct *and* how they can challenge the construction of these subjectivities opening up alternative liberatory and empowering storylines through which to live. Stories from disabled athletes who embody multiple intersecting identities in differing contexts should continue to be elucidated, helping inform policy and enhancing inclusivity. For example, Lumsdaine and Lord (2021) call for those in sport development positions to use narratives when designing and advertising their disability sport projects. A narrative turn in further social research into disability sport is therefore well warranted at a theoretical and applied level.

Sensuous Scholarship

Sensuous scholarship offers another way of revealing the grounded experiences of the disabled sporting body and the physical, psychological, emotional, social and cultural interpretations of the world in which it is located (e.g. Murphy, 1990; Sparkes, 2009). Responding to critiques of overly linguistic and incorporeal analyses of the body and ocularcentric ways of knowing in contemporary Western cultures, sensuous scholarship compels us to fully explore how we experience life as fleshy, sentient, embodied beings (e.g. Stoller, 1997; Howes, 2003, 2005). This approach focuses on all the senses and how they interplay, interact and blend with each other in structuring everyday experience, informing how we make sense of the world. In doing so, physical sensation is understood as more than a physiological response to a stimulus or structured by personal psychological experience. Rather, it is understood collectively as decorated by cultural ideology and practice as "the medium through which all the values and practices of society are enacted" (Howes, 2003: xi).

Taking this into account, scholars have recognised (e.g. Pink, 2009, 2010; Vannini et al., 2013) that sensuous scholarship should not be conceived of as just researching about the sensory body, but should emphasise "how it is experienced through a sensing, embodied subject" (Powis, 2020: 25). Such an approach reinforces how sensing and sense making cannot be separated from each other or from discourse, social interaction and performance in the creation of symbolic meaning. Analyses of how symbolic meaning is attributed to sensorial experiences have been termed as 'somatic work' by Waksul and Vannini (2008). Acknowledging the irreducibility between sensing and sense making (Vannini et al., 2013), this concept offers potential for exploring agency by analysing the dynamics between sensing, experiencing and meaning at both the individual and collective level. Uncovering sensuous experiences of disability therefore offers ways of revealing how the world is structured in restrictive and oppressive ways for individuals with impairments, but also how agency and resistance emerges through the very bodies that sense it.

In spite of these possibilities, social research into disability sport has not extended to include significant engagement with the sensorial dimensions of disability (Powis, 2020). As Howe (2011: 289) has previously commented however, greater understandings of how "our senses interpret how our bodies react with the social and the physical environment" will allow for more nuanced analyses between movement, identity and cultural interpretations of embodied difference in disability sport. This is clearly evident in examples of sensuous research that do exist. The majority of these contributions are located in visually impaired (VI) sport in which the usually dominant sense of sight is impaired. Here, Macpherson's (2009, 2011) research into a VI walking group, Hammer's (2015, 2017) accounts of VI and sighted tandem cyclists, and Powis' (2020) research into VI cricket all provide compelling examples of the power of sensuous scholarship in highlighting restriction, reproduction and oppression in disability sport as well as opportunity for empowerment, resistance, transgression.

Sensuous scholarship however should not be limited to addressing disabled athletes with sensorial impairments. While this is a start, we are all sensuous beings and as such this research should include attuning to the unique sights, sounds, smells, tastes, and touch sensed by disabled bodies in alternative sporting spaces and how they structure experience in differing ways. Such analysis could include, for example, how the odours associated with the disabled body, which have historically been stigmatising (Brittain & Shaw, 2007), are interpreted and managed in sport contexts. Alternatively, deeper analyses of touch and the way the disabled body feels under differing conditions will generate more informed understandings of disabled athletes' bodies and their location within the social structures of sport. For example, Sparkes and Brighton (2020: 426) explore the processes of embodied experiential learning undertaken by wheelchair rugby players with spinal cord injury who experience autonomic dysreflexia (AD), highlighting "the centrality of the sensory material body that feels the bio-physiological effects of AD and boosting as they occur, quite literally, in-the-flesh". Finally, as Brighton (2015) has previously commented on, embracing the senses in research matters not only theoretically, but methodologically in fostering reflexivity amongst researchers of disability sport. Sensuous scholarship, then, offers a concerted approach to exploring the carnal experiences of sensual disabled sporting bodies and the role of the senses in the construction of meaning.

As Sparkes (2017) suggests, re-thinking, re-feeling and re-engaging with the senses enlightens our interpretations of ways of being in sport, leisure and recreational activities by moving beyond constructionist or symbolic analysis and (re) connecting with primal ways of knowing and so should be creatively embraced in future research.

Post-Humanism

Post-humanism is best articulated through discourse that highlights what it means to be human and therefore unpacks what until recently we have taken for granted. For too long, society has prioritised a particular way of being human but, as we head deeper into the 21st century, scholars are beginning to question this. In some realms of sport studies, this may be termed new materialism. This term is used as a collective for a range of contemporary perspectives that focus on the materiality of the world, both in the social and natural contexts. The connection between post-humanism and new materialism is the questioning of the humanity and the material that we engage with.

Posthuman readings of the world are not new (Barad, 2003; Latour, 2004), but of late there has been an upswell of interest in this approach across the arts, humanities and social sciences (Herbrechter, 2013) which has led to much innovative work. In the field of physical cultural studies, a subdiscipline of the social science of sport, post-humanism and new materialism have been used to good effect (Howe & Morris, 2009; Markula, 2019;). In the field of disability studies there has been a growing interest in post-humanism (Goodley et al., 2014; Murray, 2020), particular related to ableism (Campbell, 2009; Cherney, 2019). In terms of research within disability sport the use of post-humanism is in its infancy (Silva & Howe, 2019; Howe & Silva, 2021, Monforte et al., this volume).

Crip studies, a sub-field of post-humanism, has also produced high-quality contributions. This theory or rather methodological approach to studying disability is the result of intersectional identity politics that combine disability studies with queer studies (McRuer, 2006, 2018). Like the other approaches to post-humanism highlighted above, it draws upon arts, humanities and social science perspectives to crip the world – that is to look at the world differently. It centres the research often using a collage of approaches to understand the lifeworlds of people who experience disability. In the realm of disability sport research, Danielle Peers is a leading advocate for the need to crip disability sport and we are lucky to have them involved in this current collection (see Chapter 7).

Reflections

In this chapter, we sought to provide a comprehensive overview of the historical origins of the disability studies movement in order to help social scientists in disability sport be mindful when locating their research. We have also aimed to explore the plurality of theories that are available to research disability sport and the lives of disabled athletes in order to expand our understandings of them. Each of these approaches has their uses. Researchers should therefore carefully consider which theory they should employ and why it most suits the specific phenomena under study. We also encourage researchers to not be transfixed by one approach, but be original, brave and creative in exploring through theoretical eclecticism. This is particularly important in 'post-qualitative' research (Monforte & Smith, 2021). Clearly there are many more theories that could be used to shed light on disability sport which we have not had space to include here. For example, the application of Bauman's liquid modernity (see Campbell, 2013; Brighton et al., 2021) or critical realist approaches might be particularly useful in exploring disability sport in the future. We urge others to take up the mantle here and reveal the extent of their value in further theorising the field and the lives of disabled athletes. Equally, be cautious of theory. For some (e.g. Shakespeare, 2014; Barnes, 2020) over theorisation serves to muddy the waters of political intent. We should therefore be sceptical of theoretical musings that replace activism, liberation, empowerment of disabled people. As Goodley (2017: 30) reinforces "a dalliance with social theory and complex language might obscure the very things research was meant to understand; the very conditions research should seek to reveal". Importantly therefore, whatever theory chosen in researching disability, it should be employed in a transformative, openly ideological way with the emancipation, empowerment, and political interests of disabled people foregrounded.

Note

1 Due to the multiple works and methods undertaken, we acknowledge that it is too simplistic to label these theorists as simply 'poststructuralists'.

References

Abberley, P. (1996). Work, Utopia and impairment. In Barton, L. (Ed.), *Disability and Society: Emerging Issues and Insights*. Harlow, Longman, pp. 61–82.

Abrams, T. (2016). Cartesian dualism and disabled phenomenology. *Scandinavian Journal of Disability Research*, 18(2): 118–128, doi:10.1080/15017419.2014.995219

Allan, V., Evans, M. B., Latimer-Cheung, A. E. & Côté, J. (2020). From the athletes' perspective: A social-relational understanding of how coaches shape the disability sport experience. *Journal of Applied Sport Psychology*, 32(6): 546–564.

Allen-Collinson, J. & Evans, A. (2019). To be or not to be phenomenology: That is the question. *European Journal for Sport and Society*, 16(4): 295–300, doi:10.1080/16138171.2019.1693148

Apelmo, E. (2012). Falling in love with a wheelchair: Enabling, disabling technologies. *Sport in Society*, 15(3): 399–408. doi:10.1080/17430437.2012.653208

Apelmo, E. (2017). *Sport and the Female Disabled Body*. London: Routledge.

Apelmo, E. (2018). 'You do it in your own particular way.' Physical education, gender and (dis)ability. *Sport, Education and Society*, 24(7): 702–713. doi:10.1080/13573322.2018.1452198

Ashton-Shaeffer, C., Gibson, H.J., Autry, C.E. & Hanson, C.S. (2001). Meaning of sport to adults with physical disabilities: A disability sport camp experience. *Sociology of Sport Journal*, 18(1): 95–114. doi:10.1123/ssj.18.1.95

Barad, K. (2003). Posthumanism Performativity: toward an understanding of how matter comes to matter. *Signs: Journal of Women in Culture and Society*, 28: 3 doi:10.1086/345321

Barnes (1990). *Cabbage Syndrome: The Social Construction of Dependence*. Lewes: Falmer.

Barnes, C. & Mercer, G. (1996). *Exploring the Divide: Illness and Disability*. Leeds: Disability Press.

Barnes, C. & Mercer, G. (2003). *Disability: Key Concepts*. Cambridge: Polity Press.

Barnes, C. (2020). Understanding the social model of disability: Past present and future. In N. Watson & S. Vehmas (Eds.). *The Routledge Handbook of Disability Studies* (pp. 14–31). London: Routledge.

Brighton, J. (2015). Researching disabled sporting bodies: Reflections from an 'able'-bodied ethnographer. In I. Wellard (Ed.), *Embodied Research in Sport*. London: Routledge, 163–177.

Brighton, J. (2018). Disability, spinal cord injury, and strength and conditioning: Sociological considerations. *Strength and Conditioning Journal*, 40(6): 29–39 doi:10.1519/SSC.0000000000000419

Brighton, J. (2021). Growth and adversity in disability sport following spinal cord injury. In R. Wadey, M. Day & K. Howells (Eds), *Growth Following Adversity in Sport*. London: Routledge.

Brighton, J., Townsend, R., Campbell, J. & Williams, T.L. (2021). Moving beyond models: Theorizing disability in the sociology of sport. *Sociology of Sport Journal*, 38(4): 386–398. doi:10.1123/ssj.2020-0012

Brittain, I. (2004). Perceptions of disability and their impact upon involvement in sport for people with disabilities at all levels. *Journal of Sport and Social Issues*, 28(4): 429–452.

Brittain, K.R. & Shaw, C. (2007). The social consequences of living with and dealing with incontinence – A carers perspective. *Social Science & Medicine*, 65(6): 1274–1283.

Butryn, T. M. & Massuci, M. A. (2003). It's not about the book: A cyborg counternarrative of Lance Armstrong. *Journal of Sport and Social Issues*, 27(2): 124–144.

Bundon, A. & Hurd Clarke, L. (2015). Honey or vinegar? Athletes with disabilities discuss strategies for advocacy within the Paralympic movement. *Journal of Sport and Social Issues*, 39(5): 351–370.

Bickenbach, J. (2020). The ICF and its relationship to disability studies. In N. Watson & S. Vehmas (Eds.), *The Routledge Handbook of Disability Studies* (pp. 45–54). London: Routledge.

Bourdieu, P. (1977). *Outline of a Theory of Practice*. Trans. Richard Nice. Cambridge, UK: Cambridge University Press.

DePauw, K., Bonace, B. & Karwas, M. (1991). Women and sport leadership. *Journal of Physical Education, Recreation & Dance*, 62(3): 32–34.

Campbell, F. K. (2009). *Contours of Ableism: The Production of Disability and Ableness*. London: Palgrave Macmillan.

Campbell, N. (2013). In times of Liquid Modernity: Experiences of the Paralympic Student-Athlete. Unpublished Doctoral dissertation: University of East London.

Chase, S. E. (2005). Narrative inquiry: Multiple lenses, approaches, voices. In N.K. Denzin & Y.S. Lincoln (Eds.), *The Sage Handbook of Qualitative Methods* (3rd ed, pp. 651–679). Thousand Oaks, CA: Sage Publications.

Cherney, J. L. (2019). *Ableist Rhetoric: How We Know, Value, and See Disability* (Vol. 11). University Park, Pennsylvania: Penn State Press.

Cockain, A. (2020). Reading (readings of) UK Channel 4's 2012 and 2016 Paralympic advertisements: On the undecidability of texts and dis/ability itself. *Journal of Literary & Cultural Disability Studies*, 14(3): 261–279.

Corker, M. (1999). Differences, conflations and foundations: The limits to 'accurate' theoretical representation of disabled people's experience? *Disability & Society*, 14(5): 627–642.

Davis, L.J. (2002). *Bending over Backwards: Disability Dismodernism and Other Difficult Positions*. New York: New York University Press.

Day, M.C. & Wadey, R. (2016). Narratives of trauma, recovery, and growth: The complex role of sport following permanent acquired disability. *Psychology of Sport and Exercise*, 22: 131–138.

DePauw, K.P. & Gavron, S.J. (2005). *Disability Sport* (2nd ed). Champaign, IL: Human Kinetics.

Diedrich, L. (2001). Breaking down: A phenomenology of disability. *Literature and Medicine*, 20(2): 209–230.

Finkelstein, V. (1996). Outside, 'Inside Out'. *Coalition*, April, 30–36.

Frank, A.W. (1995). *The Wounded Storyteller*. Chicago, IL: University of Chicago Press.

Frank, A. W. (2000). The standpoint of storyteller. *Qualitative Health Research*, 10(3): 354–365.

French, S. (1993). Disability, impairment or something in between? In J. Swain, V. Finkelstein, S. French & M. Oliver (Eds.), *Disabling Barriers—Enabling Environments* (pp. 17–25). London: Sage Publications, Inc; Open University Press.

Garland-Thomson, R. (1997). *Extraordinary Bodies: Figuring Physical Disability in American Literature and Culture*. New York: Columbia University Press.

Garland-Thomson, R. (2002). Integrating disability, transforming feminist theory. *NWSA Journal*, 14(3): 1–32.

Garland-Thomson, R. (2005). Feminist disability studies. *Signs: Journal of Women in Culture and Society*, 30(2): 1557–1587.

Goffman, E. (1963). Embarrassment and social organization. In N.J. Smelser & W.T. Smelser (Eds.), *Personality and social systems* (pp. 541–548). John Wiley & Sons Inc. doi:10.1037/11302-050

Goodley, D. (2011). *Disability Studies: An Interdisciplinary Introduction*. London: Sage

Goodley, D. (2013). Dis/entangling critical disability studies. *Disability & Society*, 28(5): 631–644.

Goodley. D. (2014). *Dis/Ability: Theorising disablism and ableism*. London: Routledge.

Goodley, D. (2017). *Disability Studies: An Interdisciplinary Introduction* (2nd ed.). London: Sage.

Goodley, D. (2020). *Disability and Other Human Questions*. London: Emerald Group Publishing.

Goodley, D., Lawthom, R. & Runswick-Cole, K. (2014). Posthuman disability studies. *Subjectivity*, 7(4): 342–361.

Grenfell, M.J. (Ed.). (2014). *Pierre Bourdieu: Key Concepts*. London: Routledge.

Gubrium, J. & Holstein, J. (2009). *Analysing Narrative Reality*. London: Sage.

Hammer, G. (2015). Pedaling in pairs toward a 'dialogical performance': Partnerships and the sensory body within a tandem cycling group. *Ethnography*, 16(4), pp. 503–522.

Hammer, G., 2017. Performing the sensory body in a tandem cycling group: Social dialogues between blindness and sight. In Andrew C. Sparkes (ed.), *Seeking the Senses in Physical Culture* (pp. 101–119). London: Routledge.

Hardin, M. & Hardin, B. (2004). The 'supercrip' in sport media: Wheelchair athletes discuss hegemony's disabled hero. *Sociology of Sport Online*, 7(1).

Haslett, D., Fitzpatrick, B. & Breslin, G. (2017). The psychological influences on participation in wheelchair rugby: A social relational model of disability. *Auc Kinanthropologica*, 53(1): 60–78.

Herbrechter, S. (2013). *Posthumanism: A Critical Analysis*. London: Bloomsbury.

Howe, P.D. (2008). From inside the newsroom: Paralympic media and the production of elite disability. *International Review for the Sociology of Sport*, 43(2): 135–150.

Howe, P.D. (2011). Cyborg and supercrip: The Paralympics technology and the (dis)empowerment of disabled athletes. *Sociology*, 45(5): 868–882. doi:10.1177/0038038511413421

Howe, P.D. & Jones, C. (2006). Classification of disabled athletes: (Dis)empowering the Paralympic practice community. *Sociology of Sport Journal*, 23(1): 29–46.

Howe, P.D. & Morris, C. (2009). An exploration of the co-production of performance running bodies and natures within 'running taskscapes'. *Journal for Sport and Social Issues*, 33(3): 308–330.

Howe, P.D. & Silva, C.F. (2017). Challenging 'normalcy': Possibilities and pitfalls of Paralympic bodies. *South African Journal for Research in Sport, Physical Education and Recreation*, 39(1:2): 191–204.

Howe, P. D. & Silva, C. F. (2021). Cripping the dis§abled body: Doing the posthuman tango, in through and around sport. *Somatechnic*, 11(2): 139–156. doi:10.3366/soma.2021.0348

Howes, D. (2003). *Sensual Relations: Engaging the Senses in Culture and Social Theory*. Michigan: University of Michigan Press.

Howes, D. (Ed.). (2005). *Empire of the Senses*. London: Berg.

Hughes, B. & Paterson, K. (1997). The social model of disability and the disappearing Body: Towards a sociology of impairment. *Disability & Society*, 12(3), 325–340. doi:10.1080/09687599727209

Jones, C. & Howe, P.D. (2005). The conceptual boundaries of sport for the disabled: classification and athletic performance. *Journal of the Philosophy of Sport*, 32(2): 133–146.

Kitchin, P. J. & Howe, P. D. (2013). How can the social theory of Pierre Bourdieu assist sport management research? *Sport Management Review*, 16(2): 123–134.

Latour, B. (2004). How to talk about the body? The normative dimension of science studies. *Body & Society*, 10(2–3): 205–229. doi:10.1177/1357034X04042943

Lindemann, K. (2010). Cleaning up my (Father's) mess: Narrative containments of "leaky" masculinities. *Qualitative Inquiry*, 16(1): 29–38. doi:10.1177/1077800409350060

Lumsdaine, G. & Lord, R. (2021). (Re)creating a healthy self in and through disability sport: Autoethnographic chaos and quest stories from a sportswoman with cerebral palsy. *Disability & Society*, 1–20. doi:10.1080/09687599.2021.1983415

Macbeth, J.L. (2009). Restrictions of activity in partially sighted football: Experiences of grassroots players. *Leisure Studies*, 28(4): 455–467.

Macbeth, J.L. & Powis, B. (this volume). What are we doing here? Confessional tales of non-disabled researchers in disability sport. In B. Powis, J. Brighton & P.D. Howe (Eds.), *Researching Disability Sport: Theory, Method, Practice*. London: Routledge.

Markula, P. (2019). What is new about new materialism for sport sociology? Reflections on body, movement, and culture. *Sociology of Sport Journal*, 36: 1–11.

Macpherson, H. (2009). The intercorporeal emergence of landscape: Negotiating sight, blindness, and ideas of landscape in the British countryside. *Environment and Planning A*, 41(5): 1042–1054.

Macpherson, H. (2011). Guiding visually impaired walking groups: Intercorporeal experience and ethical sensibilities. In M. Paterson & M. Dodge (Eds.), *Touching Place: Placing Touch* (pp. 131–150). Aldershot: Ashgate.

McRuer, R. (2002). Critical investments: AIDS, Christopher Reeve, and queer/disability studies. *Journal of Medical Humanities*, 23(3): 221–237.

McRuer, R. (2006). *Crip Theory: Cultural Signs of Queerness and Disability*. New York: New York University Press.

McRuer, R. (2018). *Crip Times: Disability, Globalization, and Resistance*. New York: New York University Press

Meekosha, H. & Shuttleworth, R. (2009). What's so critical about critical disability studies? *Australian Journal of Human Rights*, 15(1): 47–75. doi:10.1080/1323238X.2009.11910861

Merleau-Ponty, M. (1945). *Phenomenology of Perception* (2002 Reprint). London: Routledge Classics.

Mercer, G. (2002). Emancipatory disability research. In C. Barnes, M. Oliver, & L. Barton, (Eds.), *Disability Studies Today* (pp. 228–249). Cambridge: Polity Press.

Mitchell, D. & Snyder, S. (Eds.). (1997). *The Body and Physical Difference: Discourses of Disability*. Ann Arbor: University of Michigan Press.

Mitchell, D.T. & Snyder, S.L. (2020). Minority model: From liberal to neoliberal futures of disability. In N. Watson and S. Vehmas (Eds.), *The Routledge Handbook of Disability Studies* (pp. 45–54). London: Routledge.

Monden, K. R., Trost, Z., Catalano, D., Garner, A. N., Symcox, J., Driver, S., Hamilton, R. G. & Warren, A. M. (2014). Resilience following spinal cord injury: A phenomenological view. *Spinal Cord*, 52(3): 197–201.

Monforte, J. & Smith, B. (2021). Conventional and postqualitative research: An invitation to dialogue. *Qualitative Inquiry*, 27(6): 650–660.

Monforte, J., Smith, B. & Pérez-Samaniego, V. (2021). 'It's not a part of me, but it is what it is': The struggle of becoming en-wheeled after spinal cord injury. *Disability and Rehabilitation*, 43(17): 2447–2453.

Morris, J. (1991). *Pride against Prejudice: A Personal Politics of Disability*. London: Womens Press Ltd.

Morris, J. (1992). Personal and political: A feminist perspective in researching physical disability. *Disability, Handicap and Society*, 7(2): 157–166.

Moola, F.J. & Norman, M.E. (2012). Transcending 'hoop dreams': Toward a consideration of corporeality, crossroads and intersections, and discursive possibilities in disability and theory. *Qualitative Research in Sport, Exercise and Health*, 4(2): 284–295. doi:10.1080/2159676X.2012.685103

Murphy, R.F. (1990). *The Body Silent*. New York: Norton.

Murray, S. (2020). *Disability and the Posthuman: Bodies, Technology and Cultural Futures*. Liverpool: University of Liverpool Press.

Oliver, M. (1990). *Politics of Disablement*. Macmillan International Higher Education.

Oliver, M. (1992). Changing the social relations of research production. *Disability, Handicap and Society*, 7(2): 101–114.

Oliver, M. (1996). *Understanding Disability: From Theory to Practice*. London: Macmillan.

Papadimitriou, C. (2001). From dis-ability to difference: Conceptual and methodological issues in the study of physical disability. In S.K. Toombs (Ed.), *Handbook of Phenomenology and Medicine* (pp. 475–492). Dordrecht: Springer.

Paterson, K. & Hughes, B. (1999). Disability studies and phenomenology: The carnal politics of everyday life. *Disability and Society*, 14(5): 597–610. doi:10.1080/09687599925966

Peers, D. (2012a). Interrogating disability: The (de)composition of a recovering Paralympian, *Qualitative Research in Sport, Exercise and Health*, 4(2): 175–188. doi:10.1080/2159676X.2012.685101

Peers, D. (2012b). Patients, athletes, freaks: Paralympism and the reproduction of disability. *Journal of Sport and Social Issues*, 36(3): 295–316. doi:10.1177/0193723512442201

Perrier, M-J., Smith, B. & Latimer-Cheung, A. E. (2013). Narrative environments and the capacity of disability narratives to motivate leisure-time physical activity among individuals with spinal cord injury. *Disability and Rehabilitation*, 35(24): 2089–2096.

Pickering Francis, L. (2005). Competitive sports, disability, and problems of justice in sports. *Journal of the Philosophy of Sport*, 32(2): 127–132.

Pink, S. (2009). *Doing Sensory Ethnography*. London: Sage.

Powis, B. (2020). *Embodiment, Identity, and Disability Sport: An Ethnography of Elite Visually Impaired Athletes*. London: Routledge.

Purdue, D. E. J. and Howe, P. D. (2015). Plotting a Paralympic field: An elite disability sport competition viewed through Bourdieu's sociological lens. *International Review for the Sociology of Sport*, 50(1): 83–97.

Riessman, K. (2008). *Narrative Methods for the Human Sciences*. London: Sage.

Shakespeare, T. (2006). *Disability Rights and Wrongs*. London: Routledge.

Shakespeare, T. (2014). *Disability Rights and Wrongs Revisited*. London: Routledge.

Shakespeare, T. & Watson, N. (1997). Defending the social model. *Disability & Society*, 12(2): 293–300.

Shakespeare, T. & Watson, N. (2001). The social model of disability: An outdated ideology? Exploring theirs and expanding methodologies. *Research in Social Science and Disability*, 2: 9–28.

Shakespeare, T. & Watson, N. (2010). Beyond models: Understanding the complexity of disabled people's lives. In S. Scambler & G. Scambler (Eds.), *New Directions in the Sociology of Chronic and Disabling Conditions* (pp. 57–76). London & New York: Palgrave Macmillan.

Sherry, M. (2016). A sociology of impairment. *Disability & Society*, 31(6): 729–744.

Shildrick, M. (2020). Critical disability studies: Re-thinking the conventions for the age of postmodernity. In N. Watson & S. Vehmas (Eds.), *The Routledge Handbook of Disability Studies* (pp. 32–44). London: Routledge.

Silva, C. F. & Howe, P. D. (2012). The [in]Validity of *supercrip* representation of Paralympic athletes. *Journal for Sport and Social Issues*, 36(2): 174–194. doi:10.1177/0193723511433865

Silva, C. F., & Howe, P. D. (2019). Sliding to reverse Ableism: An ethnographic exploration of (dis) ability in sitting volleyball. *Societies*, 9(2): 41.

Smith, B. (2013). Sporting spinal cord injuries, social relations and rehabilitation narratives: An ethnographic creative non-fiction of becoming disabled through sport. *Sociology of Sport Journal*, 30(2): 132–152.

Smith, B. & Bundon, A. (2018). Disability models: Explaining and understanding disability sport in different ways. In I. Brittian & A. Beacom (Eds.), *The Palgrave Handbook of Paralympic Studies* (pp. 15–34). London: Palgrave MacMillan.

Smith, B., Bundon, A. & Best, M. (2016). Disability sport and activist identities: A qualitative study of narratives of activism among elite athletes' with impairment. *Psychology of Sport and Exercise*, 26: 139–148. doi:10.1016/j.psychsport.2016.07.003

Smith, B. & Perrier, M.J. (2014) Disability, sport and impaired bodies: A critical approach. In R.J. Schinke & K. R. McGannon (Eds.), *The Psychology of Sub-culture in Sport and Physical Activity: Critical Perspectives* (pp. 95–106). London: Routledge.

Smith, B., & Sparkes, A. C. (2002). Men, sport, spinal cord injury, and the construction of coherence: Narrative practice in action. *Qualitative Research*, 2(2), pp.143–171.

Smith, B. & Sparkes, A.C. (2004). Men, sport, and spinal cord injury: an analysis of metaphors and narrative types. *Disability and Society*, 19(6), pp. 613–626.

Smith, B. & Sparkes, A.C. (2005). Men, sport, spinal cord injury and narratives of hope. *Social Science & Medicine*, 61(5), pp. 1095–1105.

Smith, B. & Sparkes, A.C. (2008a). Changing bodies, changing narratives and the consequences of tellability: A case of becoming disabled through sport. *Sociology of Health & Illness*, 30(2), pp. 217–236.

Smith, B. and Sparkes, A.C. (2008b). Narrative and its potential contribution to disability studies. *Disability & Society*, 23(1), pp. 17–28.

Smith, B., & Sparkes, A.C. (2009a). Narrative analysis and sport and exercise psychology: Understanding lives in diverse ways. *Psychology of Sport and Exercise*, 10(2): 279–288.

Smith, B. & Sparkes, A.C. (2009b). Narrative inquiry in sport and exercise psychology: What can it mean, and why might we do it? *Psychology of Sport and Exercise*, 10(1): 1–11.

Smith, B., & Sparkes, A. C. (2011). Exploring multiple responses to a chaos narrative. *Health: An Interdisciplinary Journal for the Study of Health, Illness and Medicine*, 15(1), pp. 38–53.

Sparkes, A. C. (2009). Ethnography and the senses: Challenges and possibilities. *Qualitative Research in Sport, Exercise and Health*, 1(1): 21–35. doi:10.1080/19398440802567923

Sparkes, A.C. (2017). *Seeking the Senses in Physical Culture: Sensuous Scholarship in Action*. London & New York: Routledge.

Sparkes, A.C., Brighton, J. & Inckle, K. (2014). Disabled sporting bodies as sexual beings: Reflections and challenges. In J. Hargreaves & E. Anderson (Eds.), *Routledge Handbook of Sport, Gender and Sexuality* (pp. 199–208). London: Routledge.

Sparkes, A.C. & Smith, B. (2002). Sport, spinal cord Injury, embodied masculinities and the dilemmas of narrative identity. *Men and Masculinities*, 4(3): 258–285.

Sparkes, A.C., & Smith B. (2003). Men, sport, spinal cord injury and narrative time. *Qualitative Research*, 3(3): 295–320.

Sparkes, A.C. & Smith, B. (2005). When narratives matter: Men, sport and spinal cord injury. *Journal of Medical Ethics*, 31(2): 81–88.

Sparkes, A.C. & Smith, B. (2011). Inhabiting different bodies over time: Narrative and pedagogical challenges. *Sport, Education and Society*, 16: 357–370.

Sparkes, A.C., & Smith, B. (2012). Narrative analysis as an embodied engagement with the lives of others. In J. Gubrium & J. Holstein, (Eds.), *Varieties of Narrative Analysis* (pp. 53–73). London: Sage.

Sparkes, A.C. & Smith, B. (2014). *Qualitative Research Methods in Sport, Exercise and Health: From Process to Product*. Abingdon & New York: Routledge.

Sparkes, A., Brighton, J. & Inckle, K. (2017a). Imperfect perfection and wheelchair bodybuilding: Challenging ableism or reproducing normalcy? *Sociology*, 52(6): 1307–1323.

Sparkes, A.C., Brighton, J. & Inckle, K. (2017b) 'It's a part of me': An ethnographic exploration of becoming a disabled sporting cyborg following spinal cord injury. *Qualitative Research in Sport, Exercise & Health*, 10(2): 151–166.

Sparkes, A., Brighton, J. & Inckle, K. (2017c). Imperfect perfection and wheelchair bodybuilding: Challenging ableism or reproducing normalcy? *Sociology*, 52(6): 1307–1323.

Sparkes, A.C. & Brighton, J. (2020) Autonomic dysreflexia and boosting in disability sport: Exploring the subjective meanings, management strategies, moral justifications, and perceptions of risk among male, spinal cord injured, wheelchair athletes. *Qualitative Research in Sport, Exercise and Health*, 12(3): 414–430.

Stoller, P. (1997). *Sensuous Scholarship*. Philadelphia, PA: University of Pennsylvania Press

Stone, E. & Priestley, M. (1996). Parasites, pawns and partners: Disability research and the role of non-disabled researchers. *British Journal of Sociology*, 47(4): 699–716.

Thomas, C. (1999). *Female Forms: Experiencing and Understanding Disability*. Buckingham: Open University Press.

Thomas, C. (2002). The 'disabled' body. M. Evans & E. Lee (Eds.), *Real Bodies* (pp. 64–78). Basingstoke: Palgrave MacMillan.

Thomas, C. (2004). Rescuing a social relational understanding of disability. *Scandinavian Journal of Disability Research*, 6(1): 22–36.

Thomas, C. (2007). *Sociologies of Disability, 'Impairment', and Chronic Illness: Ideas in Disability Studies and Medical Sociology*. London: Palgrave MacMillan.

Thomas, N. & Smith, A. (2009). *Disability, Sport and Society: An Introduction*. London: Routledge.

Townsend, R. C., Smith, B. & Cushion, C. J. (2016). Disability sports coaching: Towards a critical understanding. *Sports Coaching Review*, 4(2): 80–98.

Tremain, S. (2002). On the subject of impairment. In M. Corker & T. Shakespeare (Eds.), *Disability/Postmodernity: Embodying Disability Theory* (pp. 32–47). London & New York: Continuum.

Tremain, S. (2005). Foucault, governmentality and critical disability theory: An introduction. In S. Tremain (Ed), *Foucault and the Government of Disability* (pp. 1–26). Michigan: University of Michigan Press.

Tremain, S. (2006). *Foucault and the Government of Disability*. Ann Arbor: University of Michigan Press.

Vannini, P., Waskul, D. & Gottschalk, S. (2013) *The Senses in Self, Society and Culture: A Sociology of the Senses*. New York and London: Routledge.

Van Hilvoorde, I. & Landeweerd, L. (2008). Disability or extraordinary talent Francesco Lentini (three legs) versus Oscar Pistorius (no legs). *Sport, Ethics and Philosophy*, 2(2): 97–111.

Vehmas, S. & Watson, N. (2014). Moral wrongs, disadvantages, and disability: A critique of critical disability studies. *Disability & Society*, 29(4): 638–650.

Waksul, D.D. & Vannini, P. (2008). Smell, odor, and somatic work: Sense-making and sensory management. *Social Psychology Quarterly*, 71(1): 53–71. doi:10.1177/019027250807100107

Wendell, S. (1996a). *The Rejected Body: Feminist Philosophical Reflections on Disability*. London: Routledge.

Wendell, S. (1996b). Towards a feminist theory of disability. In L.J. Davis (Ed.), *The Disability Studies Reader* (pp. 260–279). London: Routledge.

Wheeler, G.D. (2004). Ethical aspects in sports participation. In E. Kioumourtzoglou & K. Politis (Eds.), *Paralympic Games from 1960 to 2004*. Athens: Organising Committee for the Olympic Games. Athens: International Olympic Committee.

Yoshida, K.K. (1993). Reshaping of self: A pendular reconstruction of self and identity among adults with traumatic spinal cord injury. *Sociology of Health and Illness*, 15(2): 217–245.

Chapter 3

Cultural Politics, Disability Sport and Physical Activity Research

P. David Howe

I have for as long as I can remember been fascinated with the political meaning in and around physical bodies. Growing up, to borrow a phrase from the British television show *Little Britain*[1] '*as the only spaz in the village*', I was made constantly aware – whether through teasing, bullying and/or exclusion – that the physical difference in my body mattered. It had a significance that, at a young age, I was unable to make sense of. My parents made me believe I was singled out as marginal to groups because others were jealous of the life I had. While this was a complete fallacy, it enabled me to survive my youth. As I approach old age – closer to the end of my life than the beginning – I am able to be reflective of my own material positioning within this lifeworld.

> Disabled people are often conceived of as anything but socio-political actors. It is also within this culture, and again without much academic resistance, that disabled people are researched, rehabilitated, treated, operated on, incarcerated, and trained, as if all of these are natural events and not social and political ones.
>
> (Titchkosky, 2003: 38)

When I decided to explore the significance of cultural politics, or rather revisit it for this current volume on *Researching Disability Sport*, I was annoyed to find that I had not explicitly defined it in the monograph I wrote entitled *The Cultural Politics of the Paralympic Movement* (Howe, 2008a). This is ironic and sloppy as the first thing I tell my students is "to define the definables". Definables being all the significant terms in any argument. This approach was the hallmark of my undergraduate training in social anthropology and philosophy. I still endeavour to utilise it today because it is important that your audience (whether that be a professor in a course, your peers, or the general public) understand the dissemination of ideas both simple and complex, because the act of communication is why we write.

Due to my oversight in not defining cultural politics years ago, perhaps because I felt the term was self-explanatory, I will explain it here. Cultural politics, simply (and clearly to me at least!) describes the fact that politics at all levels is heavily

DOI: 10.4324/9781003153696-4

influenced by specific cultural practices. In other words, if the International Paralympic Committee (IPC) had been developed by traditional tribal societies in sub-Saharan Africa, its form would be distinct from the Euro-centric organisation that was developed in the 1980s. Of course, I have chosen a stark analogy here, but it serves as a useful reference. Neo-colonialism (Nkrumah, 1965) in this case associated with sport and the development of its international infrastructure, such as the IPC, have been built upon the oppression of non-Western cultural values (Wolf, 1982). This continues in spite of (or dare I say because of) the Universal Declaration of Human Rights that was a hallmark of diplomacy post World War II. From here we see the speeding up of new forms of neo-colonialism through the process of globalisation (Giulianotti, 2015) and neo-liberalism (Silk and Andrews, 2012) as the world becomes smaller because of the advancement of movement and communication technologies. In this context, sport can be understood in what Maguire (2011) calls the global media sport complex.

The cultural politics of contemporary sport and physical activity is a minefield where high-performance national sporting federations and government sporting agencies have political influence. At the international level, federations and highly commercialised professional sports leagues (think of the English Premier League [soccer] or any one of a number of North American professional sports leagues) are held to account by bigger influencers than national or international governance. They are held to task by multi-national corporations that in a time of neo-liberalism hold the balance of power (Silk and Andrews, 2012). In this case the corporations are driving the car from the backseat, in hopes that no one will notice. Students and colleagues in the social sciences and humanities are likely to know this already, but I think reiterating the cultural politics surrounding sport and physical activity is useful because it gives us a platform from which to explore in more detail how this landscape impacts upon individuals who experience disability.

In order to explore the relationship between the cultural politics and disability sport we must first address some of the fledgling arguments within disability studies. One word of caution before we proceed. I believe the personal is political (Howe, 2018). As a former Paralympic athlete and as an outspoken advocate for the needs of people who experience disability to have voice (and I am well aware of the privilege it is to have my own), for the largely able-bodied audience of this volume, some of what I have to say may cause discomfort – and it should! I suggest you work through it by reflecting on your own positionality in this vital field of research. Bear with me – my attacks are not personal but rather are designed to illuminate the insidiousness of cultural politics surrounding the ideology of ableism.

Grounding the Critique in Robust Disability Studies

Much of the high-quality research that is in the diverse field of disability studies has in recent years preferred the term 'critical' disability studies. While there are many scholars that use the term to good affect (see Goodley, 2014, as well as some of the scholars in this volume), I worry that the less insightful will assume they are critically engaged – simply because the term is an adjective front and centre in their description of the work they are doing. As our field of scholarship expands, there is an increased likelihood of poor-quality research obscured by an up-to-date rhetoric. If I were more influential in the field of critical disability studies, I would push for a name change to *neo* disability studies which more accurately reflects the new focus of enquiry. Perhaps because I am an aging scholar in a related subfield, when I am writing as the only author of a publication, I prefer to refer to the field as simply disability studies.

I have long preached that a great grounding for critical engagement into the field of the cultural politics of disability sport can be grounded in three foundational texts: Goffman's *Stigma: notes on the management of spoiled identity* (1963); Murphy's *The Body Silent* (1987) and Oliver's *The Politics of Disablement* (1990). Some readers may be disappointed that these texts are all written by white male academics. I am aware of this privilege (one which I share), but these are all high-quality writings in this field, which only has a relatively brief history. Much excellent feminist scholarship developed from these seminal works (see Garland-Thompson, 1997; Thomas, 1999). Goffman was most certainly abled bodied at the time he wrote *Stigma*. Murphy's ethnographic text chronicles the moment he acquired his impairment to his death (the book was finished by his widow and fellow anthropologist Yolanda Murphy) as his body became completely silent. Oliver's treatise of political activism that brought the social model of disability to a diverse audience was written by him as an established academic who experienced disability. For me, these books are foundational because they poked my internal political fire at significant points in my own academic development and can provide a robust grounding for students and scholars alike (Kerr & Howe, 2017) to move the political agenda forward. However, there has been a desire to keep politics out of issues surrounding people who experience disability.

> Our culture is only too ready to separate its images of disability and disability discourse from any sense of the social and political organization of the meaning of disabled people's lives. Disabled people's lives can be understood as being led side-by-side with an unexamined cultural temptation to obliterate disability from social thought.
>
> (Titchkosky, 2003: 39)

In his landmark work *The Politics of Disablement* (1990) Oliver makes a conscious attempt at formulating a social understanding of disablement based on the theoretical insights of Marx and Gramsci. Though disability sport and physical activity does not feature in the text, the argument highlights that the Western construction of disability is an individual medicalised problem, which enables society at large to marginalise and control many of those who experience disability. This work made a vital contribution to allowing social scientists to re-evaluate the research on disability from a critical though increasingly unfashionable perspective. With the increased interest in post-modern and post-structural accounts of identity formation (Riddell and Watson, 2003), Oliver's overtly structural analysis has fallen out of favour. However, a collective understanding of a community still has value in attempting to determine if there are common experiences that are shared.

> The hegemony that defines disability in a capitalist society is constituted by the organic ideology of individualism, the arbitrary ideologies of medicalisation underpinning medical intervention and personal tragedy theory underpinning much social policy. Incorporated also are ideologies related to the concepts of normality, able-bodiedness and able-mindedness
>
> (Oliver, 1990: 44)

Therefore, if research were to abandon an agenda for equity and the redistribution of goods and services in favour of a focus upon diversity and difference, we might find ourselves in a situation where the limited critique of structural inequalities may impact upon how the people who experience disability can be represented (Riddell and Watson, 2003: 2). I am not suggesting here that individual identity is not important rather individual identity, which in the case of athletes who experience disability is partly determined by type and degree of impairment, is less significant when looking at how sport and physical activity are organised.

For scholars within the multidisciplinary field of disability studies, Oliver's historical material account of the creation of the 'problem' of disability led to its conceptualisation as a social constraint. The resulting 'social model of disability', which was initially developed in the 1960s, was brought to a wider audience in the publication of *Fundamental Principles of Disability* (UPIAS, 1975), a political statement of intent by the Union of the Physically Impaired Against Segregation. These ideas were subsequently shared through the work of Oliver (1990, 1996) and others (Barnes, 1991; Thomas, 1999).

> In our view, it is society which disables physically impaired people. Disability is something imposed on top of our impairments by the way we are unnecessarily isolated and excluded from participation in society. Disabled people are therefore an oppressed group
>
> (Oliver, 1996: 22)

If disability is a social construction, a product of medicalisation, as those who advocate a social model of disability suggest, it is perhaps not surprising that so little attention within disability studies has been paid to the practice of sport which has traditionally classified bodies on medical grounds.

The Category of Disability

The notion of the categorisation of impairments that leads directly to a marginal position in society stems from the work of Goffman (1963). Categorising the body based on its degree of difference places it on a continuum where one trait may make an individual less marginalised than someone else who exhibits another different trait. *Stigma: Some Notes on the Management of Spoiled Identity* (1963) was one of the first studies that drew attention to the nature of the problem of the stigmatisation of different people. Some critics (Barnes, 1991; Oliver, 1990) have argued that the role of studies of stigma was an attempt to medicalise disability in order to classify it in respect to the predominate views of normality. However, these scholars fail to see the value in the categorisation along medical lines as a way of making sense of difference (Kerr and Howe, 2017). For this reason, Goffman's work on stigma is useful when exploring the categorisation or rather classification of para-athletes who experience disability. After all, the practice of classifying for sport is largely a medical one that can, if not properly managed, lead to stigmatisation and alienation because it can ultimately create a hierarchy of bodies. Turner's conceptualisation of 'liminality' (1967, 1969) is also useful since it positions stigmatised individual at the margins of society. Murphy in *The Body Silent* (1987) utilises the concept of liminality suggesting

> 'Betwixt and Between,' is actually a neat description of the ambiguous of the disabled. ... The long-term physically impaired are neither sick nor well, neither dead nor fully alive, neither out of society nor wholly in it. They are human beings but their bodies are warped or malfunctioning, leaving their full humanity in doubt. They are not ill, for illness is transitional to either death or recovery. Indeed, illness is a fine example of nonreligious, nonceremonial liminal condition. The sick person lives in a state of social suspension until he or she gets better. The disabled spend a lifetime in a similar suspended state.
>
> (Murphy, 1987: 131)

Liminality therefore allows us to see people who experience disability not as entirely marginal but on the edge of society. There is a 'symbolic order' (Douglas, 1966) where those who exhibit normal bodies and behaviours are given priority. The concept of liminality illuminates the position of the people who experience disability in society. In order to improve the position of people who experience disability, those working within disability studies have often adopted an emancipatory paradigm for their research. To this end Barnes (1992) suggests,

> Emancipatory research is about the systematic demystification of the structures and processes which create disability, and the establishment of a workable 'dialogue' between the research communitas and the disabled people in order to facilitate the latter's empowerment.
>
> (1992: 122)

This approach to research is explicitly politically driven and is implicitly at the heart of many of the chapters in this current volume. As Charlton (1998) has suggested in the title of his thought-provoking work *Nothing about us Without us*, it is paramount that we all remember this mantra – even those of us who experience disability because we can be ableist from time to time (See Silva, this volume). The engagement with emancipatory research is of vital important if we are to prioritise the elimination of ableism by embarking on the exploration of social issues that impact upon people who experience disability from the perspective of explicit advocacy.

Move to Explicit Advocacy

In a number of academic outlets (Howe, 2008a, 2008b, 2018) I have talked personally about my involvement in the Paralympic movement. But what I have not been explicit about is the detail of my first attempt to seek an office to help enact political change. My writing may be devoid of this narrative in part because of my lack of success in achieving any worthwhile lasting change.

Some of my earliest memories revolve around 'passing as normal' so that the teasing and bullying of me would stop. My body was not normal in my small-town community (or anywhere for that matter) and so I was ever so conscious of trying to hide my difference (Goffman, 1963). While things improved when I became an adult and I realised I have had a very privileged life, I am still unable to celebrate my experience of disability the way so many high-profile advocates do. This is of course a potential failing on my part, but it is also an acknowledgement that we all live in an able-bodied world that is enshrined in an ideology of ableism (Goodley, 2014; Naro-Redmond, 2020). It was not until after I had attended the Barcelona 1992 Paralympic Games that my unease with the Paralympic movement (Howe, 2008a, 2008b) began to boil over. I was frustrated on two fronts that I still find problematic today. First, the IPC was (and unfortunately still is) governed by the ethos of an able-bodied moral majority that situates people who experience disability as inferior. Second, and just as importantly, the athletes in the Paralympic village seem to be placed in a hierarchy (Sherrill, 1999) based upon the degree to which their body was distant from the societal norm. Those whose bodies were closer to the norm were seen as legitimate Paralympic athletes and others were not. Ultimately, it is the bodies that are cyborgs (Howe, 2011; Silva and Howe, 2012; Howe and Silva, 2017) and the most able that continue to have a privileged position within parasport.

My frustration with what I saw as the marginal position of severely impaired bodies in the Paralympic movement forced me to take direct political action. This action was not a storming of the Bastille as was the case in the French Revolution, but it was much more modest. While in the dining hall at the 1996 Paralympic Games in Atlanta, USA – which were extremely poorly organised – I saw a poster advertising elections for an athlete's representative to the IPC Athletics committee. This official election was done live with athletes who wished to have the role delivering a speech of up to 10 minutes in length and then a number of rounds of voting took place until there was a final ballot between two candidates. I went along to the meeting to see who was running for the position. My intent had not been to run but support the individual I thought would do the best for the athletes in my sport. When it became clear that a high-profile male T54 wheelchair racer (who competed in the Olympic demonstration 1500m in both 1996 and 2000) was likely to be the winner of the election – I begrudgingly put myself forward. I was fearful that this athlete with Hollywood good looks, a chiselled torso and a desire to have closer ties with mainstream sport – for athletes like himself – needed to be stopped. We were the last two athletes on the final ballot, and I was able to convince the audience (voters) that I would represent a larger demographic of our membership if I was elected – so I got the position.

I do not remember experiencing any joy associated with my election victory as later that afternoon I met the IPC Athletics Committee and realised what a struggle my four-year tenure would be. This technical committee was made up of representatives from the International Sports Organisation for the disabled (IOSDs). These federations – Cerebral Palsy International Sport and Recreation Association (CP-ISRA), International Blind Sport Association (IBSA), International Stoke Mandeville Wheelchair Sports Federation (ISMWSF), International Sport Organisation for the Disabled (ISOD)[2] and the International Sports Federation for Persons with Intellectual Disability (INAS-FID)[3] – were established with the explicit intention of creating opportunities for people who experience disability and using sport as a vehicle for their empowerment. As well as these members, the committee executive was made up of individuals who were also athletics officials. This proved problematic. While they all had international experience in organising and running athletics events, these skills (and the dispositions that developed alongside them) acted as a fire-retardant foam to any athlete-centred development that might be a result of such a committee. Key for this committee executive was running well organised and efficient track and field athletic competitions, which meant that the executive at least was willing to sacrifice diversity in classification.

Classification has long been a significant political issue in the Paralympic movement (Howe and Jones, 2006; Howe, 2008a; Purdue and Howe, 2013). In 2008, I went so far as to suggest in a title of a paper that classification is the *Tail is Wagging the Dog* (Howe, 2008b). I still believe that the cultural politics surrounding the parasport classification system has far too great an influence upon the opportunities of para-athletes to experience sport at the highest level. Over my time on the IPC Athletics committee, I was constantly trying to stop the erosion of competitive opportunities for athletes who would not get them outside of parasport. It was a political battle I constantly felt I was losing – because the committee felt its mandate was to run an efficient IPC athletics meet whenever they were called upon. The only significant change I was able to help initiate was the inclusion of race running[4] as a demonstration event at the 1998 IPC World Athletics Championship in Birmingham, UK, and at the Sydney 2000 Paralympic Games. This athletic discipline allows athletes who have severe balance issues to use a three wheeled support frame to propel themselves around the track. The invention of this discipline is important for the inclusion of more athletes with high support needs within the athletics program of IPC sport events but, at the time of writing, it had still not made its debut as a full medal event at the Paralympic Games.

After my term ended as athlete's representative at the Sydney 2000 Paralympic Games, I was appointed as the Athletics Technical lead for CP-ISRA where my stated aim was to ensure the greatest opportunity for athletes with cerebral palsy at IPC events. This included the athletes who used racerunning frames. My tenure in this position lasted until the Athens 2004 Paralympic Games but, judging by the fact that there was an increased erosion of competitive opportunities for athlete with cerebral palsy, I realised I was unsuited to such political roles. It was at this time – having retired from competitive sport in 2003 – I decided my contribution to the politics of the Paralympic movement would be to insight awareness of cultural issues that had political consequences for people who experienced disability and wished to engage in high performance sport. Whether as an academic I have been successful in this form of political resistance is yet to be fully revealed. But I and like-minded academic critics (many of whom have also written in this volume) realise that igniting the spark that starts a revolution takes time.

I can hear you saying – an interesting story but how do I as a researcher integrate the cultural politics that surrounds the lifeworld of individuals who experience disability into my research? If you have read this book from the introduction until now you will be aware of some potential options laid out in Chapter 2. To explore the significance of cultural politics that surrounds disability I personally am drawn to the work of the social theorist Michel Foucault that offers further salience to a discussion regarding the cultural politics of categorisation of various bodies (Foucault, 1977).

Foucault's Governmentality: A Lens for Illuminating Cultural Politics

Importantly, Foucault's work can be used to explore the political issues around classification that have been highlighted above. The work of Foucault has been shown by scholars working in the field of sport studies to provide an appropriate critique of the objectification of the sporting body, particularly as it relates to scientific classification and dividing practices (Markula and Pringle, 2006: 25–26). The process of classifying an athlete for involvement within parasport, for example, may be seen as the scientific classification of an organism that ultimately leads in some way to its marginalisation; being separated from their social environment because of the distinctive nature of classification and the manner in which parasport is practised. This act of classification is overtly political since that processing of the body into a particular class is a form of segregation. In order to make sense of the political transformations within parasport, it is important here to briefly outline Foucault's conceptualisation of governmentality and highlight its utility for researchers.

Governmentality is a useful way of exploring the control that social institutions such as those in parasport have over individuals. This concept links Foucault's technologies of discipline found in *The Birth of the Clinic* (1975) and *Discipline and Punish* (1977) and his later work on sexuality that more explicitly focuses upon the technologies of the self (Markula, 2003; Markula and Pringle, 2006). Governmentality 'incorporates both techniques or practices of self-government and the more apparent forms of external government – policing, surveillance and regulatory activities carried out by agencies of the state or other institutions for strategic purposes' (Lupton, 1995: 9). In other words, society uses individual consciousness to perpetuate the status quo. Individual choice is as important as the structure of society. More explicitly, governmentality for Foucault 'refers to a 'mentality' or way of thinking about the administration of society, in which the population is managed through the beliefs, needs desires, and choices of individuals' (Smith-Maguire 2003: 307).

The process of classification within parasport is perhaps the most important manner in which athletes are governed. The approaches taken by individual IOSDs vary, partly because some of the impairments are sensory and others are physical, but the principles behind the advent of each system are the same: the creation of an equitable sporting environment (Howe and Jones, 2006; Howe, 2008b). My time working on behalf of athletes in the context of IPC athletics, highlighted above, is perhaps best understood using Foucauldian governmentality because it allows us to see cultural politics in action.

The work of Foucault is not only linked to the body but also the associated issues of power and knowledge construction. Like most scholars, Foucault's project shifted focus throughout his lifetime. His early work was concerned with the technologies of dominance and it is this work that has the most salience exploring parasport. In my experience, parasport athletes can be understood as having body politic, to borrow from Scheper-Hughes and Lock (1987), that is they are regulated and surveyed to establish that that they are acting correctly. All the ruminations and posturing that occurred while I was part of IPC athletics was to control the bodies of athletes who experience disability. And, importantly, this was and is still done by the able-moral majority who are making the rules and controlling political discourse within the IPC and in broader society (Purdue and Howe, 2013; Howe and Silva, 2018, 2021a; Silva and Howe, 2018, 2019) as a form of domination.

Again, Foucauldian thinking is central here. As Andrews (1993) suggests, the development of disciplinary practice

> revolved around the emergence of a cluster of disciplinary institutions which, in terms of structure and ideology, promoted the ethos of discipline. Institutions such as prisons, hospitals, and schools increasingly came to the fore, augmented by complementary structures of knowledge and related human sciences that rationalized and legitimated the agenda of social discipline
>
> (1993, 156)

Parasport today can be seen as a disciplinary institution on two fronts. The IPC's rules of classification are a clear case of discipline, but also the manner in which parasport athletes are trained and then subjected to normative judgement is another example of discipline. For example, the way in which coach-athlete relationships are structured can clearly be seen as a disciplinary institution where the athlete's body is in part controlled through the training process (Pronger, 2002).

"The technologies of domination, principally the act of discipline, are important in critically examining sporting and physical activity practices for those experiencing disability because they attempt, often successfully, to normalize their moving bodies (Rail and Harvey, 1995)." Following on from this point, Cole et al. state

> [B]odies are never simply trained but are subjected to normative judgments (which include an ethical dimension), or what Foucault called divided practices. At least dividing practices are forces of "normalisation" that produce and exclude through reference to a norm. Techniques of normalization distinguish the normal from the pathological, or the normal from the threatening.
>
> (2004: 212)

This act of normalisation that is part of society generally has had an influence on research within the field of disability studies, particularly when related to service provision for people with a disability (Tyne 1992: 34). In service provision, normalisation can be seen as a good thing if it leads to the empowerment of those who experience disability, but it so rarely does. The adoption of 'care in the community' as a primary vehicle for the assimilation or normalisation of people who experience disability can be seen to have an impact upon the way in which sporting and physical activity practices have developed. Research conducted by Williams (1994a, 1994b) suggests that sporting practice is a useful way to socialise individuals who experience disability. But socialisation to what end? The process of normalisation to someone who physically lacks normality can be problematic.

It is clear that able and disabled 'bodies are invested with power relations, making them the legitimate target of the interventions of medicine, education and economics' (Smith-Maguire, 2002: 299). In other words, technologies of dominance shape the world in and around sporting and physical activity practices engaged in by people who experience disability, such as classification systems used within parasport (Howe, 2008b). Yet, the IPC also has a desire to control the social messages coming from advocates' research outputs. Let me give you an example.

Advocacy through Scholarship

During the 2013 IPC's VISTA Sport Science Conference, held in Bonn, Germany, I was told quietly by one of the organisers that I should avoid talking to the then IPC President Sir Philip Craven because he was disappointed that I was an invited speaker at the event. The reason given was something that I had written had brought the IPC into disrepute. I was shocked by this revelation for two reasons; first I always tried (and continue to do so) to end my publications on a positive note with suggestions for a better future. The second and perhaps more important reason is that, though I might try, the audience for my research outputs is not that widespread or influential. At the London 2012 Paralympic Games, I had worked as a journalist and a couple of pieces I wrote for an online magazine had focused on contentious issues related to classification (Howe, 2012a, 2012b). Perhaps this is what was being referred to. These pieces highlighted problems with ableism within the IPC's track and field athletics classification system.

Standing over canapés during VISTA 2013, the issues raised in these publications were not the concern of the President. While I was asked to avoid Sir Philip, I took it upon myself to engage with him directly – this I felt was an ideal advocacy movement. It turned out that he had his attention drawn to a paper entitled *Who's in and who is out? Legitimate bodies within the Paralympic Games* (Purdue and Howe, 2013) that I had written with a former PhD student. Sir Philip asked me if I was 'the' P. David Howe who co-authored this piece (as I only use the initial of my first name when I publish). I acknowledged that I was the author and he told me the article had the potential to be harmful to the IPC. In the ensuing discussion, Sir Philip acknowledged that he had not read the piece, but he was worried about the inflammatory nature of the title. I asked him to read the abstract and conclusion and he obliged. It turns out that Sir Philip agreed with the premise of the paper – that the IPC has to advocate for elite sporting opportunities for ALL its classifiable athletes – but he was still annoyed with the provocative title. As we parted company, I suggested that if the journal article had not had such a provocative title, the piece would not have been brought to his attention and we would not have had this important discussion.

The brief event highlighted above can be seen as a snapshot of cultural politics in action. An interaction between a two former Paralympians – one with power and influence within the IPC, the other a researcher who is eager to learn and to educate – but the power differential is significant. Both myself and Sir Philip were aware that the world we are engaged in is an able-bodied one where people who experience disability are often referred to as special because that masks their oppression.

Fast forward to 2021 and the IPC (under a new president) helped to launch a global initiative known as #Wethe15 that is designed to celebrate the inclusion of the 15% of the world's population that experience disability (Howe and Silva, 2021b). This for me is a real frustration. Not because I do not believe in inclusion – I believe the goal of #Wethe15 is worthwhile – but rather because launching this movement at the Opening Ceremony of the Tokyo 2020 Paralympic Games (held in 2021) missed the point that the Paralympic Games are exclusionary and high-performance sport is only accessible to a limited number of people who experience disability. In other words, by using the Tokyo 2020 Games as a launch pad for this new global movement, #Wethe15 may have shoot itself in the foot. If only those behind #Wethe15 had taken the time to read high quality research in disability studies in general and disability sport and physical activity cultures specifically – like the high-quality material captured in the rest of this current volume.

Summary

As a student and/or researcher interested in exploring disability sport and physical activity culture for the first time, it is important to remember that the landscape of the field is writ large with cultural politics. Be mindful that in the social world, not all developments are 100% positive and that while you might be of an age where disability sport and physical activity cultures seem to be readily available and highly celebrated, I encourage you to look 'behind the veil' to observe, record and articulate the unseen. It is particularly important that we all do this in the best interests of those who experience disability. Even if you have personal experience of disability, as I have, there is a desire to believe that you are immune to the smoke screen of ableism (Silva, this volume). I certainly am not. We all need to be reflective thinkers in order to robustly unpack the cultural politics around us.

Notes

1 In the BBC Show, comedian Matt Lucas played a character Daffyd Thomas, who claims to be "the only gay in the village' https://en.wikipedia.org/wiki/Little_Britain.
2 In September 2004, International Wheelchair and Amputee Sport Association (IWAS) was formed when ISMWSF and ISOD merged two federations that have been part of the Paralympic movement since its inception.
3 INAS-FID - This federation was rebranded as Virtus in 2019.
4 See https://en.wikipedia.org/wiki/Racerunning

References

Andrews, D. L. (1993) 'Desperately seeking Michel: Foucault's denealogy, the body, and critical sport sociology', *Sociology of Sport Journal*, Vol. 10: 148–167.
Barnes, C. (1991). *Disabled people in Britain and discrimination: A case for anti-discrimination legislation*. London: Hurst & Co.
Barnes, C. (1992) 'Qualitative research: Valuable or irrelevant', *Disability, Handicap and Society*, Vol. 7:115–124.
Charlton, J. (1998) *Nothing about US without US: Disability, oppression, and empowerment*. London: University of California Press.
Cole, C. L., Giardina, M. D. and Andrews, D. L. (2004) 'Michel Foucault: Studies of power and sport', in Giulianotti, R. (ed.) *Sport and modern social theorists*. Basingstoke, U.K., Palgrave MacMillan.
Douglas, M. (1966) *Purity and danger*. London: Routledge.
Foucault, M. (1975) *The birth of the clinic: An archeology of medical perception*. London: Vintage Books.
Foucault, M. (1977) *Discipline and punish: The birth of the prison*. London: Hammonworth.

Garland-Thompson, R. (1997) *Extraordinary bodies: Figuring physical disability in American culture and literature*. New York: Columbia University Press.

Giulianotti, R. (2015) 'Sport and globalisation', in Giulianotti, R. ed. *Sociology of sport handbook*. London: Routledge. pp. 440–451.

Goffman, E. (1963) *Stigma: 'Notes on the management of spoiled identity'*. New Jersey: Penguin Books.

Goodley, D. (2014), *Dis/ability studies: Theorising disablism and ableism*, London: Routledge.

Howe, P. D. (2008a) *The cultural politics of the paralympic movement: Through the anthropological lens*. London: Routledge.

Howe, P.D. (2008b) 'The tail is wagging the dog: Classification and the paralympic movement', *Ethnography*, Vol. 9 (4): 499–518.

Howe, P. D. (2011) 'Cyborg and Supercrip: The paralympics technology and the (dis) empowerment of disabled athletes', *Sociology*, Vol. 45 (5): 868–882.

Howe, P.D. (2012a) 'Pistorius shouldn't be allowed to compete at the Paralympics' September 5. https://theconversation.com/pistorius-shouldnt-be-allowed-to-compete-at-the-paralympics-9278

Howe, P. D. (2012b) 'Crossing the line: Are Richard Whitehead's moves illegal?' September 7. https://theconversation.com/crossing-the-line-are-richard-whiteheads-moves-illegal-9407

Howe, P. D. (2018) 'Athlete, anthropologist and advocate: Moving toward a lifeworld where difference is celebrated', *Sport and Society: Culture, Commerce, Media, Politics*, Vol. 21(4): 678–688. doi:10.1080/17430437.2016.1273628

Howe, P. D. and Silva, C. F. (2017) 'The cyborgification of paralympic sport', *Movement & Sport Sciences*. https://doi.org/10.1051/sm/2017014.

Howe, P. D. and Silva, C. F. (2018) 'The fiddle of using the Paralympic Games as a vehicle for expanding [dis]ability sport participation', *Sport and Society: Culture, Commerce, Media, Politics*, Vol. 21(1): 125–136. doi:10.1080/17430437.2016.1225885.

Howe, P. D. and Silva, C. F. (2021a) 'Cripping the dis§abled body: Doing the posthuman tango, in through and around sport', *Somatechnic*, Vol. 11(2) 139–156. doi:10.3366/soma.2021.0348

Howe, P. D. and Silva, C. F. (2021b) '#WeThe15 was misguided in using the Tokyo Paralympic Games to Launch a disability inclusion revolution' September 2. https://theconversation.com/wethe15-was-misguided-in-using-the-tokyo-paralympic-games-to-launch-a-disability-inclusion-revolution-166725

Kerr, S. and Howe, P. D. (2017). 'Using disability studies to ground high-quality paralympic research', *Diagoras: International Academic Journal on Olympic Studies*, Vol. 1, 117–134. Retrieved from http://diagorasjournal.com/index.php/diagoras/article/view/10

Lupton, D. (1995) *The imperative of health: Public health and the regulated body*. London: Sage.

Maguire, J. (2011) 'The global media sports complex: Key issues and concerns', *Sport in Society*, Vol. 14(7–8): 965–977. doi:10.1080/17430437.2011.603552

Markula, P. (2003) 'The technologies of the self: Sport, feminism, and foucault', *Sociology of Sport Journal*, Vol. 20: 87–107.

Markula, P. and Pringle, R. (2006) *Foucault, sport and exercise: Power, knowledge and transforming the self*. London: Routledge.

Murphy, R. F. (1987) *The body silent*. New York: Norton.

Naro-Redmond, M. R. (2020) *Ableism: The causes and consequences of disability prejudice*. Oxford: Wiley Blackwell.

Nkrumah, K. (1965) *Neo-Colonialism, The Last Stage of Imperialism*. London: Thomas Nelson & Sons, Ltd.

Oliver, M. (1990) *The politics of disablement*. London: Macmillan.
Oliver, M. (1996) *Understanding disability: From theory to practice*. London: Macmillan.
Pronger, B. (2002) *Body fascism: Salvation in the technology of physical fitness*. London: University of Toronto Press.
Purdue, D. E. J. and Howe, P. D. (2013) 'Who's in and who is out? Legitimate bodies within the Paralympic Games', *Sociology of Sport Journal*, Vol. 30(1): 24–40.
Rail, G. and Harvey, J. (1995) 'Body at work: Michel Foucault and the sociology of sport', *Sociology of Sport Journal*, Vol. 12: 164–179.
Riddell, S. and Watson, N. (2003) 'Disability, culture and identity: Introduction', in Riddell, S. and Watson, N. (eds.), *Disability, culture and identity*. Harlow: Pearson Education. pp. 1–18.
Scheper-Hughes, N. and Lock, M. (1987) 'The mindful body: A prolegomenon to future work in medical anthropology', *Medical Anthropology Quarterly*, Vol. 1(1): pp 6–41.
Sherrill, C. (1999) 'Disability sport and classification theory: A new era', *Adapted Physical Activity Quarterly*, Vol. 16: 206–215.
Silk, M. L. and Andrews, D. L. (2012). 'Sport and the neoliberal conjuncture', in Andrews, D. L. and Silk, M. L. (eds.), *Sport and neoliberalism: Politics, consumption, and culture*. Philadelphia: Temple University Press. pp. 1–19.
Silva, C. F. and Howe, P. D. (2012) 'The [in]validity of Supercrip representation of paralympic athletes', *Journal for Sport and Social Issues*, Vol. 36(2): 174–194.
Silva, C. F. and Howe, P. D. (2018) 'The social empowerment of difference: The potential influence of parasport', *Physical Medicine and Rehabilitation Clinics of North America*, Vol. 29(2): 397–408. doi:10.1016/j.pmr.2018.01.009
Silva, C. F. and Howe, P. D. (2019) 'Sliding to reverse ableism: An ethnographic exploration of (dis)ability in sitting volleyball', *Societies*, Vol. 9: 41. doi:10.3390/soc9020041
Smith-Maguire, J. (2002) 'Michel Foucault: Sport, power, technologies and governmentality', in Maguire, J. and Young, K. *Theory, sport and society*. London: Elsevier Science. pp. 293–314.
Thomas, C. (1999) *Female forms: Experiencing and understanding disability*. Buckingham: Open University Press.
Titchkosky, T. (2003) *Disability, self, and society*. London: University of Toronto Press.
Turner, V. (1967) *The forest of symbols*. Ithaca: Cornell University Press.
Turner, V. (1969) *The ritual process: Structure and anti-structure*. Chicago: University of Chicago Press.
Tyne, A. (1992) 'Normalisation: From theory to practice', in Brown, H. and Smith, H. (eds.), *Normalisation: A reader for the Nineties*. London: Routledge.
UPIAS (1976) *Fundamental Principles of Disability: Being a Summary of the Discussion Held on 22nd November, 1975 and Containing Commentaries from Each Organisation*. Union of the Physically Impaired Against Segregation. Disability Alliance.
Williams, T. (1994a) 'Disability sport socialisation and identity construction', *Adapted Physical Activity Quarterly*, Vol. 11: 14–31.
Williams, T. (1994b) 'Sociological perspectives on sport and disability: Structural-functionalism', *Physical Education Review*, Vol. 17(1): 14–24.
Wolf, E. R. (1982). *Europe and the people without history*. University of California Press.

Chapter 4

What Are We Doing Here?
Confessional Tales of Non-Disabled Researchers in Disability Sport

Jess Macbeth and Ben Powis

Introduction

Social scientific research on disability sport has never been more popular. As evident in this edited collection, this burgeoning field is theoretically and methodically diverse and spotlights a multiplicity of intersectional experiences. There is also diversity amongst those who are doing this research with non-disabled and disabled researchers making valuable contributions to sociological understandings of disability sport. However, the growth of the field does not necessarily equate with an increase of diverse voices; as disability becomes a mainstream focus for sociologists of sport, we are seeing an influx of 'tourist' researchers who have limited knowledge of the state-of-the-art and adopt an uncritical approach to the research process. In particular, there is a dearth of literature that explicitly engages with authors' non-disabled/disabled identity and their positionality. Yet, this is not a new issue: over a decade has passed since Macbeth's (2010) research note in Leisure Studies revealed that detailed reflexive accounts of researchers' experiences were scarce. In conclusion, Jess asserted:

> Open and honest debate about what we do well, mistakes we make and ways of improving research in this field will help both disabled and non-disabled researchers to better represent the lived experiences of sport and leisure in the lives of disabled research participants.
>
> (484)

A handful of non-disabled scholars have offered detailed insights on entering and navigating disability sport spaces (Smith, 2008; Berger, 2009; Brighton, 2015; Brighton & Williams, 2018; Powis, 2018; Campbell, 2020). Engaging with debates in disability studies about the place of non-disabled researchers, their accounts discuss inclusive, emancipatory and participatory approaches, positionality, empathy, and a range of methodological and ethical dilemmas. This chapter offers a brief review of this work before presenting our own confessional tales (Sparkes, 2002; Van Maanen, 2011) of being non-disabled researchers in disability sport. This popular form of writing often reveals the researcher's

DOI: 10.4324/9781003153696-5

'human qualities' (Van Maanen, 2011), including foibles and character flaws, and is in explicit contrast to realist accounts of conducting fieldwork. Through our self-reflective vignettes, we intend to demystify the research process and use our reflections as a platform to discuss three particularly interesting issues for us: 1) positionality; 2) asking about impairment; and 3) giving back. In doing so, we hope to add to these important methodological discussions and trigger dialogue between disabled and non-disabled researchers and their disabled co-researchers or research participants.

Non-Disabled Researchers in Disability Sport Spaces

In the title of this chapter, we ask: *what are we doing here?* While it's a question that many qualitative researchers contemplate when planning a new study or entering the field for the first time, it holds particular significance in disability studies literature. Twenty-five years ago, Robert Drake (1997), a non-disabled researcher, posed the same question of his role in the disability movement. He reflected upon his disability policy research and discussed the legitimate roles for non-disabled people in this space, including as researchers who expose disabling practices and bring about societal change. In response, Fran Branfield (1998), a disabled researcher, reframed Drake's question and queried: "what are *you* doing here?" She argued that the relationship between non-disabled people and the disability movement was untenable and warned against the hijacking and reappropriation of disability studies by non-disabled academics. Not all non-disabled researchers of disability sport demonstrate an awareness of, or engagement with, Drake and Branfield's arguments, but for others the debate still resonates. Questioning one's place in disability research is more than introspection; it requires an acute awareness of the social and political tensions that mark this process.

Whether as an *advocate* (Powis, 2018), an *ally* (Quinn et al., 2020) or a *progressive partner* (Campbell, 2020), a small number of non-disabled researchers have sought to conceptualise their role in disability sport spaces. Campbell (2020), who cites Stone and Priestley's (1996) call for partners rather than parasite researchers, acknowledges that her presence as a non-disabled person within the disabled community is at the "perpetuated exclusion of others" (616). Despite her longstanding involvement in disability sport, she reinforces that her experiences do not qualify her to speak on behalf of disabled people. In Powis' (2018) discussion of his advocacy, Ben makes a similar point: "being an advocate is not speaking for a marginalised individual or group, it is letting their voices be heard" (257). He contends that social research can be a transformative platform for disabled people to share their stories and engender positive change – but only when participants are valued as experts and research is conducted in an inclusive and accessible way. However, identifying as an advocate or a progressive partner *per se* is insufficient. In their reflexive pieces, both authors discuss the theoretical and methodological challenges they faced when putting their standpoints into practice, including the role of gatekeepers and the complexities of providing disabled people with a 'voice'.

Brighton and Williams (2018) argue that non-disabled scholars should clarify their rationale and motivations for researching disabled people at the outset of any study. The authors encourage researchers to consider: "why are they interested in disability, what questions they want to answer, if they share any of the experiences they are investigating, and how their own embodiment influences their relationships with others and perspectives on their work" (29). Reflecting upon their research with people who have experienced spinal cord injury, both authors explain how their personal and professional experiences supported the development of a 'disability consciousness' (Berger, 2009). They refer to their *empathy* (Brighton) and *compassion* (Williams) for disabled people, and outline an empathetic approach to disability sport research in which researchers position themselves in their participants' place and seek to compassionately explore their experiences. Although the idea of putting yourself in another's body is problematic (Smith, 2008; Sparkes and Smith, 2012), this process of corporeal reflexivity is vital. And, while we should respect that other *is* Other (Sparkes and Smith, 2012), researchers must tune into their own embodiment to understand their connectedness to their participants.

In *Hoop Dreams on Wheels* (2009), Berger recounts his naivety upon entering the field of disability sport research. He describes a hostile encounter at a sociology conference, where a disabled session moderator excluded him from open discussions because he was non-disabled. Significantly, it wasn't until Berger shared that he has a daughter with cerebral palsy that the moderator accepted that he was well-intentioned and had a legitimate interest in disability research. As Berger acknowledges: "a little bit of self-disclosure goes a long way" (8). While his comment reveals an apparent acceptance of this situation, it raises questions about how much non-disabled researchers must *give away* of themselves to justify their presence in disabled spaces. Disclosure of personal details is also a way of building trust and rapport for any researcher. In his ethnographic research with wheelchair basketball players, Brighton (2015) disclosed his lived experiences of *bodily vulnerability* with his participants as an act of reciprocity. He argues that his gradual sharing of stories about his body and impairment eased participants' initial scepticism and fostered more open, empathetic relationships. As an ostensibly non-disabled researcher, Brighton's experiences serve to breakdown a disabled/non-disabled binary – both for the disabled athletes in his study and for the reader. His reflexive account captures the embodied, intimate nature of ethnography and stands out as the most *lived* depiction of access and positionality in disability sport research. While there are similarities in their experiences of self-disclosure, Brighton's confessional tale tells us significantly more about being a non-disabled researcher than Berger's 'neat' anecdote about his initial experiences of accessing the field. In the next section, our own confessional tales further explore the issues raised by Brighton and provide similarly candid accounts of the research process.

Our Confessional Tales

Ben

And that was that. Ten months in the field. Friendships built, in-jokes crafted, rail replacement services negotiated, and then it's over. No final farewell or big celebration; just the ending of a training weekend and "See you around, mate". I kept in touch with some of the participants over the following few years, however that eventually ended. Nevertheless, in reflecting upon my research experiences now, I am still left with a nagging feeling: I hope they didn't read my findings. Not because I unfairly characterised the participants or misrepresented their opinions, but because they might not like the stories that I have told.

As a non-disabled researcher in a disabled sporting space, there is a weight of responsibility to listen to *authoritative knowers* and conduct research that *gives back* to disabled people. Yet, while striving for these principles, what if participants accuse each other of cheating? Or disclose incidents of bullying? Or describe half of their teammates as 'second-class' citizens? When the authoritative knowers contradict each other and provide conflicting versions of events, where does that leave notions of *member checking, emancipation* or *co-production*? While my research did *give back* – I produced a key findings document for the governing body which outlined the players' recommendations for change – I took more than I gave.

No matter the anonymity I offered or the pseudonyms that the participants selected for themselves, the players and coaches would have been able to recognise each other in my writing. I didn't disclose certain elements of their biographies, including nature of impairment, but the small squad size meant it was impossible to anonymise their stories. And, even if I could have, it would have meant removing the richness from their experiences and leaving a lifeless husk of a transcript. What is the point of asking the authoritative knowers about their experiences, just to sanitise them afterwards? My outsider-turned-insider status and ethnographic knowledge of the space meant that, perhaps for the first time, the players were asked questions that *mattered* by an interviewer. I knew they would give compelling, even controversial answers, and engage with notions of power, inequality and injustice- but for whose benefit? Beyond the players' initial emotional release of sharing their experiences, I was the sole benefactor. Like a thief in the night, I took their stories and ran back to the safety of academia. In pursuit of critical sociological research, the participants were left to pick up the pieces.

Jess

Off I set, a keen Research Fellow fresh out of my PhD and into the unfamiliar world of partially sighted football. I wasn't interested in this area because of my own, or a loved one's, lived experience of visual impairment. I had, at that point, no lived experience of disability or significant interaction with disabled people (as far as I knew). What I did have was a passion for football and an interest in the sporting experiences of marginalised groups. So, with the World Championship on my doorstep and access to gatekeepers secured, I negotiated an 'insider' role as Team Co-ordinator with the England Squad. But how would I fit in with a squad of male partially sighted footballers? How would I relate to them and them to me? How would they perceive me and my interest in their experiences?

My tournament role got me as close as I could, at least as a female who was not partially sighted. I stayed in the same hotel, travelled and ate with the players, had tournament accreditation, was pitch-side during training and matches, attended squad meetings, socialised in the hotel lobby during downtime, and partied on the night of the final. Feelings of insiderness sometimes intensified: like when I was invited to sit in the back of the minibus with players rather that my usual 'tour guide' position by the driver. In other moments my outsiderness was blatant: like when being female denied me access to an emotionally charged changing room.

The players seemed flattered by my interest in them. Some had never been asked about their experiences of partial sighted football before, some had only just started playing, and others had frustrations to vent. I juggled the roles of tournament 'volunteer' (whilst being paid a university wage) and researcher. Being on the fringes of the squad, I also became confidante. But my lack of knowledge of visual impairment was something I perceived as a barrier between us. I knew the players' classification, something disabled athletes can never hide, and I wanted to know more. But no research methods module had taught me how to broach this and I felt awkward. I wasn't sure how, when or even whether, to ask. So, when players volunteered their impairment stories during casual conversations, it was a huge relief, my elephant had left the room.

Our reflections pose more questions than answers, but it is not the aim of this chapter to provide a 'how to' guide for non-disabled researchers. We are certainly not experts, and each new research project presents another learning curve as we make very modest steps towards developing our "disability consciousness" (Berger, 2009 Brighton and Williams, 2018) in a landscape that is in flux. The next section blends examples from our own experiences with accounts by other non-disabled researchers to examine positionality, asking about impairment, and giving back.

Positionality

Of all the topics discussed by non-disabled researchers when reflecting on their sociological studies of disability sport, positionality has been afforded most attention. Whilst some researchers offer only a cursory declaration of non-disabled status, others devote entire papers (as reviewed earlier) to reflexive accounts of positionality and its impacts. As conversations within disability studies have moved on from categorising researchers as either an insider or outsider (Macbeth, 2010), non-disabled researchers of disability sport have also begun to offer important critical reflections on complex and fluid identity positions that work to dismantle the impairment-based insider-outsider binary. For example, Campbell (2020:613) has recently identified herself as an inside-outsider pracademic, a position which "abandons the constructed dichotomies of being inside or outside a group, and instead embraces and explores the complexity and richness of the space between entrenched perspectives".

Non-disabled researchers have reflected on the situational identities and dynamic nature of positionality experienced during research. The richest insights have emerged from observational and ethnographic projects that illuminate the embodied nature of these approaches. Some non-disabled researchers negotiated access to position themselves 'inside' disability sport spaces, specifically to undertake research (e.g. Macbeth & Magee, 2008; Brighton, 2015; Powis, 2020). This involved taking on a reciprocal role which moves them from a position of outsider to experiencing varying degrees of situationally dependent insiderness. In contrast, other non-disabled researchers held pre-existing professional or voluntary roles 'inside' disability sport contexts prior to conducting research (e.g. Brighton & Williams, 2018; Campbell, 2020; Quinn et al., 2020), and their experiences within these established roles have provided the inspiration for subsequent research projects.

Although most non-disabled researchers endorse an empathetic approach, whilst acknowledging the challenges this brings (Smith, 2008; Brighton, 2015), there is a consensus that they cannot truly know how disabled athletes (the authoritative knowers) experience impairment and disability. As asserted by Campbell (2020:616), "a list of vocations and contributions does not qualify me to assume any right to speak on, for or on behalf of any marginalised community". But it is crucial to acknowledge the diversity of impairment and disabled people as a heterogenous group. As Shakespeare (2006:195), and others in the field of Disability Studies before him, argue:

> Just because someone is disabled does not mean they have an automatic insight into the lives of other disabled people. One person's experience may not be typical, and may actively mislead them as to the nature of disability… someone with one impairment may have no more insight into the experience of another impairment than a person without any impairment… The idea that having an impairment is vital to understanding impairment is dangerously essentialist.

There is the common assumption that 'outsiders' are likely to possess faulty preconceptions of research participants which can result in the misrepresentation of everyday actions (Fletcher, 2014: 249–250). However, in line with Shakespeare's (2006) argument, we cannot assume that disabled people, even those who have similar impairments, possess preconceptions of each other that are accurate. Berger (2009:127) recognises this when asserting that, "the notion of a common disability identity is so elusive", posing the question "what do people with such varying impairments that develop at varying times over the life course really have in common?" Our research with visually impaired (VI) athletes has exposed misconceptions that players within and across sight classes have of each other and this can cause tensions between teammates (Powis, 2020; Powis & Macbeth, 2020). Assumptions about how each other's impairment effects play out in the dynamic and embodied practice of sport can also be exacerbated by the classification system (as discussed in the next section). We tentatively propose that a non-disabled researcher engaging in rich discussions about the intricacies of disabled participants' lived sporting experiences may have a greater insight than another disabled person with a different (or even a similar) impairment. So where does this leave us in terms of positionality? Does it, as Harvey (2013:91) suggests, "call[s] into question the relevance of whether a researcher is disabled or not"?

When it comes to examining our relational positionality (as non-disabled), the extent to which research participants embrace a disabled identity can also muddy the waters. The possibility that "…not all perceived disabilities are disabilities to the people experiencing them" (Richards, 2008:1719) presents another way that the disabled/non-disabled dichotomy can be fractured. It is also apparent that there are athletes who are eligible and competing within 'disability sport' who reject a disabled identity. In his research on VI cricket, Powis (2018:254) revealed that "the majority of participants did not identify as disabled", with some working to disassociate themselves from their ('more') disabled peers and align themselves more closely with a non-disabled identity. Based on the assumption that Ben was not VI (despite not openly declaring this), one partially sighted participant stressed that "I am much more similar to you, in terms of the way I do things, as I am to a blind person" and a blind participant explained that his aspirations in life "would be similar to yours and not similar to someone else who is visually impaired" (Powis, 2018:255). These remarks are consistent with Campbell's (2008) explanation of internalised ableism which can manifest itself in two primary strategies: dispersal from other disabled people, and emulation of ableist norms. The internalisation of ableism resurfaces in the next section where we discuss the process of 'asking about impairment'.

To summarise this section, whilst it is important to reflect on the differences between ourselves and research participants, there is also a danger that we forget our commonalities. Reflecting on their research, Brighton and Williams (2018) provide an important reminder of the "multiple or intersecting identities" that non-disabled researchers and disabled research participants embody, recognising that we are all also "gendered, sexed, raced and classed". In our own work we have shared aspects of identity with research participants, and rapport has developed on this basis. For example, Ben recognised that, whilst he is not VI, his "status as a young male cricket player with similar interests and cultural references as any of the players was vital to developing… trusting and fruitful relationships" (Powis, 2018:255). In a research project with VI children and their families, Jess could relate to experiences of being a mother and introducing young children to sport, but not having VI children (British Blind Sport, 2020). In our project on the impact of COVID-19 on VI runners, we were both able to share experiences of running prior to and during the pandemic, Jess could relate to gendered aspects of running raised by female participants, but neither of us had experience of being a VI runner (or guide runner). So, whilst identities associated with impairment and disability are central to the relationships we form with research participants, there are other aspects of our identities that we share, offering elements of insiderness to each other's worlds and lived experiences.

Asking About Impairment

As researchers with our own sporting backgrounds, asking disabled research participants about their sporting biographies and experiences has always been safe ground. But asking questions about impairment was unchartered territory for us both when we embarked on our first projects with VI athletes. We had anxieties about the impact on participants, whether such questions would be too intrusive, catch them off guard or evoke memories of past traumatic experiences. Moreover, we were mindful of Kitchin's (2000:34) assertion that "disabled people will only tell partial stories to a non-disabled researcher for fear of embarrassment or lack of empathy" and that they can therefore have a tendency "to make situations seem better than they really are".

But we were also apprehensive that what we asked, the way we asked it, and how we engaged in discussions about impairment, might expose our own limited knowledge. We were conscious that revealing a "misunderstanding of the nature of disability" (Barton, 1992:99) had the potential to frustrate participants and leave them wondering 'what are *you* doing here?' In early projects, we both adopted the strategy of structuring interview questions to enable stories of impairment to naturally evolve. We usually began by asking about sporting biography and experiences of sport in family and school contexts. In their responses, participants would refer to impairment, offering us licence to probe further with more specific questions. Another benefit of this approach was that it usually meant we could follow our participants' leads and mirror their use of preferred language and ways of identifying themselves (Peers et al., 2014). On the face of it, this could all be regarded as good ethical practice but, on reflection, it was also to some extent a tactic to avoid asking about impairment directly. So, how can we explain our reluctance to broach the subject of impairment with participants? We think the answer lies in a complex combination of theoretical influences, classification in disability sport, and internalised ableism.

As revealed in her confessional tale, Jess' first project on partially sighted football (2004) was opportunistic and she entered this unfamiliar disability sport space equipped with only a brief dip into the field of disability studies. Influenced by the social model, her research focused on the social and political factors shaping the socialisation experiences and career paths of players (Macbeth and Magee, 2006). But this approach reinforced the dualism between impairment and disability, with the impaired body effectively medicalised and reduced to biology (Terzi, 2004). Disability sport research has drawn heavily on the social model, but as criticisms of it have acknowledged, the impaired body is increasingly recognised as pivotal to experiences of disability in sporting contexts (Smith & Bundon, 2018; Powis, 2020). This, however, doesn't make asking about impairment any less complex.

The centrality and complexity of classification in disability sport also has an impact on athletes' and researchers' interpretations of impairment. The process of undergoing classification brings impairment to the fore, and the specific sport class allocated to elite disabled athletes is in the public domain. This can result in athletes being subjected to, and engaging in, various forms of surveillance (Peers, 2012; Powis & Macbeth, 2020). As a researcher, knowing the sport class of an athlete could be naively assumed to provide sufficient information about the nature of their impairment. But, as our more recent work with VI athletes has revealed, sight classes can do as much to obscure as they do to reveal the nuances of visual impairment and its impact on individual sporting experiences (Powis & Macbeth, 2020). Ben's work has uncovered how the medicalised process of classification has unintended social consequences with sport classes becoming an established aspect of athletes' social identity (Powis, 2020). Moreover, Goodley and Tregaskis (2006:638) assert that impairment is "relational, constructed, and negotiable", and for disabled athletes, the classification process plays a significant role in this process. The interplay between classification, impairment and identity in disability sport makes asking disabled athletes about impairment a complex sociological endeavour, particularly for non-disabled researchers with no lived experience of impairment.

This leads us to consider the impact of internalised ableism on discussions of impairment with research participants. Throughout our projects on VI sport, we have encountered participants who align with an affirmative understanding of disability (Swain & French, 2000). In contrast, others appear to have internalised the ableist viewpoint, described by Campbell (2008: 153) as "a belief that impairment (irrespective of type) is *inherently* negative" [original emphasis]. Such identity construction can be impacted by various factors, including: whether an athlete's impairment is congenital or acquired (and how long ago) (Powis, 2020); the extent to which their impairment is visible or hidden, and; the social contexts (including research interviews) in which they 'perform' identities. Participants in our projects have engaged in various strategies of dispersal from other disabled people and emulation of ableist norms (Campbell, 2008). In light of this, asking about impairment is difficult to navigate, but engaging in such discussions can illuminate the complexities of identity formation for disabled athletes. Furthermore, Campbell (2008: 151) asserts "we are all, regardless of our subject positions, shaped and formed by the politics of ableism" and as non-disabled researchers we need to reflect on how our own ableist assumptions might frame the questions we ask, our interactions with disabled research participants and interpretations of their impairment stories.

It is difficult to appreciate the extent to which it is the subject matter, our status as non-disabled researchers, or a combination of both, which makes asking about impairment a tricky path to negotiate. Similar reflections from other researchers, particularly disabled researchers, would enable comparisons.

Our recent project on the impact of COVID-19 on VI runners has given us the opportunity to reflect on how our approach to these conversations has evolved. As our understanding of visual impairment has developed, we are more confident of becoming relatively authoritative knowers, at least to the extent that we can as non-disabled researchers without lived experience of impairment. Our interview strategy tends to remain the same as in early projects and we have generally experienced a willingness from participants to discuss (visual) impairment in the hope that our research will raise awareness and have a positive impact. It is to a discussion of the aims and impacts of our research that the chapter now turns.

Giving Back

Our final area of discussion, which is also a central theme in Ben's confessional tale, is the act of *giving back*. In his vignette, Ben explores the promise of reciprocity and acknowledges that, for his participants, the potential cost of sharing their experiences outweighed the benefits of taking part in the study. This was not a mutual exchange; Ben's doctoral research was principally conducted for academic and professional gain. While the players were given an outlet to share their thoughts and opinions, any social or institutional changes resulting from the study were not guaranteed. Similarly, Jess also intended to give her participants voice and use her findings to influence key policymakers. Yet, when she shared her academic publications with the governing body, they argued that her research was one-sided and did not acknowledge their good work in developing disability football (see Macbeth, 2010). In both our experiences, giving back was a hopeful gesture rather than an expected outcome. But can reciprocity ever be more than an aspiration? Is it the responsibility of disability sport researchers to conduct mutually beneficial research? And do participants always want something in return? In this section, we problematise the act of giving back in a research setting and consider the harm of giving back 'badly' (Hammett et al., 2019). We also discuss the turn to co-production in UK academia (Bell & Pahl, 2018) and explore the possibilities and pitfalls of this approach for future disability sport scholarship.

Drawing upon their experiences as non-disabled academics, Brighton and Williams (2018) include *give back* in their guidelines for researching disabled peoples' experiences of sport and physical activity. The authors urge researchers to provide something of 'real value' to their participants and refer to their own examples of giving back, including challenging ableism through sharing participants' stories, and working with stakeholders to inform policy and education. While these examples demonstrate the diverse ways in which researchers can give back, the notion of real value is ambiguous. The act of giving back often presupposes what participants need or want from the research process without consultation (Finney, 2014), thus 'value' is defined from the researcher's perspective. It is also not a static process; it is both time and context dependent (Diver & Higgins

2014). Significantly, acts of giving back may be fleeting and, despite speculative promises of long-term impact, only benefit participants in the short term.

Notwithstanding the laudable principles of giving back, Hammett and colleagues (2019: 380) argue that "moves to institutionalise giving back may have unintended and problematic consequences…and risks reducing what can – and should – be an ethical and potentially transformative activity to an unethical box-ticking practice". As demonstrated in Ben's confessional tale, giving back in a research setting is fraught with ethical dilemmas (Hammett et al., 2019). Firstly, whether giving back is always possible, desirable, or even appropriate. Secondly, the harmful consequences of giving back 'badly'. Finally, if research findings are suitable recompense for participants' time and knowledge. For Ben, the players in his study may have come to emotional harm if they had been involved in the process of member checking. Although they were given the opportunity to make recommendations for change and read a copy of the resulting report, academic publications were not directly shared with participants. Considering the polarising findings of the study – which he refers to in his vignette – this would have been an unsuitable and potentially harmful way of giving back.

So, how can disability sport research be reciprocal and give back in an ethical and transformative way? Currently, *co-production* offers the most viable method for meaningful collaboration during the research process. Smith and Wightman (2019: 3) define co-production as:

> …the process in which academics work alongside other stakeholders whose lives are affected by research. It means that not only research evidence is used to inform research and make decisions but also the lived experiences of stakeholders are foregrounded in the research and decision making.

The authors' discussion of co-production is based upon their experiences of *Get Yourself Active*, a project which brings together a range of stakeholders to promote physical activity to disabled people. As part of the project, an infographic of evidence-based physical activity recommendations (see Smith et al., 2019) was co-produced – involving 350 disabled adults, 10 disability organisations and 50 health professionals – and later endorsed by the UK Chief Medical Officer. However, while *Get Yourself Active* demonstrates the considerable possibilities of this approach, there is often a gap between the rhetoric and reality of co-produced research (Flinders et al., 2016). In the context of the *impact agenda*, there is a pressure to engage stakeholders throughout the research process – including analysing and interpreting data – *and* producing research which will be peer-reviewed and assessed for its academic quality (Flinders et al., 2016; Bell & Pahl, 2018; Oliver et al., 2019). According to Oliver et al. (2019: 4), there are multitude of 'costs' involved in co-production: practical costs, personal and professional costs to researchers, costs to research, costs to stakeholders and costs to the research profession. The authors posit a cautious approach to co-production and encourage researchers to reflect upon their motivations for adopting this method. Much like the act of giving back, if co-production is only employed performatively for the researcher or institution's benefit, the inequalities of the research process will be further exacerbated.

Significantly, we need a range of eclectic critical methodologies (Danieli & Woodhams, 2005) to develop the field and further our knowledge of disability sport – including both participatory and researcher-led approaches. Giving back is of vital importance, but it cannot and should not be a defining principle of *all* disability sport research. There must be space for criticality and the opportunity to conduct *research for research's sake* (Shakespeare, 1996). However, this is not to say that 'non-participatory' methods should disregard participants' needs; we need to embed reciprocity in ways that are wanted by our stakeholders, while also recognising that collaboration can take many forms.

Conclusion

When we began researching disability sport, there was very little by way of introspective accounts by non-disabled researchers navigating this space. Since then, the works reviewed in this chapter have provided valuable insight into a range of issues, considerations, and dilemmas that non-disabled researchers have faced, and the strategies employed to manage them. Frank confessions within this emergent body of literature have revealed mistakes that can shock those who haven't, or reassure those who have, encountered similar experiences. In this chapter we focused on positionality, asking about impairment, and giving back, as they reflect the areas that have caused us most discomfort. There were of course other themes that we could have covered, but there was not space to do them justice. We hope that other researchers of disability sport are encouraged to lay themselves bare and add to the conversation.

We are also conscious that the chapter is likely to have stimulated more questions than it has answered. One that has always surfaced in our conversations is: do disabled researchers have similar anxieties and experiences? In 2004 (n.p.) Tregaskis called for disabled researchers to break the "orthodoxy of concealment" within the field of Disability Studies more broadly. Although David Howe and Danielle Peers have provided detailed insights into their 'insider' statuses, confessional tales from disabled researchers in disability sport are notably absent. While this reflects the troubling under-representation of disabled researchers in Higher Education (Brown & Leigh, 2018), it may also be the result of disabled researchers never being asked "what are you doing here?" As we've demonstrated in this chapter, this question does not have to be a hostile cross-examination; instead, it can be an invitation for purposeful reflection. Our answers should also be more than a simple justification of place, they should reflect on how our status in relation to disability informs the decisions we make throughout the research process. Whatever form they take, our accounts should be insightful enough to inform the research practice of novice and experienced researchers alike. If more researchers engaged in the writing of confessional tales, we think social scientific research on disability sport would be richer for it.

References

Barton, L. (1992) 'Introduction'. *Disability, Handicap and Society*, 7(2), 99–99. DOI: 10.1080/02674649266780131

Bell, D.M. & Pahl, K. (2018) 'Co-production: Towards a utopian approach'. *International Journal of Social Research Methodology*, 21(1), 105–117.

Berger, R.J. (2009) *Hoop dreams on wheels: Disability and the competitive wheelchair athlete*. London: Routledge.

Branfield, F. (1998) 'What are you doing here? 'Non-disabled' people and the disability movement: A response to Robert F. Drake'. *Disability & Society*, 13(1), 143–144.

Brighton, J. & Williams, T. (2018) 'Using interviews to explore experiences of physical disability in sport and physical activity'. In: Medcalf, R. & Mackintosh, C. (eds.) *Researching difference in sport and physical activity*. London: Palgrave, pp. 25–38.

Brighton, J. (2015) 'Researching disabled sporting bodies: Reflections from an 'able'-bodied ethnographer'. In: Wellard, I. (ed.) *Researching embodied sport: Exploring movement cultures*. London: Routledge, pp. 163–177.

British Blind Sport (2020) Motor Competence in Children & Young People with Visual Impairment – Interim Report. Available from: https://britishblindsport.org.uk/wp-content/uploads/2021/10/CYP-Final-Interim-Report-With-Cover.pdf

Brown, N. & Leigh, J. (2018) 'Ableism in academic: Where are the disabled and ill academics?' *Disability & Society*, 33(6), 985–989. DOI: 10.1080/09687599.2018.1455627

Campbell, F.A.K. (2008) 'Exploring internalized ableism using critical race theory'. *Disability & Society*, 23(2), 151–162. DOI: 10.1080/09687590701841190

Campbell, N. (2020) 'Gatekeepers, agency and rhetoric: An academic's reflexive ethnography of 'doing' a (failed) adaptive CrossFit project'. *Qualitative Research in Sport, Exercise and Health*, 12(4), 612–630. DOI: 10.1080/2159676X.2019.1645727

Diver, S.W. & Higgins, M.N. (2014) 'Giving back through collaborative research: Towards a practice of dynamic reciprocity'. *Journal of Research Practice*, 10(2), Article M9. http://jrp.icaap.org/index.php/jrp/article/view/415/401

Danieli, A. & Woodhams, C. (2005) Emancipatory research methodology and disability: A critique. *International Journal of Social Research Methodology: Theory & Practice*, 8(4), 281–296. DOI: 10.1080/1364557042000232853

Drake, R.F. (1997) 'What am I doing here? 'Non-disabled' people and the disability Movement'. *Disability & Society*, 12(4), 643–645.

Finney, C. (2014) 'Doing it old school: Reflections on giving back'. *Journal of Research Practice*, 10(2), Article N3.

Fletcher, T. (2014) "Does he look like a Paki?' An exploration of 'whiteness', positionality and reflexivity in inter-racial sports research'. *Qualitative Research in Sport, Exercise and Health*, 6(2), 244–260. DOI: 10.1080/2159676X.2013.796487

Flinders, M., Wood, M. & Cunningham, M. (2016) 'The politics of co-production: Risks, limits and pollution'. *Evidence & Policy*, 12(2), 261–279. DOI: 10.1332/174426415X14412037949967

Goodley, D. & Tregaskis, C. (2006) 'Storying disability and impairment: Retrospective accounts of disabled family life'. *Qualitative Health Research*, 16(5), 630–646.

Hammett, D., Jackson, L. & Vickers, D. (2019) 'The ethics of (not) giving back'. *Area*, 51(2), 380–386. doi: 10.1111/area.12471

Harvey, J. (2013) 'Footprints in the field: Researcher identity in social research'. *Methodological Innovations Online*, 8(1), 86–98. DOI: 10.4256%2Fmio.2013.0006

Kitchin, R. (2000) 'The researched opinions on research: Disabled people and disability research'. *Disability & Society*, 15(1), 25–47.

Macbeth, J.L. (2010) 'Reflecting on disability research in sport and leisure settings'. *Leisure Studies*, 29(4), 477–485. DOI: 10.1080/02614367.2010.523834

Macbeth, J. & Magee, J. (2006) 'Captain England? Maybe one day I will': Career paths of elite partially sighted footballers'. *Sport in Society*, 9(3), 444–462. DOI: 10.1080/17430430600673464

Macbeth, J.L. & Magee, J. (2008) 'Insider research in sports 'Fields': Getting in, building trust and establishing rapport'. *Leisure Studies Association Newsletter*, No. 79 (March), LSA.

Oliver, K., Kothari, A. & Mays, N. (2019) 'The dark side of coproduction: Do the costs outweigh the benefits for health research?' *Health Research Policy and Systems*, 17(33). DOI: 10.1186/s12961-019-0432-3

Peers, D. (2012) 'Interrogating disability: The (de)composition of a recovering paralympian'. *Qualitative Research in Sport, Exercise and Health*, 4(2), 175–188. DOI: 10.1080/2159676x.2012.685101

Peers, D., Spencer-Cavaliere, N. & Eales, L. (2014) 'Say what you mean: Rethinking disability language in adapted physical activity quarterly'. *Adapted Physical Activity Quarterly*, 31(3), 265–282. DOI: 10.1123/apaq.2013-0091

Powis, B. (2018) Transformation, advocacy and voice in disability sport research. In: Carter, T. F., Burdsey, D. & Doidge, M. (eds.), *Transforming sport: Knowledges, practices, structures*. London: Routledge, pp. 248–259. DOI: 10.4324/9781315167909-18

Powis, B. (2020) *Embodiment, identity and disability sport: An ethnography of elite visually impaired athletes*. London: Routledge. DOI: 10.4324/9780429317675

Powis, B. & Macbeth, J.L. (2020) 'We know who is a cheat and who is not. But what can you do?': Athletes' perspectives on classification in visually impaired sport'. *International Review for the Sociology of Sport*, 55(5), 588–602. DOI: 10.1177/1012690218825209

Quinn, N., Misener, L. & Howe, P.D. (2020) 'All for one and one for all? Integration in high-performance sport'. *Managing Sport and Leisure*. DOI: 10.1080/23750472.2020.1829989

Richards, R. (2008) 'Writing the othered self: Autoethnography and the problem of objectification in writing about illness and disability'. *Qualitative Health Research*, 18(12), 1717–1728. DOI: 10.1177/1049732308325866

Shakespeare, T. (1996) 'Rules of engagement: Doing disability research'. *Disability & Society*, 11(1), 115–121. DOI: 10.1080/09687599650023380

Shakespeare, T. (2006) *Disability rights and wrongs*. London: Routledge.

Smith, B. & Bundon, A. (2018) 'Disability models: Explaining and understanding disability sport in different ways'. In: Brittain, I. & Beacom, A. (eds.) *The Palgrave handbook of paralympic studies*. London: Palgrave Macmillan, pp. 15–34.

Smith, B. & Wightman, L. (2019) 'Promoting physical activity to disabled people: Messengers, messages, guidelines and communication formats'. *Disability & Rehabilitation*. DOI: 10.1080/09638288.2019.1679896

Smith, B. (2008) 'Imagining being disabled through playing sport: The body and alterity as limits to imagining others' lives'. *Sport, Ethics and Philosophy*, 2(2), 142–157. DOI: 10.1080/17511320802222040

Smith, B., Kirby, N., Skinner, B., Wightman, L., Lucas, R. & Foster, C. (2019) 'Physical activity for disabled adults'. *British Journal of Sports Medicine*, 53(6), 335–336. DOI: 10.1136/bjsports-2018-100158

Sparkes, A. (2002) *Telling tales in sport and physical activity*. Champaign, IL: Human Kinetics.

Sparkes, A. & Smith, B. (2012) Narrative analysis as an embodied engagement with the lives of others. In: Holstein, J.A. & Gubruim, J.F. (eds.) *Varieties of narrative analysis*. London: Sage, pp. 53–74. DOI: 10.4135/9781506335117.n4

Stone, E. & Priestley, M. (1996). 'Parasites, pawns and partners: Disability research and the role of non-disabled researchers'. *British Journal of Sociology*, 47(4), 699–716.

Swain, J. & French, S. (2000). 'Towards an affirmation model of disability'. *Disability & Society*, 15(4), 569–582. DOI: 10.1080/09687590050058189

Terzi, L. (2004) 'The social model of disability: A philosophical critique'. *Journal of Applied Philosophy*, 21(2), 141–157. DOI: 10.1111/j.0264-3758.2004.00269.x

Tregaskis, C. (2004) 'Identity, positionality and power: Issues for disabled researchers. A response paper to Broun and Heshusius'. *Disability Studies Quarterly*, 24(2). DOI: 10.18061/dsq.v24i2.492

Van Maanen, J. (2011) *Tales of the field: On writing ethnography* (2nd Ed). London: University of Chicago Press.

Chapter 5

Barriers to Disability Sport Research and the Global South
A Personal View[1]

Leslie Swartz

In order to introduce the issues I want to address in this chapter, I will begin by telling a small part of the story of a person who was a major influence in my life and work in the field of disability rights in Africa.

Alexander Phiri was a very young boy from a poor family in what was then Southern Rhodesia (now Zimbabwe) when he was struck by a heavy vehicle. He lost both his legs in the accident, and, as he would tell it, his family abandoned him in the hospital after the accident, not knowing how to care for a disabled child. As it happens, a nurse in the hospital became very attached to little Alister, and cared for him. Later in life, Alister would say, 'becoming disabled was the best thing that happened to me.' The nurse took him in and cared for him, educated him, gave him a place in the world. Alister became a disability activist, rising to become the Secretary General of the Southern African Federation of the Disabled (SAFOD), an umbrella organization representing Disabled People's Organizations (DPOs) in ten southern African countries. He became known internationally as the consummate disability rights campaigner, and an activist to emulate.

Alister was anything but conventional, and he did not believe in sticking by the rules when they were not helpful. One day when I was running a workshop for SAFOD at a hotel in a southern African country, we all noticed that there were no ramps in the venue, so access for wheelchair users was restricted. Within two days, at Alister's insistence, workers were on site building ramps. Alister did not wait for regulations and red tape – in the context this would have got us nowhere – and by the end of the week, the ramps were functional and being used. This practicality extended into personal kindness. As is true elsewhere in the world, there is a relationship between disability and poverty. Flouting every pompous principle about the problems of charity, Alister, with his pragmatism, always had a store of $1 notes in his shirt pocket. When people who were desperate and needy approached him, he always had something to give. This generosity extended to how he treated me. I am a white man and I work at Stellenbosch University, which historically was an institution only for white people, and strongly

DOI: 10.4324/9781003153696-6

associated with propping up the apartheid regime in South Africa (Kenney, 2016). Understandably, some people in the disability movement were wary of me and did not approve of my involvement in disability rights in Africa, warning Alister that because of my race and the not so distant history of the university with which I was associated, that I must be a racist. Just as he fought every day against the disavowal and caricaturing of disabled Africans as weak and pathetic, Alister refused to put me in a convenient box, telling me, "I judge people on what they do." He gave me a chance, a chance which led me to a career of working with and learning from people, and trying to make a contribution to social change and disability rights.

Because of his accident as a child, Alister was physically a very small man (other activists would jokingly call him 'the smallest man in the disability movement'). During a SAFOD visit to Cape Town, I took Alexander and his colleagues to lunch at a restaurant. Playing on a stereotype of African masculinity, Alexander loudly announced, "I want to eat cow". He was given, and ate all of, the biggest steak I have ever seen. I teased Alister then, as I teased him on other occasions, that he was eating far too much – this was not good for his health. His response was to order a large, sugary desert to eat.

Unlike most of the impoverished people with whom he worked, Alister had access when not travelling for work to a swimming pool and an opportunity to exercise. We discussed lifestyle issues and the fact that friends and fellow-activists routinely, it felt, died young all around us from lifestyle-related diseases. Many of them were obese and had no opportunity to exercise. Alister, in his ebullient service to others, did not look after himself, and he died of complications of type 2 diabetes at the age of 57. He was a beacon for disability rights in Africa and the world, and in the midst of an activism which was recognising that rights mean nothing if people are dying.

The world of disability sport, the world inhabited by many contributors to and readers of this book, feels in some ways on another planet from the world within which Alister worked, an often inaccessible and excluding world where the idea of sport and lifestyle issues was not even considered, or a luxury. This is the reality not just of Africa, but of the Global South more broadly – the poorer countries of the world, the countries where most people on the planet live. But of course if there is to be disability inclusion and participation globally, healthy lifestyles and physical activity must be part of the story. At present, in disability and development circles, and ten years after Alister's death, there remains surprisingly little focus on lifestyle concerns. There are many reasons for this, but one I want to deal with in this chapter is the unimaginability of the world of disability and poverty in low-income countries to the mainstream of disability sport research, dominated as that field is by people from wealthier contexts. My task in this chapter is simple: not to provide solutions to complex problems but to ask readers to gain a sense with me of the world of Alister's work. This may be a step to helping eliminate boundaries to engagement.

The world of disability in Africa which I am privileged to inhabit does seem to me to be a world away from that of the Paralympics, for example, with its excellent resources, its concerns about classification, its concern with inspiring people, and changing the world. When I think of the mission of the IPC, which in its current iteration is to **"Make for an inclusive world through Para sport"**, I am struck by the contrast between the world of the IPC and the world of DPOs in southern Africa. The wonderful audacity of the IPC is to change the world – not only is the IPC committed to making for an inclusive world, but the IPC is making a claim about how to do it - Para sport is a means to effect this change. But how does one make the whole world more inclusive, and how does one know whether one has achieved this?

Some years ago, I was very fortunate to be part of the International Olympic Committee Consensus Group on mental health in elite athletes (Reardon et al., 2019). My job as part of this meeting was to convene a subgroup to review the evidence on mental health in Paralympians (Swartz et al., 2019). When I attended the meeting of the group in Lausanne, however, I found my job was rather different and broader than I had anticipated. The convenors of the group had done a spectacular job in getting us to do most of the work before we all met in Lausanne, and this enabled us to use the few days together much more effectively that we would have done. I was the only person from Africa at the meeting, and there were very few participants from other low- or middle-income countries. The very first presentation at our meeting was by one of the many people there from the USA, and the presentation was excellent. A very sensible suggestion was that in order to meet the mental health needs of elite athletes it would be a good idea if a mental health professional like a psychologist or a psychiatrist could be embedded with each elite sports team. This is a great idea, but I pointed out that this was a view from a tiny part of the world – most low- and middle-income countries have very few mental health professionals, and this means in practice that in some countries, for example, there may be one psychiatrist for a million people. In such a context, any recommendation to embed a mental health professional within a team or group of teams would be ridiculous and bad for public mental health in that country. I found the participants at the meeting exceptionally open to what I had to say, and I was pleased that in the final consensus statement, this point as we have it is not an 'add-in' – it is up front. The world of most people, with or without disabilities, looks very different from that inhabited by those of us attending a meeting in Lausanne.

Let me give you another example. Recently, I attended a disability studies meeting in Europe. One of the keynote speakers from the UK gave a superb talk about how important it was for disability studies scholars to engage with disability in the global south – as this is where most people with disabilities live. It was an excellent talk, and I agreed with every word, but from the floor I pointed out that if disability studies is about anything, it is about the politics of voice – 'nothing about us without us' (Charlton, 1998). There was an irony in a major international disability studies meeting having a keynote speaker from the global north telling other participants from the global north that they should be speaking with and listening to people from the global south. How about having a disability studies scholar from the global south as a keynote speaker? This would be a good start. My suggestion was met with applause, and I took great comfort from that. I am not aware that this has yet been acted upon by organisers of that particular set of meetings, though it is important to honour the fact that the IPC did invite a speaker from the global south to give a keynote address – and that this address forms the basis for the current chapter.

How, then, do we get closer to the IPC vision of "making for an inclusive world"? The IPC has done a great deal, not least through the Agitos Foundation, to begin to realise this dream. This foundation describes itself as follows: "We are the leading global organisation developing sport activities for people with disabilities as a tool for changing lives and contributing to an inclusive society for all." (Agitos Foundation, n.d.). But what does this mean? The Agitos website says: "We work on a global basis, reaching more than 100 countries in every continent of the world. We focus on distributing resources and expertise to the areas where they are most needed." This is a large claim, a big vision. I want to contrast this large global vision with the much more local and ad hoc operations of locally-based DPOs, and the more common but less obvious daily struggles of ordinary people to be included in a world which does not include them.

The Three T's of Disability Inclusion in the Majority World

I often joke that there are three Ts to be aware of when thinking about disability and inclusion in the majority world. None of these will be unfamiliar to readers of this book but they take on local inflections. The three Ts are Transport, Toilets, and Time. They are linked to one another, as I shall show, but I now give examples of each.

Transport

Imagine that you are a person with a mobility impairment in rural Malawi. You get a cold, but you ignore it because it is just so difficult to get to the health facility. Your cold gets worse and eventually you have what will later be diagnosed as pneumonia. You have to get to the clinic. If you are lucky, you will have a choice – to pay a neighbour to put you in a wheelbarrow to get to the clinic, or to pay someone else to get you there by perching you on the crossbar of their bicycle (Munthali et al., 2019).

This is not uncommon in Africa. When I first got involved in disability studies, a paediatrician said to me: if you want to understand childhood disability in South Africa, put a 25kg sack of potatoes on your back and walk 10 km. I have never forgotten this, because it is so true. It also speaks to cascades of completely preventable disablement – if you are the nondisabled parent of a developmentally disabled child, with very little infrastructure, the chances are that you will disable yourself at some point through the sheer physical labour of trying to move the child around.

Here is a second example. Siyabulela Mkabile works with on issues related to parenting intellectually disabled (ID) children in Cape Town, capital of the second richest province in South Africa, and a place where there is a hospital with very good intellectual disability services. Many parents do not bring their children to care, and a substantial proportion miss appointments, according to those working in the services. There is a range reasons for this, some of which relate to differing understandings of intellectual disability, its causes and supposed "cures". But very prominent in Siyabulela's data is a much simpler story (Mkabile & Swartz, in press). Imagine that you are the parent of a child with ID who, like all children, is curious and active, and who also has somewhat atypical judgement. Just to get to the gate of the hospital with your child you have to take two minibus taxis to get to the hospital. Minibus taxis are the lifeblood of many African cities – at once miraculous, clever, and horribly dangerous. Eventually you get the child on to the first taxi, then on to the second one. The hospital is on a very busy street with chaotic traffic, and many taxis going in all directions. You get off the taxi. It's raining and visibility is not great. Your child has been cooped up with far too many people in the taxi and you yourself feel queasy. Your child runs off as soon as she is able and you are convinced she will be killed in the traffic (a not unlikely scenario). You manage to save her, and you get to the gate of the hospital, only to find that the ID service is in a building far away from the hospital entrance. Eventually, and completely exhausted, you arrive at the ID service after the time that the day's clinic has officially ended. Luckily for you, the kind service providers, though exasperated, see you and your child and book you for follow-up assessments in two weeks' time. You greatly value the service. Is it any wonder though that you miss the next appointment and become a defaulter, "lost to follow-up"?

Toilets

Access to sanitation is a major issue for many people world-wide. One in three schools globally does not have proper toilet facilities, according to UNICEF, but where there are toilets, they are often inaccessible. A recent study in Malawi (Zaunda et al., 2018) found that not a single school in a district had fully accessible toilets. A study in Guatemala (Kuper et al., 2018) similarly found that "People with disabilities in Guatemala experience greater difficulties in accessing sanitation facilities and practicing hygienic behaviours than their peers without disabilities" (p. 1)/, with older people with disabilities being at a particular disadvantage In order to feel included, to be part of the more inclusive world, which is the vision of the IPC, it helps if you can be clean and hygienic. It helps not to smell. It helps not to disgust people.

Time

Where facilities are stretched and there are few services, the issue of time comes to the fore. In a recent African study, Munthali and colleagues found that health care personnel who generally held good attitudes towards people with disabilities were reluctant to treat them because, as they said, "this one will delay us." (Munthali et al., 2019)

The issue of time interacts with other issues, including that of transport. For example, Taxi drivers in rural South Africa told Richard Vergunst and colleagues that they were very willing to accommodate wheelchair users and space in the taxi was not too much of a problem. But as taxi drivers they were always in a hurry, so, they said, of course you can use our taxis to get about but "You must carry your wheelchair" yourself and get on to the taxi as soon as possible (Vergunst et al., 2015). Similarly, some South African researchers have looked at the question of trying to get around when you are a person with a communication impairment – the process of hearing the taxi driver, or of communicating to the taxi driver where you want to go, may take longer if you have a communication or hearing impairment, and there is a danger that nobody will wait for you (Green et al., 2015).

None of these three Ts examples will be unfamiliar to anyone working in the disability field even in wealthy countries, but they are issues writ large in the majority world – we cannot assume that there is an infrastructure which makes the added benefits of Para sport to make the world more inclusive possible. There are many things, and more basic things, to think about first. Most community development work looking at creating a more inclusive world starts, appropriately enough, with some form of community meeting. Before we can have such a meeting, we have to think about who can get to the meeting, and in time. Commonly, we exclude people with disabilities before we start. It is absolutely true that some people with disabilities are hidden away from the world because of shame and stigma, and these people will probably not get to meetings. But there are also the simple practical questions of who can physically travel places.

Wanting to make the world more inclusive in the IPC sense is to a certain degree about attitudes, and also about knowledge about what non-normative bodies can do. Attitudinal issues are, of course, important. Willson Tarusarira (please see a publication on his work by Tarusarira & McKenzie, 2019) is currently working with women who have migrated from Zimbabwe to Cape Town, and who are also the mothers of disabled children. These are women who are no strangers to being blamed – for producing defective children, for bringing shame on families, for creating a situation in which other community members fear being polluted by the disabled children and hence "catching" disability, for being witches who may bewitch others, and, once they reach Cape Town, for being a drain on meagre state resources by claiming care dependency benefits. There is a litany of exclusion and punishment for causing disability. How do we make the world more inclusive for these people?

The Importance of Local Activism

In order to make the world more inclusive, it is important to start from where people are. This involves understanding what people are already doing, or trying to do, to make a more inclusive society. It involves being attuned to local factors, and to the wide range of local cultural contexts. At the start this chapter I mentioned my admiration for Alexander Phiri. One thing Alexander always did was to ask people what they did to manage, and to make things better. And we do learn surprising things if we engage even when it is difficult. Let me give you an example from my own experience. If you look at most handbooks on community development work in low-income contexts, just about every single task requires that people can see. Acutely aware of this, when doing community-based training with disability activists from ten southern African countries, when I asked participants to do mapping of their communities, I provided digital voice recorders for those with visual impairments. Before long, I was the butt of joking by the people with visual impairment at the meeting. First, they found my extreme anxiety about wanting to include them amusing and they wanted to be seen as a bit more robust than they saw me as viewing them. More fundamentally, though, they said to me, "Leslie, if you want to know what an African city looks like, the people you must ask are the blind people." We have to know where the potholes are, where the traffic drives on the pavement, where there is a danger from livestock – what do you think blind people talk about in Africa? We talk about how places look." I learned an important lesson about the strengths and adaptational abilities of disabled people in scarce-resource contexts – it was not all misery. It was also ingenuity borne out of necessity, a constant grassroots working at making the world more inclusive. In her very important contributions to how we understand ID psychologically, the British psychoanalyst Valerie Sinason (2010) discusses what she terms (in language that would no longer be used, but which was the preferred usage at the time she was writing), "secondary handicap". The term is quite complex, but it is enough to say here that one of the key senses in which Sinason uses it concerns the way in which socially excluded and isolated people may actually exaggerate their impairments and make themselves seem more impaired than they are as a result of being so excluded. At times the person with ID may implicitly be saying, "You think I am incapable and disgusting – I will become even more incapable and disgusting" – sometimes as an aggressive response to being disavowed. In my work with disability activists, I also came to see that there was also secondary ability – people becoming more resourceful because of the difficulties posed by their social isolation and the social barriers in their way.

Looking at Disability in the World

Part of understanding the local, though, is about understanding and grappling with the way we see things. Rosemarie Garland-Thomson (2009), who is a leader feminist critical disability studies in the USA, entitled what may be her most famous book rather wonderfully. The book is entitled *Staring: How we look*. I wish I had written such clever title – Garland-Thomson, who has a visible impairment, concerns herself in the book both with the question of how we look *to* others (how we appear), and how we stare *at* others – the complex dance of staring, looking away, the pride but also the shame at being looked at and the pride but shame at looking at others. She views staring as part of being human, but also as profoundly politically structured. And, not surprisingly for this chapter, whenever we have binaries along the lines of power, we have what become interlocking and mutually constitutive images of power, raising questions about who may look at whom and in what ways, whose eyes must be averted, who may frankly stare, and so on.

I do not have space to discuss this in detail, but suffice it to say that I doubt that anyone would disagree that there has historically been a politics of how men look at women, how white people look at black people, and how people with normative bodies look at those with non-normative bodies. There are of course many ways in which the looking can be structured and ordered and this is especially interesting in the case of the Para sport. This tradition started essentially through a rehabilitation gaze at Stoke Mandeville hospital in the UK. Though the role of the Paralympics remains in some central ways about health, the Paralympics today is also, like all elite sport, an important spectacle and commercially embedded enterprise (Howe, 2008).

Spectacle in a broader sense is key to understanding global disability issues and to understanding disability and decoloniality (Ned, 2022). A piece I find helpful in this regard is a short paper by Imada in which she says:

> In the broadest sense, colonialism demanded able bodyminds *(sic)* from subordinated subjects. Colonial projects imposed impossible regimes and expectations of self-regulation its subjects would not be able to perform. Thus, the colonized were **always already figured and constituted as disabled**, whether because of their perceived unproductivity as laborers; embodied racial-sexual differences; "unchaste" proclivities of their women; susceptibility to moral contagion and infectious diseases; or inability to learn. In the undulating colonial hall of mirrors, the inversion of these qualities — too much learnedness and the adoption of European manners, for example — could mean colonized people had failed to maintain the vigor of their "race." Thus, we begin to see how disability operated as a flexible and capacious concept and a very useful weapon during the incarceration, elimination, and removal of unfit colonial Others.
>
> (Imada, 2017: 1; emphasis in the original)

There's more work which we need to do theoretically on this, but I think that Imada does capture some of the historical and ongoing intertwining between racism and disablism – she suggests that Africans have been, and are, damned if they do and damned if they don't – in their "natural" state they are not fully human and in that sense, they are not fully able. But if they become educated and European then they lose their innate Africanness and hence once again are not fully human or able. This way of linking the idea of Africanness to either a primordial savagery, or its obverse, and kind of savage nobility (Lucas & Barrett, 1995) Lucas and Barrett referred to as the Arcadian versus the Barbarian image of the primitive was clearly part of the colonial project. But it has also been used by postcolonial and certainly post-apartheid African leaders – such as South African former president, Jacob Zuma, for example, said that what he termed 'clever blacks' would be concerned about his corrupt practices, but the real blacks, the true Africans would not be concerned about these things (Dimitris Kitis et al., 2018). If you hear the not so faint echo here of the populism of former USA president Donald Trump in the current era of a war on facts, you are not wrong (Swartz, 2019). But that's another story.

Several years ago, Maria Marchetti-Mercer and I published an article entitled *"Disabling Africa: the power of depiction and the benefits of discomfort"* (Swartz & Marchetti-Mercer, 2018). In this piece, we discuss our work on disability, migration, and ageing, and we tell the story of a Deaf woman, formerly a white South African, now living in a high-income country. She has access to far better services there than we can provide in South Africa, and we write of her in this way:

> As she puts it, *"When I go back to South Africa I feel disabled."* (p. 483) Speaking about her Deaf friends who have remained in South Africa she comments, *"I think they are in the wrong country"*.
>
> (p. 483)

In our article we discuss our discomfort at on the one hand wanting to acknowledge and support her reality, but on the other hand not wishing to align ourselves with a quite pernicious kind of white racist Afro-pessimism in which we reproduce problematic tropes about disability and the politics of service provision and care in what have famously been called "shithole countries" by former USA president Donald Trump.

Is it Possible to Change the World through Disability Sport?

I have gone a bit of a long (and rather academic) way round to bring us back to my central dilemma in this chapter. I do think the dilemma, to some degree, is one of spectacle, or of 'how we look'. In some senses, in preparing the chapter I set myself up to offer a view of disability in the majority world. This contrasts with what to an extent I regard as the high gloss packaging of disability which we saw especially in the 2012 London Paralympic Games, often heralded for being a key moment for disability inclusion and deservedly so (Bantjes & Swartz, 2018; Pullen, Jackson & Silk, 2020). But the language of triumph and inspiration, the implication that anyone with enough grit and determination can excel has its downsides. I am not against being inspired by things, but like many critics, including Howe (2011), I worry about how supercripping turns disability into a personal morality issue – good, strong people overcome and triumph whereas those with less grit do badly. I am not against grit, determination, and personal responsibility. A key factor, as colleagues and I have shown predicting who would get into IPC meetings and who would get medals was, unsurprisingly, not personal grit and determination but the GDP of the country from which an athlete came (Swartz et al., 2016). Para sport is expensive, and it does not take anything away from personal achievement to point out that in many cases it takes money and resources to come to be inspirational.

There is a definite parallel between disability as a spectacle and Africa as a spectacle. Recently, for example, the television channel CNN started showing programmes devoted to Africa, which they tellingly describe as "the continent you thought you knew". They set themselves up to educate the viewership, by implication, about the "real Africa". This Africa, though it does have some rehabilitated wild animals in it, seems to me to be a continent-wide shopping mall. The new Africa of CNN is an Africa of cutting-edge fashion and design, with a bit of edgy hip-hop thrown in. Here's the subtext: you thought Africa was a primitive shithole, but actually it is so modern, and you can buy it. There is certainly an element here of what the John and Jean Comaroff (2009) have called "Ethnicity Inc" – the commodification and selling of the "ethnic" as the true, genuine luxury, and there is a much longer discussion to be had here. In thinking about disability sport and lifestyle in Africa and the global south more broadly, we have to do more than reproduce or question tired stereotypes. I suggest a few ways forward in my concluding remarks.

Conclusion and Suggestions

Access to exercise and lifestyle interventions is a matter of life and death in low-income countries and contexts, and as part of the package of disability rights activities, physical activity opportunities are important. The world of disability sport, however, is (understandably) dominated by contributions from wealthier contexts. Many organisations, including the IPC, have stated their commitment to greater inclusion and greater opportunity for lifestyle changes. It is relatively easy to develop small-scale interventions in low and middle income countries; it is another and much more difficult matter to reach people who by the very nature of their impairments and the infrastructure in their countries may be hidden and distant from where many interventions take place.

There is no easy solution to this, and the path to real change for people who need it most is likely to be long and arduous. It is essential to join hands with grassroots organisations and with robust research methods to see what works and what does not work. Helping small numbers of people to become spectacular to others does not help those others with the very real life and death issues of lack of exercise and toxic lifestyles affecting disabled people in the global south. Large claims about working in many countries and inspiring the world are helpful rallying cries, but they do not necessarily reflect meaningful social change. The environmental and technical challenges of getting large numbers of excluded people moving in a rapidly urbanising global south with substantial environmental degradation are huge. These challenges and the obstacles of attitudinal barriers are mutually reinforcing – but the opportunities to chip away at real wicked problems are truly amazing.

In this regard, there is a great deal of ingenuity and expertise in the global south. I certainly saw this in the work of Alexander Phiri, for example, and see it with other colleagues. In what is effectively the failed state of Zimbabwe, people show great ingenuity in managing to live their lives – not ideally, not spectacularly, but they live (Gukurume, 2015). We need to learn from local methods and ingenuity. The pragmatism of Alexander Phiri is not unique to him.

In summary, it is crucial for people interested in physical activity and lifestyle issues in the majority world to get their hands dirty, to think globally, to work locally, and to be rigorous about allowing for the possibility – the fact – that we will get things wrong. We need to learn from successes as well as failures. Wanting something to work is a good thing – but it is not the same as knowing that it works. But whatever the barriers, doing something and trying things out are important.

Note

1 This is a revised version of a keynote address delivered at the IPC Vista Conference, 4–7 September 2019, Amsterdam.

References

Bantjes, J., & Swartz, L. (2018). "Social inclusion through Para sport": A critical reflection on the current state of play. *Physical Medicine & Rehabilitation Clinics of North America, 29*, 409–416. DOI: doi:10.1016/j.pmr.2018.01.006.

Charlton, J. I. (1998). *Nothing about us without us*. Berkeley, CA: University of California Press.

Comaroff, J. L., & Comaroff, J. (2009). *Ethnicity, Inc*. Chicago, IL:University of Chicago Press.

Dimitris Kitis, E., Milani, T. M., & Levon, E. (2018). 'Black diamonds', 'clever blacks' and other metaphors: Constructing the black middle class in contemporary South African print media. *Discourse & Communication, 12*(2), 149–170.

Garland-Thomson, R. (2009). *Staring: How we look*. Oxford: Oxford University Press.

Green, S., Mophosho, M., & Khoza-Shangase, K. (2015). Commuting and communication: An investigation of taxi drivers' experiences, attitudes and beliefs about passengers with communication disorders. *African Journal of Disability, 4*(1): 1–8.

Gukurume, S. (2015). Livelihood resilience in a hyperinflationary environment: Experiences of people engaging in money-burning (kubhena mari) transactions in Harare, Zimbabwe. *Social Dynamics, 41*(2), 219–234.

Howe, P. D. (2008). *The cultural politics of the Paralympic movement: Through an anthropological lens*. London: Routledge.

Howe, P. D. (2011). Cyborg and supercrip: The Paralympics technology and the (dis) empowerment of disabled athletes. *Sociology, 45*(5), 868–882.

Imada, A. L. (2017). A decolonial disability studies?. *Disability Studies Quarterly, 37*(3). https://dsq-sds.org/article/view/5984/4694

Kenney, H. (2016). *Verwoerd: Architect of apartheid.* Johannesburg: Jonathan Ball Publishers.

Kuper, H., Mactaggart, I., White, S., Dionicio, C., Cañas, R., Naber, J., ... & Biran, A. (2018). Exploring the links between water, sanitation and hygiene and disability; Results from a case-control study in Guatemala. *PLoS One, 13*(6): e0197360.

Lucas, R. H., & Barrett, R. J. (1995). Interpreting culture and psychopathology: Primitivist themes in cross-cultural debate. *Culture, Medicine and Psychiatry, 19*(3), 287–326.

Mkabile, S., & Swartz, L. (in press). Putting cultural difference in its place: Barriers to access to health services for parents of children with intellectual disability in an urban African setting. *International Journal of Social Psychiatry*, doi:10.1177/00207640211043150.

Munthali, A., Swartz, L., Mannan, H., MacLachlan, M., Chilimampunga, C., & Makope, C. (2019). "This one will delay us": Barriers to accessing health care services among persons with disabilities in Malawi. *Disability and Rehabilitation, 41*, 683–690. doi:10.1080/09638288.2017.1404148

Ned, L. Y. (2022). African renaissance as a premise for reimagined disability studies in Africa. *Journal of Black Studies, 53*(5), 485–504.

Pullen, E., Jackson, D., & Silk, M. (2020). (Re-) presenting the paralympics: Affective nationalism and the "able-disabled". *Communication & sport, 8*(6), 715–737.

Reardon, C. L., Hainline, B., Aron, C. M., Baron, D., Bauam, A. L., Bindra, A., Budgett, R., Campriani, J. M., Currie, A., Derevensky, J. L., Glick, I. D., Gorczynski, P., Gouttebarge, V., Grandner, M. A., Han, D. H., McDuff, D., Mountjoy, M., Polat, A., Purcell, R., Putukian, R., Rice, S., Sills, A., Stull, T., Swartz, L., Zhu, L. J., & Engebretsen, L. (2019). International Olympic Committee consensus statement on mental health in elite athletes. *British Journal of Sports Medicine, 53*, 667–699. doi:10.1136/bjsports-2019-100731

Sinason, V. (2010). *Mental handicap and the human condition: an analytical approach to intellectual disability.* London: Free Association Books.

Swartz, L. (2019). Disability and citizenship in the Global South in a post-truth era. In B. Watermeyer, J. McKenzie & L. Swartz (Eds.). *The Palgrave handbook of disability and citizenship in the Global South.* (pp. 57–65). New York: Palgrave Macmillan

Swartz, L., Bantjes, J., Rall, D., Ferriera, S., Blauwet, C., & Derman, W. (2016). "A more equitable society": The politics of global fairness in Paralympic sport. *PLoS One 11*(12): e0167481. doi:10.1371/journal.pone.0167481

Swartz, L., Hunt, X., Bantjes, J., Hainline, B., & Reardon, C. L. (2019). Mental health symptoms and disorders in Paralympic athletes: A narrative review. *British Journal of Sports Medicine, 53*, 737–740. doi:10.1136/bjsports-2019-100731

Swartz, L., & Marchetti-Mercer, M. (2018). Disabling Africa: The power of depiction and the benefits of discomfort. *Disability and Society, 33*, 482–486 doi:10.1080/02684527.2017.1400240.

Tarusarira, W., & McKenzie, J. (2019). Disability, migration, and family support: The case of Zimbabwean asylum seekers in South Africa. In B. Watermeyer, J. McKenzie & L. Swartz (Eds.). *The Palgrave handbook of disability and citizenship in the global south* (pp. 359–369). Cham: Palgrave Macmillan.

Vergunst, R., Swartz, L., Mji, G., MacLachlan, M., & Mannan, H. (2015). 'You must carry your wheelchair' – Barriers to accessing health care in a South African rural area. *Global Health Action*, 8, 29003, doi:10.3402/gha.v8.29003.

Zaunda, H., Holm, R. H., Itimu-Phiri, A., Malota, M., & White, S. (2018). A qualitative assessment of disability friendly water and sanitation facilities in primary schools, Rumphi, Malawi. *Development Southern Africa*, 35(6), 760–773.

Part II

Disability, Sport and Intersectionality

Chapter 6

Disabled Female Sporting Bodies

Reflections on (In)Visibility of disAbility in Sport

Karen P. DePauw

Sport, a highly visible and influential socio-cultural institution, is not only an integral part of society worldwide, it is found across and within cultures. Sport sociologist Donnelly (1996) wrote that sport reflects society and associated societal values; as such, sport serves as a conveyor of socio-cultural context(s), often the dominant or primary culture. In this way, a traditional paradigm of sport which privileges certain sporting bodies reproduces the status quo and therefore social inequality. Given the visibility of sport, Donnelly and others argued that sport can also provide a context for resistance and a site for social change (DePauw, 1997a; Donnelly, 1996; Sage, 1993). Sage (1993) articulated clearly that "sport and physical education are practices which are socially constructed within the culture in which they exist" (p. 153). He challenged sport scholars to be agents of change with "a grounding in an understanding the power, privilege and dominance [of sport] within society" and "social relations which underlie social inequality, sexism, racism and other types of social injustice" (Sage, 1993 p.153). Today, we would not only include ableism, homophobia, transphobia and more but also the importance of identifying and understanding intersectionality of these social identities.

Sport, especially elite competitive sport, has contributed to the social construction of the "sporting body" which in the Western world historically privileged white, heterosexual, able-bodied males from middle and upper classes (DePauw, 1997a). In his seminal work on stigma, sociologist Goffman (1963) described the "prototypical figure whom Western society constructs as its ideal and its norm" (Garland-Thomson, 1997, p. 32) as "young, married, white, urban, northern, heterosexual, Protestant, father of college education, fully employed, of good complexion, weight and height, and a recent record in sports" (Goffman, 1963, p. 128). I noted with interest the inclusion of sport in the description of the ideal figure. Although the body is not mentioned specifically, the descriptors assume an "able body". Sport has contributed to the social construction of the body, normal, and even disability (e.g., disabled body) as visualized through the sporting body. The sporting body is seen as an ideal (perfect) body and depicts athleticism and ability associated with that body – the able normal body.

DOI: 10.4324/9781003153696-8

This body and the performance must also be 'aesthetically pleasing' as articulated by Purdue and Howe (2013):

> ...aesthetically pleasing sporting performances are often those that represent purposeful, controlled bodily movement in a manner displaying, one or more of the attributes of speed, endurance, strength, and/or high levels of skill in the achievement of sport specific excellence.
>
> (p. 35)

Exploring the disabled female sporting body and disabled female experiences in sport begins with an acknowledgement of the human body at the core, understanding disability studies and feminist perspectives, and ultimately requires changing the research paradigm. The exploration in the narrative that follows includes revisiting the constructs articulated in the (in)Visibility of disAbility (DePauw, 1997a) and reflecting upon these in our current contemporary context.

The Human Body at the Core

Our current notions of ability are related to socially constructed and acceptable views of the body that are informed by the dominant cultural perspective of the "able" body. That is, the body is seen through a set of cultural default settings arrived at the wholesome adoption of ableist cultural values (Davis, 1995). As Thomas Kuhn (2012) wrote in the *Structure of Scientific Revolutions*, anomaly appears only against the background provided by the paradigm. Although the paradigm seems to be shifting, the image ...

> "[of body and disability] ... is powered by the imperative of the norm, and then is supplemented by the notion of progress, human perfectibility, and the elimination of deviance, to create a dominating, hegemonic vision of what the human body should be".
>
> (Davis, 1995, p. 35)

Because of its visibility, the human body is the focal point of identity and the means through which identity is viewed, defined and perceived (Davis, 1995; DePauw, 1997a; Garland-Thomson, 1997; Thomson, 2017). Individuals who have visible impairments and experience disability are often identified and judged primarily through their bodies because these bodies are often conspicuous. Attention is drawn to the body, and we stare at the 'extraordinary' body (Garland-Thomson, 2009). Given the cultural context in which we live, comparisons are frequently made to the normal or perfect body.

It is important to understand which bodies are visible and privileged in physical activity and sport through the framework of marginality (masculinity, physicality, sexuality) in sport (DePauw, 1997a, p. 422), by the ableist notion of body (Davis, 1995) and the "cultural rules about what bodies should be or do"

(Garland-Thomson, 1997, p. 6). The description of this body has relied upon biological essentialism, which has reinforced traditional views of body and a quest for the perfect or "ideal" body and enhanced performance.

Science and medicine together have constructed the "normal" body and the search for the perfect body. As such, it has also identified deviations from the "norm" including the female body, the colonized, racialized, the sexualized body, the HIV-infected body and the disabled body. The "disabled" body has been described as imperfect, incomplete, and inadequate, and viewed as signifying abnormality and a transgression of the ideal body (Davis, 1995; DePauw, 1997a; Garland-Thomson, 2002; Linton, 1998).

Disability Studies and Feminist Perspectives

Feminist scholars in the late 20th century (e.g., Garland-Thomson, 1997, 2002; Linton, 1998; Morris, 1992) took issue with the medical model of disability and embraced the social model of disability. Introduced by Oliver (1990), this model encouraged moving away from the medical model to a socio-cultural approach in order to acknowledge and incorporate the social identity of individuals who experience disability. This trend was enhanced by the emergence of 'disability studies' through which scholars are informed by the conversation about disability rights, access, equity and social justice. As a result, the historical and traditional static wheelchair symbol ♿ is giving way to a more active and accurate representation of wheelchair users and individuals with disabilities in general 🦼.

The object of disability studies is not the person/individual (and one's body) but the "set of social, historical, economic, and cultural processes" that control our thinking about and through the body (Davis, 1995, p. 2). Further, disability studies emerged to examine the construction and function of disability and specifically as a space to think critically about disability (Linton, 1998). These "scholarly explorations and the initiatives undertaken by the disability rights movement have resulted in new paradigms used to understand disability as a social, political and cultural phenomenon" (Linton, 1998 p. 2). In *Academic Ableism*, Dolmage articulates that disability studies take a "critical approach to disability, grounded in disability rights and foregrounding the experiences and perspectives of people with disabilities, maintaining that disability is a political and cultural identity, not simply a medical condition" (2017, p. 5).

Femininity and disability are bound together in patriarchal culture (Garland-Thomson, 1997, 2009; Thomson, 2017). The female body has traditionally been considered deviant as is currently the case for the disabled body. Garland-Thomson (1997) wrote that "strands of feminist thought most applicable to disability studies are those that go beyond a narrow focus on gender alone to undertake a broad sociopolitical critique of systemic, inequitable power relations based on social categories grounded in the body" (p. 19). Further she states:

> Many parallels exist between the social meanings attributed to female bodies and those assigned to disabled bodies. Both the female and disabled body are cast as deviant and inferior, both are excluded from full participation in public as well as economic life; both are defined in opposition to a norm that I assumed to possess natural physical superiority.
>
> (p. 19)

A feminist perspective grounded in feminist theory can be used not just to analyze gender and disability in sport but provides for social action and social change in sport. Specifically, a feminist perspective demands an understanding of the nature of sport and of disability and their interaction. A critical analysis provides not only the impact of disability on sport but the intersection of gender and disability in the context of sport requires us to view sport and disability as socially constructed and challenges us to examine the social values reproduced in society (DePauw, 1997a). This raises the issue of the traditional model of sport based upon the socially constructed ideal sporting body and the marginality that excludes those who do not "fit" within the traditional model and defines how conformity allows for inclusion. The marginality framework consists of three overlapping circles which the key ideals of sport are shown: specifically, masculinity, physicality and sexuality (DePauw, 1997a).

Accordingly, masculinity (or hegemonic masculinity [Connell, 1995]), in this context, was defined by able-bodied heterosexual males demonstrating characteristics of strength, courage, independence and more. Within the construct of masculinity came specific articulation of femininity and biological identification as female. Physicality was defined as able-bodied physical ability or prowess. Sexuality was defined as the socially accepted view of heterosexuality. Traditionally, males and females were included in sport unless they crossed the line of socially acceptable masculinity/femininity, physicality and sexuality. 'Masculine' looking women and effeminate males were not always welcome in sport and their social identities remained hidden in most cases historically. Transgender individuals were actively excluded historically, and women athletes had to be tested to prove they were female (DePauw, 1997b). For individuals with disabilities whose impairment was not apparent or performance was not negatively impacted but still conformed to the other two ideals, they were allowed to compete (e.g., post-polio equestrian in 1924 Helsinki; Wheelchair archer in 1984 [DePauw & Gavron, 2005]).

This marginality framework can be used to understand the conditions by which an athlete is a 'fit' and is included in sport or is excluded from or marginalized within sport (DePauw, 1997a). Although the boundaries of these constructs have been crossed in the case of para-athletes (physicality), and LGBTQ+ athletes (sexuality) competing at the highest levels, the three constructs and the intersection of these continue to be markers of marginality. Boundaries were crossed with the inclusion of wheelchair athletes in the 1984 Olympics Games (demonstration events were held until 2004). Not only was the traditional notion of able-bodied physicality crossed but female wheelchair users were allowed to compete. In addition to competing in the World Wheelchair Games and Paralympics, wheelchair athletes were also competing in major (able-bodied) international sporting events, such as the Boston Marathon (initially only males, then females), which seemed the most acceptable sport, especially in that the athletes' upper bodies depicted strength and power and appeared less different in physicality. Although not discussed publicly at the time, the performances of these wheelchair athletes were likely to be more aesthetically pleasing and therefore, more acceptable than those with more severe physical impairments. Another boundary that was crossed was sexuality especially seen through individuals competing as an openly LGBTQ+ athlete (i.e., Dover in 1988) in the Olympics. Until recently, most LGBTQ+ athletes have 'come out' after ending their competitive careers. The intersection of these three ideals/constructs is also at play here including Paralympians who compete openly (Wikipedia, n.d.).

There is yet another example of 'fit' and marginality – the case of Oscar Pistorius. Specifically, the controversy around Pistorius, a world record holder sprinter, and his participation in both the Paralympics and Olympics. Because he competed with technologically advanced protheses, he was considered 'too-able' and having unfair advantage. His performance was threatening to sport and the cultural assumptions about normal bodies (Burkett, McNamee & Potthast; 2011; Corrigan, Paton, Holt, and Hardin, 2010; Wolbring, 2008)

As stated above, members of socially marginalized groups have been not only excluded from sport but also marginalized within sport (DePauw, 1997a). Given the social constructs of normal, body and able-bodied-ness and the perceptions of the sporting body (perfect, sculpted, beautiful), I reflected on the exclusion of athletes with impairments, their entrée into the sporting world, and pondered if the physical performances of these athletes could be seen and be accepted as sport and valued as such. In the case of individuals with disabilities and the spectacle of the body, I argued the (in)Visibility of disAbility in sport in the following three ways:

1. Invisibility of disability in sport – excluded from sport
2. Visibility of disability – visible in sport as **disabled** athletes
3. (in)Visibility of disAbility – visible as **athletes**

Prior to the mid-20th century, individuals with impairments were mostly excluded from sport. Opportunities (grass roots through competitions) to participate were limited and when available, they were in segregated settings (e.g., wheelchair basketball, World Games for the Deaf, Special Olympics). Opportunities for females were fewer than for males.

Significant progress has been made. There are many more opportunities that span from the local to the international levels and athletes with disabilities and disability sport programs are visible to the broader sporting world. Perhaps most significant is the development of the Paralympics and their incorporation into the highly visible sporting world of the Olympics. The Paralympic movement has been touted as a catalyst for disability rights (Blauwet & Willick, 2012), an agent of change, empowerment, and gender parity (Dean, Bundon, Howe & Abele, 2021; Purdue & Howe; 2012; Silva & Howe, 2018). Although much of this has been positive and about social change, the Paralympics still follows the model of marginality proposed by DePauw (1997a) excluding athletes with impairments who do not conform to the ideals of masculinity, physicality and sexuality.

The visibility of athletes with disabilities has increased significantly throughout the 21st century but has yet to reach the level that society can readily 'see' the performance and athletic achievements as sport and sporting ability and not just relegated to the category of disability sport. As one example, we could change the language using the modifier of 'disabled' in referring to athletes participating in the Paralympic Games; why not state athletes competing in the Paralympic Games like their counterparts of athletes competing in the Olympic Games. Visibility as athletes can be achieved when the focus is on difference not deviation from the norm (Silva & Howe, 2018) as demonstrated in the 2021 commercial by Fitbit entitled *What's Strong with Me* which features individuals with their own bodies (not the ideal sporting body) participating in physical activity, including a female with missing hand engaged in the sport of mountain climbing (Fitbit, 2021).

Disabled Female Sporting Body

The disabled female body is subject to the socially constructed ideals of masculinity, physicality and sexuality as proposed originally by DePauw (1997a) and the intersection of these constructs. And therefore, the disabled female body continues to be marginalized and, at times, invisible as a sporting body. Since the early beginnings of disability sport in the late 1880s and especially throughout the 20th century, individuals with disabilities actively fought for their right to participate in sport (DePauw & Gavron, 2005). Currently, many individuals with disabilities do have access to physical activity and sport from the local level to the highly competitive international arena (e.g. Paralympics). Although much progress has been made, there is still much work to be done because sport still reflects and often reproduces the values, norms and standards of society or dominant culture (Donnelly, 1996). Thus, some individuals remain marginalized from and in sport because they are not viewed by society as physically ideal for sport because of the normative standards of femininity and ability (Hardin & Hardin, 2005, Hargreaves & Hardin, 2009): specifically, female athletes and athletes with disabilities.

Female athletes with disabilities are dually challenged by being female and having a disability (Blinde & McCallister, 1999; DePauw & Gavron, 2005; DePauw, 1997a; Hardin & Hardin, 2005). In their study, Blinde and McCallister (1999) found that the dual forces of sexism and ableism (disability

Disabled Female Sporting Bodies 91

discrimination) (see Silva this volume) impact the experiences of women with physical disabilities. These forces have led to the situation in which women with disabilities experience a "double jeopardy" (Benefield & Head, 1984; Blinde & McCallister, 1999; Deegan & Brooks, 1985; Hanna & Rogovsky, 1993; Wendell, 1989).

Female Athletes with Disabilities

Despite these constraints to participation in sport, female athletes with disabilities have participated in competitive sport for more than a century. Dating back to the early 1900s, this history is little known and mostly unrecognized. Historically, female athletes with disabilities have been found in disability sport and able-bodied sport but only became more visible in the 1960s. The early examples include deaf women who competed in the First International Silent Games (Paris, France) in 1924; Liz Hartel (post-polio, Denmark) who won a silver medal in dressage at 1952 Olympics; women who competed in the first U.S. National Wheelchair Games (New York); and female athletes with disabilities who competed in the first International Games for the Disabled (now known as the Paralympics) in Rome, Italy in 1960. Additional firsts include Sharon Rahn Hedrick as the first women to win the women's wheelchair division of the 1977 Boston Marathon, Neroli Fairhall (NZ) as the first wheelchair athlete to compete in the 1984 Summer Olympics (archery), Jean Driscoll honored as Sudafed Female Athletes of the year in 1991, Tanni Grey Thompson (Great Britain and Northern Ireland) named Sunday Times 1992 Sportswoman of the Year by Her Majesty the Queen, Monique Kalkman (the Netherlands) earned the title of Amsterdam's 1994 Sportswomen of the Year, and Marla Runyon, a legally blind runner (USA) competed in the 2000 Olympic Games after successfully competing in the 1992 and 1996 Paralympic Games. These examples demonstrate that female athletes with disabilities were successful in the early days of elite competitive sport and recognized for their achievements (DePauw & Gavron, 2005).

Although participation has increased, females with disabilities in sport remain underrepresented in major sport competitions like the Paralympics. Data gathered in the last decade+ indicate the following for the Summer Paralympics (WSF, 2017, 2018):

- The 2008 Beijing Paralympics included 1383 female athletes compared to 2568 male athletes
- The 2012 London Paralympics increased to 1523 (35.4%) females and 2736 males
- The Rio 2016 Paralympics Games increased by 11.3% to 1669 female athletes with disabilities (38.7%) which was more than double the 1996 Atlanta Games (790 female participants) and up from 990 women (25.5%) in 2000
- Biggest number of women ever at the Paralympics – there are 1,853 female athletes at Tokyo 2020, a near 11 per cent increase on Rio 2016

- First Paralympic Winter Games (1976) included 37 women (18.7%) which increased to 21% of the Winter Paralympics in 2002
- At the most recent Paralympic Winter Games in 2018 women accounted for 23.6% of athletes

Although the numbers and percentages have increased for both Summer and Winter Paralympic Games, there remains a gender equity concern in that competition opportunities for female Paralympians lag behind their male counterparts. Specifically, Dean, Bundon, Howe, and Abele (2021), who conducted a study of IPC and NPC initiatives to encourage the participation of women in the Paralympic movement, found that the "rhetoric of gender balance is there, but the practice is not" (p. 7) leaving much work to be done.

Disabled Female Athletes' Participation and Experiences

A comprehensive study of the sport participation of females with disabilities was undertaken in Australia by Taylor, Darcy and Lock (2012). They investigated the constraints to and the benefits of participation in physical activity and sport. They found that of the 266 women who responded, 86% of them were active in sport especially those who were more independent and less dependent upon assistance. Significant among the findings were a series of constraints related not necessarily to one's impairment but interpersonal (no one to participate with) and structural (government support). Key benefits included a sense of achievement, improved health, sense of belonging, companionships, and time with friends.

Although participation of female athletes with disabilities has increased, their experiences are not well documented or studied or even understood. It is important to state that while we can be informed by the literature on the female able-bodied sporting experiences, generalizing from able-bodied sport to disability sport, ignores, denies, or erases the significance of women's experiences within disability sport (Olenik, 1995). Olenik and colleagues (1995) provided the first analysis of the issues and barriers facing female disabled athletes and a foundation for understanding their experiences. Specifically, the purpose of the study was to invite the voices of the female athlete to be heard and to reveal the reality of her experience in sport. Among the findings are the following:

- The women wanted to compete in elite sport and found competition challenging and exciting.
- Although successful in sport, society failed to view them as athletes.
- Lack of financial resources made it difficult to sustain their participation.
- Disability sport was not perceived by society as a "normal" or real sport.
- The sport system was designed after the able-bodied male model and therefore not inclusive of the intersectionality of gender and disability.
- Coaches were skilled in sport or disability but not both.
- The sport of choice for these women differed from those practiced by able-bodied females and promoted by the sport organizations.

In brief, these athletes expressed their concerns about the lack of female athletes and administrators, the traditional model of sport (male, able-bodied), and societal views of disability sport. This study initiated the process of identifying barriers and inequities in disability sport (sport) facing female athletes with disabilities. Although not specifically stated, marginality in sport by gender and disability was a barrier.

In a related study of physical fitness and sport, Blinde and McCallister (1999) explored the daily experiences of women with physical disabilities. Participants in the study perceived the gap between sport and physical fitness activity and disability as less for men with physical disabilities than for women with physical disabilities. The women with disabilities identified a gap between males and females with disabilities, a contradiction between the values of sport and physical fitness activity and perceptions of disability, and lack of societal expectation of female with disabilities participation in fitness and sport. The authors identified three main reasons for participation: maintaining functionality, social factors, and psychological factors. They concluded that their participation in fitness and sport created "additional dynamics, as the forces of sexism and disability discrimination intersect with the societal construction of sport and physical fitness activity" (p. 8).

In their recent analysis, Hammond and Macdougall (2020) reported a limited number of studies that focused on the motivations for sport participation for female athletes with a disability (e.g., Caddick & Smith, 2014; Cottingham et al., 2018). In contrast, they identified more research that was conducted on the barriers to participation in sport (e.g., lack of social support, role models, funding, and programs) that girls and women with disabilities experience (e.g., Phillips, et. al, 2018). These studies confirmed the double jeopardy that the female athletes with disabilities face by having a disability and being female (Blinde & McCallister, 1999; Garland-Thomson, 2002; Hammond & Macdougall, 2020).

As described in an essay by Kirakosyn and Geijer (2017), Brazilian female Paralympians faced a number of obstacles in recognition for their athletic achievements including insensitivity to the maternity and child-rearing needs, unequal recognition in comparison to their male counterparts and fewer competitive opportunities. The authors argued that these obstacles contributed to their underrepresentation in Paralympic sport and, at the same time, the female athletes suggested that their experiences as participants in Paralympic sport have made them more resilient. With increasing visibility of female athletes with disabilities, more opportunities will be available although women will still face barriers due to socioeconomic, cultural, political and ideological barriers (Hargreaves, 2000; Seal, 2014).

The portrayal of female athletes with disabilities in the sport media has been studied. One of the first studies was undertaken by Hargreaves and Hardin (2009) through which they explored the attitudes and perceptions of female wheelchair athletes about sport media. The purpose was to hear the voices of and to seek the perspectives of female wheelchair athletes to understand the "interlaced meanings embedded in disability, gender and sexuality" (Garland-Thomson, 2002, Hargreaves & McDonald, 2000) in sport media. Based upon their analysis, the participants indicated that they were tired of the media stereotypes about gender and disability, and they believed that the media is partially responsible for the lack of coverage of women and individuals with disabilities in sports media.

These findings reinforced the results of a study by Hardin, Lynn and Walsdorf (2006). The authors investigated the relationship among images of sport, disability, gender and race in four U.S. women's sport/fitness magazines. These magazines were assumed to provide an empowering space for women including women with disabilities. The study concluded that by failing to include athletes with disabilities, the magazines failed to 'break free from a male/ableist hegemonic body standard'.

The first cross-cultural analysis of the photographs from the 2008 Paralympics was conducted by Buysse and Borcherding (2010). This study was designed to examine photographs from 12 print newspapers in five countries during the Beijing Paralympics. They examined the number and type of the photographs and the content of each to determine how athletes with disabilities were portrayed. They concluded that the newspaper coverage including photographic coverage continued to "ignore and symbolically hide athletes with disabilities". They argued that the lack of coverage served to reinforce the notion that athletes with disabilities are not valued for their athletic ability. In addition, the results indicated that female athletes were marginalized even further by the use of passive poses. Their findings supported the marginality framework in sport through socially constructed ideals of physicality, masculinity and sexuality (e.g., DePauw, 1997a; Garland-Thomson, 2002).

Changing the Paradigm of Disability Sport Research

Disability sport research has included females in the research studies of athletes with disabilities, but in fewer numbers and few studies have addressed the lived experiences and the voices of female disabled athletes. To date, most of the studies have focused upon female athletes with disabilities and their participation in sport (and physical fitness) primarily, benefits of participation, barriers to participation and media coverage. These have focused more on the influence of sport (and physical activity) upon girls and women with disabilities, although some have raised questions about the model of sport and marginality. This latter approach provides the opportunity to explore the inclusion of marginalized individuals in sport, especially girls and women with disabilities, as agents of change through the lens of a critical feminist analysis (Apelmo, 2016; DePauw, 1997b).

In her research study, Apelmo (2016) explored young Swedish women's lived experience of the body, "which, on the one hand, is viewed as deviant – the disabled body – and, on the other, is viewed as accomplished – the sporting body" (p. i). Specifically, she interviewed females with disabilities about the subject position of their bodies as deviant and accomplished, as well as being marginalized, stereotyped, and othered by their gender and body in the context of the historical model of sport. Her research was situated in four research fields: sociology of the body, feminist research, sport sociology and disability studies. I would argue that this research is not only interdisciplinary but emancipatory in nature examining the disablement of females in sport.

Consistent with Apelmo (2016), disability sport research requires an examination of the underlying assumptions of body, disability and sport as well as some underlying assumptions about research (DePauw, 2000). Historically, individuals with disabilities have been the objects of research and study but not the "purveyors of the knowledge base of disability" (Snyder & Mitchell, 2010, p. 198). Based upon the medical model, disability was viewed as a problem in need of a solution rather than an important form of critical knowledge.

The paradigm for research must move away from the medical model (an ableist approach) to a socio-cultural model. Essentially the research questions need to be changed to capture more of the experiences of individuals with disabilities, especially females. Their experiences are different and significantly impacted not only by the intersection of gender and disability but also by sexuality. Disabled bodies are often seen as non-gendered and therefore individuals with disabilities as asexual (Apelmo, 2017; DePauw, 1997a). Significant gaps could be addressed and significant insights if the research questions are posed with emancipatory and participatory research in mind. Morris (1992) and Garland-Thomson (2002) have called for emancipatory and participatory research especially for understanding gender and disability.

In rethinking research, Fine (2019) challenges researchers to engage in "anti-ableist work that centers disability justice" (p. 661) through the lens of critical disability studies. Specifically, she calls for research which focuses on:

- Contest normalcy, stratification, and binaries. Scholars must challenge the categorization that are grounded on the normativity and especially the normal body and associated ability (e.g., classification). Greater attention must be also paid to the intersection of race, class, gender, sexuality and nation status.
- Theorize and organize through intersectionality. Acceptance and understanding of ableism as social oppression and its disparate consequences must be theorized and studied from the intersectional framework (e.g. access to sport and equipment).
- Design critical participatory inquiry projects that center the experience and expertise of disabled persons. Participatory (emancipatory) research must be conducted with female athletes with disabilities among theorists, researchers, participants and 'wisdom holders'.
- Performances of lives and solidarities, curated at the membrane of social sciences and art. Scholars must think beyond the body performances in sport and to explore beyond the boundaries to enable critical conversations about ableism in popular discourse.

- <u>Design policy for transformation, not simply accommodation, integration or inclusion</u>. Scholars must acknowledge ableism (explicit, implicit) in sport and seeks way to transform sport to be more accessible and inclusive.

Researching disability sport requires an examination of the underlying assumptions of body, disability, gender and sport, to understand these in context and investigate new ways of thinking and knowing. Rethinking disability sport research requires us to consider the following:

1. How research questions are often a reflection of the dominant culture in alignment with masculinity, sexuality and ability and even little about the intersection of these constructs.
2. Emancipatory research which challenges the assumptions of body, ability, and quantitative research must be undertaken.
3. Participatory research is critical to posing and answering research questions about the experiences of female athletes with disabilities.
4. Research questions about para sport must be constructed to avoid ableism.

Inasmuch as one of the values of disability sport research is to see how sport has changed and how sport could be changed (social transformation of sport), research questions need to be reframed around the question of marginality and inclusion and the experiences of those marginalized in and from sport. Although some progress has been made, much work is needed because indeed marginality is still present. The research on female disabled athletes has reinforced this – as to why there remain more men than women in sport – but if we were to hear the voices of those marginalized, we could then offer some hope for change.

According to Hendren (2020), disability can be viewed in the context of the intersection of the body and the built world. She writes that the built world presumes that there is only one way a body can be – similar to Garland-Thomson's (1997) notion of disability as "corporeal deviance – not so much a property of bodies as a product of cultural rules about what bodies should be or do" (p. 6). Further, she writes that we should focus our sights on flexible cultures, systems, and technologies and to see what a body can do. Inasmuch as sport is a built world, I would argue that sport can also be a site for resistance to the status quo and social change, (DePauw, 1997a; Donnelly, 1996) and as such, in sport we can see what the disabled female body can do.

Concluding Comments

It is important for researchers to problematize participation in sport by confronting the "ideals of acceptable physicality within the limits of masculinity-femininity and sexuality" (DePauw, 1997a, p. 422). Female athletes with disabilities have continued to fight for inclusion and to resist the marginalization. In this chapter, I have shared my musings about gender and disability (marginality of physicality and masculinity) but the third construct of marginality in sport sexuality and gender identity must also be considered and incorporated into research. Rethinking research is a very challenging and difficult task but must be done. We have the opportunity to bridge important gaps between disability studies and sociology of sport and to engage a cultural studies – feminist approach to disability sport research. Then perhaps we could really see what the female body can do in sport and society.

References

Apelmo, E. (2016). *Sport and the female disabled body*. Routledge.
Benefield, L., & Head, D.W. (1984). Discrimination and disabled women. *Journal of Humanistic Education and Development*, 23(2), 60–68.
Blauwet, C., & Willick, S.E. (2012). The Paralympic Movement: Using sports to promote health, disability rights, and social integration for athletes with disabilities. *PM&R*, 4(11), 851–856.
Blinde, Elaine M. & McCallister, Sarah G. (1999). Women, disability, and sport and physical fitness activity: The intersection of gender and disability dynamics. *Research Quarterly for Exercise and Sport*, 70 (3), 303–312.
Burkett, B., McNamee, M., & Potthast, W. (2011). Shifting boundaries in sports technology and disability: Equal rights or unfair advantage in the case of Oscar Pistorius?. *Disability & Society*, 26(5), 643–654. doi:10.1080/09687599.2011.589197
Buysse, J.M., & Borcherding, B. (2010). Framing gender and disability in sport: A cross-cultural analysis of photographs from the 2008 Paralympic Games. *International Journal of Sport Communication*, 3, 308–321.
Caddick, N., & Smith, B. (2014). The impact of sport and physical activity on the well-being of combat veterans: A systematic review. *Psychology of Sport and Exercise*, 15(1), 9–18.
Colquhoun. D. (1991). Health based physical education: The ideology of healthism and victim blaming. *Physical Education Review*, 14, 5–13.
Connell, R. W.(1995). *Masculinities*. Cambridge: Polity.
Corrigan, T.F., Paton, J., Holt, E., & Hardin, M. (2010). Discourses of the "too abled": Contested body hierarchies and the Oscar Pistorius case. *International Journal of Sport Communication*, 3(3), 288–307.
Cottingham, M., Hums, M., Jeffress, M., Lee, D., & Richard, H., (2018). Women of power soccer: Exploring disability and gender the first competitive team sport for powerchair users. *Sport in Society*, 21(11), 1817–1830.
Davis, L.J. (1995) *Enforcing normalcy: Disability, deafness, and the body*. London: Verso.
Dean, Nikolaus A., Bundon, Andrea, Howe, P. David, & Abele, Natalie. (2021). Gender Parity, False Starts, and Promising Practices in the Paralympic Movement. *Sociology of Sport Journal*. Advance online publication. doi:10.1123/ssj.2021-0030.
Deegan, M.J., & Brooks, N.A. (Eds.). (1985). *Women and disability: The double handicap*. New Brunswick, NJ: TransactionBooks.
DePauw, K. (2000). Social-cultural context of disability: Implications for scientific inquiry and professional preparation. *Quest*, 52, 358–368.
DePauw, K., & Gavron, S. (2005). *Disability and sport*. Champaign: Human Kinetics.
DePauw, K.P. (1997a). The (in)visibility of disAbility: Cultural contexts and sporting bodies. *Quest*, 49(4): 416–430.

DePauw, K.P. (1997b). Sport and physical activity in the life-cycle of girls and women with disabilities. *Women in Sport and Physical Activity Journal*, 6(2), 225–237.
DePauw, K.P. (1999). Girls and women with disabilities in sport. *Journal of Physical Education, Recreation & Dance*, 70(4), 50–52.
Dolmage, J.T. (2017). *Academic ableism: Disability and higher education*. Ann Arbor Michigan: University of Michigan Press.
Donnelly, P. (1996). Approaches to social inequality in the sociology of sport. *Quest*, 48, 221–242.
Fine, M. (2019). Critical disability studies: Looking back and forward. In Bogart, K.R. & Dunn, D. (Eds). Special Issue: Ableism. Journal of Social Issues, 75(3), 972–984.
Fine. M., & Asch, A. (1988). Disability beyond stigma: Social interaction. Discrimination, and activism. *Journal of Social Issues*, 44, 3–21.
Fitbit (2021). *What's strong with me?* [online video] Available from: https://www.youtube.com/watch?v=m3C17KDdHwE
Garland-Thomson, R. (1997). *Extraordinary bodies: Figuring physical disability in American culture and literature*. New York: Columbia University Press.
Garland-Thomson, R. (2002). Integrating disability, transforming feminist theory. *NWSA Journal*, 14, 1–32.
Garland-Thomson, R. (2009). *Staring: How we look*. Spain: OUP USA.
Goffman, Erving (1963). *Stigma: On the Management of Spoiled Identity*. Englewood, NJ: Prentice Hall.
Hammond, A., & Macdougall, H. (2020). Developing sport for women and girls with a disability. In *Developing Sport for Women and Girls* (pp. 57–68). Abingdon, Oxfordshire: Routledge.
Hanna, W.J., & Rogovsky, B. (1993). Women with disabilities: Two handicaps plus. In M. Nagler (Ed.), *Perspectives on disability* (2nd ed., pp. 109–120). Palo Alto, CA: Health Markets Research.
Hardin, M., & Hardin, B. (2005). Performance or participation ... pluralism or hegemony? Images of Disability & Gender in Sports 'n Spokes Magazine. *Disability Studies Quarterly*, 25 (4), 11.
Hardin, M., Lynn, S., & Walsdorf, K. (2006). Depicting the sporting body: The intersection of gender, race and disability in women's sport/fitness magazines. *Journal of Magazine Media*, 8(1), 105–117.
Hargreaves, J. (2000). *Heroines of sport: The politics of difference and identity*. Abingdon and New York: Routledge.
Hargreaves, J., & McDonald, I. (2000). Cultural studies and the sociology of sport. In J. Coakley and E. Dunning (Eds.), *Handbook of Sports Studies* (pp. 48–60). London: Sage.
Hargreaves, J.A., & Hardin, B. (2009). Women wheelchair athletes: Competing against media stereotypes. *Disability Studies Quarterly*, 29(2).
Hendren, S. (2020). *What can a body do? How we meet the built world*. New York: Penguin.
Kirakosyna, L., & Geijer, S. (October 26, 2017). "Disabled Femininities" in Paralympic Sport: Exploring the Narratives of Brazilian Female Paralympians*. Available from https://blogs.lt.vt.edu/reflectionsandexplorations/2017/10/26/disabled-femininities-in-paralympic-sport-exploring-the-narratives-of-brazilian-female-paralympians1/ March 28, 2021
Kuhn, T.S. (2012). *The structure of scientific revolutions*. Chicago, Illinois: University of Chicago press.
Linton, S. (1998) *Claiming Disability: Knowledge and Identity*, New York: NYU Press.

Morris, J. (1992). Personal and political: A feminist perspective on researching physical disability. *Disability, Handicap, & Society*, 7, 157–166.

Oliver, M. (1990). Critical texts in social work and the welfare state the politics of disablement. Recuperado de https://disability-studies. leeds. ac. uk/library

Purdue, D.E., & Howe, P.D. (2012). See the sport, not the disability: Exploring the Paralympic paradox. *Qualitative Research in Sport, Exercise and Health*, 4(2), 189–205.

Purdue, D. E., & Howe, P. D. (2013). Who's in and who is out? Legitimate bodies within the Paralympic Games. *Sociology of Sport Journal*, 30(1), 24–40.

Sage, G. H. (1993). Sport and physical education and the new world order: Dare we be agents of social change? *Quest*, 45(2), 151–164.

Seal, E.L. (2014). *Juggling Identities: Elite Female Athletes' Negotiation of Identities in Disability Sport*. PhD thesis, University of Bath, UK.

Silva, C.F., & Howe, P.D. (2012). The (in) validity of supercrip representation of Paralympian athletes. *Journal of Sport and Social Issues*, 36(2), 174–194.

Silva, C.F., & Howe, P.D. (2018). The social empowerment of difference: The potential influence of para sport. *Physical Medicine and Rehabilitation Clinics of North America*, 29(2), 397–408.

Snyder, S.L., and Mitchell, David T. (2010). *Cultural locations of disability*. Chicago: University of Chicago Press.

Taylor, T., Darcy, S., & Lock, D., (2012). *Females with a disability and participation in sport. Malaysian Journal of Sport Science and Recreation (MJSSR)*, 8(1), 1–14.

Thomson, R.G. (1996). *Freakery: Cultural spectacles of the extraordinary body*. New York and London: NYU Press.

Thomson, R.G. (2017). *Extraordinary bodies: Figuring physical disability in American culture and literature*. New York, United States: Columbia University Press.

Wendell, S. (1989). Toward a feminist theory of disability. *Hypatia*, 4, 104–124.

Wikipedia (n.d.). LGBT athletes in the Olympic and Paralympic Games [Online]. Available from: https://en.wikipedia.org/wiki/LGBT_athletes_in_the_Olympic_and_Paralympic_Games

Wolbring, G. (2008). Oscar Pistorius and the future nature of Olympic, Paralympic and other sports. *Scripted*, 5, 139.

Women's Sports Foundation (June 2017). Women in the Olympic and Paralympic games: An analysis of participation, leadership, and media coverage. Available from http://www.womenssportsfoundation.org/

Women's Sports Foundation (November 2018). Women in the 2018 Olympic and Paralympic winter games: An analysis of participation, leadership, and media coverage. Available from http://www.womenssportsfoundation.org/

Chapter 7

Playing, Passing, and Pageantry

A Collaborative Autoethnography on Sport, Disability, Sexuality, and Belonging

Stephanie Wheeler and Danielle Peers

DANIELLE In wheelchair basketball, the "backpick" is a technique in which an athlete plants the back of their wheelchair against the front of yours, and maneuvers in front of you to block (or fatigue you during) your progress up the court. As a queer, non-binary, disabled[1] person, I have been metaphorically back-picked throughout my athletic and academic careers; the ubiquitous barriers make even the simplest tasks exhausting. But I have trained for this. As a Paralympic athlete, I was literally backpicked constantly. I became especially familiar with the back of Stephanie Wheeler's head. She was the best backpicker in the world; no one made me push harder. Everything about Stephanie's character and commitments, however, is the opposite of a backpick. Stephanie is not a human who blocks progress, rather she is one who creates momentum. On court, the only thing I feared more than seeing her energetic ponytail in front of my stopped chair was how a hoop from her could fire up her team and swing a game. Off the court, her passion, similarly, made every space feel more welcoming (and way more fun). So, it is not surprising that Stephanie has become not only the first queer, female, disabled college coach (that I know of) but one who has been extremely successful in creating welcoming spaces, removing barriers, and nurturing the creation of extremely skilled, affirmed, and actualized athletes. In short, there is no way I could have said no to the opportunity to story my career alongside Stephanie's.

STEPHANIE: I do an activity yearly with my student-athletes in which they close their eyes and imagine the greatest teammate they've ever had. Words that connect to their imagery range from supportive, to hard working, to advocate, to relationship builder, to servant, to authentic. As a queer, disabled woman, I've had some incredible teammates in life, in sport, and in my career that embody those traits. There are also people who I would have loved to call a teammate.

Danielle is one of those people. On court, I became incredibly familiar with the diverse ways that Danielle could score that would lift their team to a world championship victory (and incredibly familiar with looking up at the flick of their wrist that punctuated the end of their perfect shot). Over

DOI: 10.4324/9781003153696-9

time, I learned that off the court, their greatness as a teammate shone brighter than their world MVP trophy ever could. Great teammates invariably make any experience more welcoming, more fun, more connected, and more authentic. It's not surprising to me that Danielle is the greatest of teammates in any community they are in, whether it's academia, sport, activism, or life. Danielle, I've always wanted to be your teammate on court. Now, I'm so grateful to be your teammate in storytelling.

STEPHANIE AND DANIELLE As Paralympians we have both told some version of our stories multiple times, often to researchers and journalists wanting to 'give us voice.' Most often, we heard a very different version of our stories amplified to the world: Stories of pity and overcoming; Stories of uncomplicated Paralympic empowerment; Stories of homogenous disability experiences, identities, and desires. "Stories about us are boring. As predictable and ubiquitous as they are dangerous … If we didn't know us better, we would bore us" (St. Pierre & Peers, 2016, p. 1). After a while, we learned to tell the story they wanted to hear. We dutifully recited the scripts—and the selves—they expected. We smiled pretty and were crowned inspirational; the blunted tiaras and stories rubbing us raw in all of the places they were never meant to fit. How come every time someone tries to give us voice something feels like it has been taken? Autoethnography exists because Othered people got angry when researchers and authors benevolently 'told the truth' about our lives in ways that cast our truths as quaint fictions. We write autoethnography because we could not squish our bones to fit the straight and narrow scripts into which we were cast, perpetually recast, and eventually cast away. Collaborative autoethnographies exist because it feels so lonely to be crowded by so many untold stories. We must tell these stories to each other, and with each other to make space for more complex, affirming, and possible narratives … and lives. This collaborative autoethnography is precisely this kind of collective, storied journey.

Methods

STEPHANIE AND DANIELLE According to Ellis, Adams and Bochner (2010), "autoethnography is an approach to research and writing that seeks to describe and systematically analyze personal experience in order to understand cultural experience" (sec. 1). Like ethnography more generally, autoethnography centers around the study of cultures and socio-cultural phenomena (Ngunjiri, Hernandez & Chang, 2010, p. 3). It emerged, however, in critical opposition to widespread forms of positivist ethnography that tended towards white male scholars perpetuating sexist and racist ideas while claiming to 'objectively' study what they constructed as other people's 'primitive' cultures (Ellis, Adams & Bochner, 2010, sec. 1). In contrast, autoethnography seeks to study phenomena from one's own "socio-cultural context," by analyzing "how the context surrounding self has influenced and shaped the make-up of self and how the self has responded to, reacted to, or resisted forces innate to the context" (Ngunjiri, Hernandez & Chang, 2010, p. 3). Although solo-authored autoethnographies are the norm, collaborative autoethnographies have sought more intersectional cultural analyses by curating 'conversations' between multiple stories and selves (e.g., Avner et al., 2014; Ngunjiri, Hernandez & Chang, 2010).

In contrast to the positivist ethnographies it sought to resist, autoethnography is most often undertaken from critical and post-structuralist paradigms that often embrace subjective knowledges and axiological investments in social justice (see Peers, 2018a). There is nonetheless a spectrum of practice between what Anderson (2006) articulates as more analytical versus more evocative approaches. We are both drawn to evocative writers who, to quote Norman Denzin (2006), seek "to change the world by writing from their hearts" (p. 423). In this chapter, we use creative writing styles to place our experiences in conversation with each other, and with relevant literature, in ways that attempt to disrupt dominant discourses of disability, queerness and parasport, while offering space to imagine multiple, contested meanings and ways forward.

Like many autoethnographies, the primary 'data' for us were our memories of past experiences, augmented through past writings, and through a process of collaborative interviewing. That is, we met for two recorded three-hour zoom sessions, wherein we traded stories and asked each other questions about our experiences at the intersections of gender, sexuality, disability, and parasport. These sessions were then transcribed verbatim. Following Braun and Clarke's (2006) thematic analysis, both authors inductively coded the transcripts based on underlying, latent meanings, identifying major themes to be storied in this chapter. We then met several more times to discuss these stories and themes, and to identify which of these—when put thoughtfully in relation to each other—would offer the most complex, insightful, evocative, and useful critique. This was followed by months of solo writing, and weekly meetings where we supported each other in crafting compelling autoethnographic narratives, and in weaving in relevant theories and literatures. The result is the following "storied conversation": a collaborative autoethnography about (para)sport, disability, sexuality, gender, religion, pageantry, passing, and the expansive pleasure of both monkeybars and belonging.

A Storied Conversation

STEPHANIE Some of my most vivid childhood memories revolve around sports, running, jumping, and playing outside with my friends. I loved recess and being outside with my friends in kindergarten. The playground was my home, the one place where I felt free. To this day, that first whiff of sweetness in the air every spring brings back memories of the honeysuckle that lined our school's playground and the freedom and joy I found there. After my accident during the summer before first-grade, the playground that I loved so much was no longer a place of freedom and fun, only a reminder that my six-year-old body was broken and didn't belong. I watched and counted as my friends jumped rope. I tried hanging on the monkey bars, but my teacher quickly grabbed me and said it wasn't safe. I longed for the freedom that I used to find on the playground. But more than anything, I longed for an escape from the new ways that people were looking at me, treating me: a new kind of freedom from pity.

Growing up in the South, religion permeated every part of my life, though I never identified with or felt tied to the dogma of it. I lived across the street from a Baptist church. Each Sunday, I watched the teams of women in their primped pastel dresses, rise out of their cars, put their shoulders back, smooth the wrinkles out of their perfectly pressed dresses, and parade up the stairs and into the front door of the church. I felt a moral imperative to be there. As a young teenager, I would search my closet for my pinkest Sunday dress, roll across the street, and enter the hidden, segregated, 'accessible' door at the back of the church into a place that was supposed to love and accept me. That Sunday roll across the street was always filled with dread; I knew what was coming. When you are the kid in a small town who was in a car accident, became paralyzed, and lost her mom, you get used to the "look." I've seen it and felt it in my body thousands of times, but most often in church.

Pity comes in many shapes and sizes. You get the look from across the room from people who knew your mom, the patronizing smile that says "I'm so glad that you're out"; but the most brazen form of pity is the one that makes folks approach you head on, like they are on a mission, emboldened by the presupposition that I feel broken, that I need to be healed. Sometimes, there was an ask, other times more a demand "let me pray for you." As I learned much, much later, this dynamic:

> reveals more about the able-bodied culture doing the asking than about the bodies being interrogated. A system of compulsory able-bodiedness repeatedly demands that people with disabilities embody for others an affirmative answer to the unspoken question, Yes, but in the end, wouldn't you rather be more like me?
>
> (McRuer, 2006, pp. 399–400)

At the time, however, I was made to feel that it was entirely about my apparently broken body, and since I always went to church alone, the pressure to allow the prayer for my healing fell solely on my shoulders. Amidst the flush of shame, the words "sure" somehow escape my throat. Their hands on me. Wincing. The counting of hour-long seconds. My body curling in on itself. The shrinking of my bones futile as they perched on my stubbornly large, hot pink wheelchair, somehow growing larger in the crowded isles of the church. Finally, the relief of the "amen." And the shame hangover for allowing it to happen. This invasion of space and autonomy, over time, ingrained in me that I wasn't whole, that something was wrong with me, that my body wasn't made to take up space. At church, shame and regret had me looking for the exit as quickly as possible; but escaping pity is not so easy.

When I was 10, the greatest antidote to the claustrophobia of shame and pity was getting out of my small southern town into the anonymity, freedom, and adventure of the big city. Having grown up in a town with no malls or fun restaurants, I longed for the monthly visits with my maternal grandmother, Nana. We would go shopping, rent movies and eat at my favorite greasy burger spot, Sonic. It felt so exciting that you could eat outside, where I felt free to move about. And those yummy, greasy burgers, hot dog, fries, and onion rings tasted of freedom ... until that one Saturday. If I close my eyes, I can feel the heaviness of the summer evening air on my skin, smell the grease permeating the air, and feel the heavy, sweaty nausea of shame climbing up from my stomach. There were many times that I've been prayed for and prayed on (perhaps, preyed upon?) by benevolent Christians, but this one sticks with me. I can feel the look of pity on the woman's face as she fervently strides towards me, as if she is on an evangelical mission to convert my body to nondisabled. As she approaches, I feel my body curl in shame, wanting to be small; just wanting to disappear. I know how this is going to go. Though not confined to a building, there still are no exits here. She passes right by me, and addresses my Nana instead: "Hello, I just feel compelled to come over and ask, can I pray for her and her healing?" Just when you think it couldn't get worse, no recognition that I am human, that I am a person with agency, only a being who is broken. My Nana, also without acknowledging the curled-up shame of my body, lets this happen. Everything gets blurry for me after that. That is how trauma works. I am not sure how my Nana agrees. I am not sure if she ever addressed me. I do remember the woman placing her hands on my legs as she prayed. Breaking through the shame in that brief moment were the twin affects of rage—for being touched without consent—and dark humor—laughing that in trying to heal my legs, she was several feet off the mark of the injury.

At 12 years old, I finally found my freedom. The moment I picked up a basketball, I fell deeply in love with the sport, and in love with who I was becoming—and unbecoming—as I trained.

Each dribble pushed away the oppression of pity and brought back the freedom of the playground. On the basketball court I no longer felt like disappearing. In fact, I wanted to be noticed. Those who had once treated me as broken told me I was strong, marveled at my speed. Their admiration uncurled that shamed little girl. At least until the next person laid hands. The more praise I received for my talent and ability, the more my self-worth became linked to "overcoming" my disability in the eyes of others. Over time, I began to internalize my supercripdom; I believed I could overcome my disability (see Clare, 2009). I was convinced that I wasn't like "those other disabled people."

DANIELLE I feel, well, ashamed to admit that your story resonates with my first experience of wheelchair basketball. At that point, I still didn't know that all of my pain and weakness were related to a disease, and I didn't think I knew anyone who had a disability. So I walked into my first practice as a potential "AB²" recruit. I distinctly remember watching people transferring from their day chairs into their spacey-looking sports chairs. And yeah, I remember feeling pity for them. I mean, I didn't try to heal any of them or anything, but I felt pity. I am sure they could feel it ooze from me. And then we got on the court, and the athletes I had pitied were backpicking me and scoring on me. The pity evaporated into some kind of supercrip cloud. Eli Clare (2009) writes of supercripdom as a mountain we all feel like we have to climb, at great cost to ourselves and other disabled people, "because down at the base of the mountain waits a nursing home" (p. 12). That is, the alternative to the supercrip was a socially constructed world of social devaluation, isolation, and desolation. Three years after that first practice, I was diagnosed with muscular dystrophy and started using a daychair. I quickly learned to wield the supercrip too. It deflected the pity, to some degree. But sooner or later I started to feel the sharp edge of that tool hurting me and the movements I cared about. In the words of feminist singer- songwriter Ani Difranco (1993), "every tool is a weapon, if you hold it right." Supercrip was a hard climb, but the alternative felt like a very slippery slope down.

STEPHANIE: Exactly, the sport that had offered me protection and freedom from pity now required me to perform disability in a way that reproduced ableist norms. I trained hard not just to perform on court at my best, but to perform disability off the court in a way that didn't elicit pity. The dominant narrative in my head and heart was never about ableism or why I felt the need to perform disability a certain way. It was always about the believe-it-or-not disability overcoming story (Clare, 2009, p. 3). And I reveled in it. I learned the script far too well. And I feel shame about this now, but in one academic interview I was quoted as proudly saying "being an empowered woman is how you project yourself to the world. The world is your canvas. How you paint yourself on that canvas" (Hardin, 2007, p. 47). But in reality, I was never fully in charge of how other people saw or treated me. I lived in spaces that expanded and shrank with the turn of an ableist cliché, a pitying or inspirational look, the hurtful placing of a 'healing' hand.

DANIELLE The expansion and contraction you describe is at the heart of what brought me to sport. Growing up (gender)queer, I never thought I would live to 20. I did not think I was going to die; I did not want to die; I just couldn't imagine any kind of life I wanted to live. Until college, I had never seen an adult with whom I could identify, a future to which I could aspire, or a way of living to which I was willing to capitulate. In the absence of an imaginable life destination, sport kept me going. It gave me purpose, granted solace, offered protection.

After a brutal chastisement from my fifth-grade teacher about my 'unladylike' behavior, I spent recess throwing a quiet, dangling tantrum on the monkeybars. The expansiveness in my armpits and hips unfurled my nauseous, contracted, shame-shaped ball of a body. My best friend literally hung around beside me, in silent solidarity for a child's forever, before he asked if I wished I were a boy. My burning palms squeaked nervously against the wet, grimy bars. The sweaty metal smelled and tasted of dirty pennies. There was gravity to the moment. Something truer than I had ever thought found its way to voice: "I don't want to be a boy. I'm just not a girl either." I never believed I was born into the wrong body. Even now as an out trans non-binary person with life-threatening impairments, I feel lovingly for, in, and of my body. But it was clear that family and teachers—and increasingly peers—believed I was inhabiting my body in very wrong ways, and that this was somehow offensive to them, and therefore dangerous for me.

In junior high, basketball replaced the monkey bars. On the court was where my joints and my soul felt most expansive. I also quickly learned that sport served as useful camouflage for whatever I was. A tight pony-tail, sweats, and no makeup were permissible—though not exactly popular—for athletes in school hallways. The endless tournaments proved legitimate excuses for opting out of dangerous hetero mating rituals. I wasn't too queer for all of that—I could usually convince others and myself—I was just too busy.

STEPHANIE As you were telling that story, I thought back to the first time I was asked if I was a lesbian, which by the way, was by my Nana. I laugh now when I think back on it, because I also used sport as my shield, to deflect and opt out of the dreaded, persistent "do you have a boyfriend" question. I vividly remember visiting home from college and my Nana predictably asking "well, do you have a boyfriend?" Almost habitually, I replied that I didn't, because training kept me too busy. This time, though, she jumped off script and—she took a (much too) long and pointed look at my pony-tail, gym clothes, unkempt eyebrows, and lack of makeup, and asked—almost matter-of-factly—"well, are you a lesbian"? "Nope. Nope. No, definitely not. I'm a basketball player. I don't have time for that, and this is just what we wear!"; I stumbled through the lies with a quickness that distracted my Nana's gaze—and my own—away from my personal life. Being an athlete was also freeing because it shielded me from performing the hyper-feminine standards expected of Southern women. Country singer-songwriter Kacey Musgraves (2015) evokes (and defies) these expectations in her song (and later my mantra) "Pageant Material."

> There's certain things you're s'posed to know
> when you're a girl who grows up in the south
> … And my mama cried when she realized,
> I ain't pageant material.

My athletic way of dressing and my lack of time for dating, were part of the sporty uniform that on one hand, kept me from having to perform "pageant" femininity, and on the other, mostly protected me from questions about (and questioning my own?) sexuality.

DANIELLE So it seems that our devotion to basketball let us both 'follow our arrow' in terms of gender presentation, while flying mostly under the radar. But the flipside is that it made my gender a potentially hypervisible target for teammates with whom I was spending hundreds of hours off court in locker rooms, and team vans, and team-building. Surviving sport, off- court, took everything I had including my ethics: ducking homophobic jokes through complicit laughter, deflecting dating talk through fictitious or utilitarian boyfriends, making myself fit into hyper-feminine pre-game dress codes because "we don't want them to think we are a bunch of dykes do we?" Sport gave me something to live for and just enough breathing room to survive undetected through school. But I did not survive unscathed.

STEPHANIE Part of what made us both fall in love with sport was the way it helped us pass as a more acceptable or valued kind of person outside of sport. To access these 'perks' we both had to pass within sport as a hyper-able, gender-conforming athlete. We made ourselves smaller or made ourselves seem bigger, so we could fit into deeply homophobic, transphobic, and ableist sporting cultures. But fitting in is the opposite of belonging (Brown, 2017).

DANIELLE There were some explicit structural barriers to us bringing our whole selves. For example, I coached for a program that had policies against gay coaches. But for the most part we learned that we could not bring our full selves, that we didn't belong, through microaggressions (Eales & Goodwin, forthcoming; Gearity & Metzger, 2017; Wing Sue et al., 2007). Microaggressions "are brief and commonplace daily verbal, behavioral, or environmental indignities, whether intentional or unintentional, that communicate hostile, derogatory, or negative … slights and insults toward people of color" and other marginalized people (Wing Sue et al., 2007, p. 271). Microaggressions result in significant cumulative harm, and in people feeling unwelcomed and unsafe (Eales, forthcoming). Although parasport often considers itself inherently "inclusive" microaggressions throughout our parasport careers taught us otherwise.

Sometimes people were very explicit about me not being welcome; times where they threatened or insulted me to my face. For the most part, these happened when I played on men's teams.

When I outplayed men, some would lash out with homophobic and transphobic slurs or threats. I even had a male teammate flash me after a game, in front of our teammates. It was clearly an attempt to humiliate me, so I responded in kind, announcing that it was too small for me to see.

The development of quick comebacks is usually a sign that you have had far too much to come back from. Most of the words these men called me were intended to harm, but I had come to own those words as compliments (see Clare, 2009). F**king D*ke, after all, just means lesbian having sex. But the threats of physical and sexual violence felt very real, and in the end, it made me quit playing in American men's leagues.

STEPHANIE That sounds really familiar. I never played on a men's team; in that way, my career is really unusual. My most vivid experiences are being on a women's team playing in a men's league, which was a very violent, gendered experience. I had teammates who were threatened with sexual violence and other bodily harm for outperforming men on the court. It became a very unsafe space for us to be as a team.

DANIELLE I have to say that I rarely experienced those kinds of microassaults—that is, microaggressions that are explicit and meant to harm (Wing Sue et al., 2007)—when I played in gender-mixed Canadian leagues, or in women's leagues. I was lucky that there had been some out lesbians on the Canadian national team before me, and they had made the space much more tolerant, for gay women at least. The microaggressions on the national team were more microinsults: things that people said that were demeaning or devaluing but were not intended to harm me (Wing Sue et al., 2007). But the harm, over time, became very real. The day I made the national team I was told by a teammate that I should not 'flaunt' my sexuality so much, because I'd never get signed by a sponsor: You can be gay, you just can't act gay. I learned that I might not be welcome by hearing what teammates and coaches said about other athletes who did not perform femaleness and homonormativity in the ways our gay athletes had. My coaches and teammates made up transphobic and homophobic nicknames for queer players on other teams, like "the man," or "the butch." My teammates would sneer at how open they were, calling them 'gross' or inappropriate when their girlfriends sat on their lap between games. I felt shame because in a way they were saying these things about me, and also because I never defended those other athletes. These kinds of things made it very clear to me that this was not a safe place for me to be myself. I could be gay, but not queer, and certainly not genderqueer.

STEPHANIE I can certainly say that my team had some of the same reactions to those same athletes. And as a young athlete, I jumped on that bandwagon as well. Looking back, I also feel ashamed for having participated in this harm. There are so many moments that can signal to athletes that they are unwelcome or unsafe. In my national team experience, it wasn't any overt anti-gay sentiment; it was moments where religion was brought into the field of play. The same religion that curled my body; the religion that pitied me. Some team members were super religious. Like, 'God wanted us to win,' religious. Before every game they wanted the team to hold hands and pray as a team bonding experience, except, I didn't feel bonded. I felt like an outsider. But I chose to conform. My nervous, sweaty palm gripped my teammate's hand. I dissociated, my thoughts focusing instead on game scenarios.

DANIELLE Having grown up catholic and queer, I am pretty sure that would have made me quit the team.

STEPHANIE Yeah, that moment taught me that I did not want to create an environment where my athletes felt like outsiders on our team. Bringing religion into sport felt incredibly alienating. In my life religion shrank; Basketball expanded ... and that was even before my sexuality was in the picture. As I was in my coming out process, it was hard to decide when to come out and to whom because I feared losing my sense of belonging. At the time, I had two other teammates who I suspected were dating, but they weren't out. So, I thought that maybe those teammates would be ok with me being gay, even though they weren't out themselves.

DANIELLE Did it worry you that they felt like they couldn't be out?

STEPHANIE Yes, very much so. I feel shame that my teammates felt they couldn't say anything to me about being gay. Did I make the environment unsafe? What could I have done to create safety? These questions haunted me as I was coming out.

Basketball saved and shielded me from pity, as it saved and shielded you. It was a soft landing before it became a sharp tool. It's where I got to make my chosen family and where, for the first time in my life, I experienced true belonging. My life has been so intricately intertwined with sport; I felt that if I did anything to lose my friends, my sport or my sense of belonging, it would feel like losing everything. That's what made it gut wrenching to come out. They were my chosen family. Coming out to my biological family was hard because I did not want to be disowned. But I didn't live with my biological family. I lived in that sporting space. It was the space that most affirmed me.

The teammate that was the hardest to come out to was one I was actually really close with and loved very much. She was Southern and religious, so all of my previous experiences made me scared to tell her. I kept it from her for months and then finally, with some liquid courage in my system, I told her. It was a massive relief and I'm so grateful that she accepted and loved me. But no one should have to feel that afraid to bring who they are and whom they love to their family - biological, chosen, sporting. People need to know they are welcomed and safe before having to potentially sacrifice it all or hide themselves away out of fear.

DANIELLE Yes! This is why we need to counter all of the microaggressions of sport with microaffirmations. That is,

> small acts, which are often ephemeral and hard-to-see, events that are public and private, often unconscious but very effective, which occur wherever people wish to help others to succeed. Microaffirmations are tiny acts of opening doors to opportunity, gestures of inclusion and caring, and graceful acts of listening.
>
> (Rowe, 2008, p. 46)

When I first came to wheelchair basketball, there was this one athlete on my team whom I read as gay. So I'd be talking about my girlfriend around her, in hopes of having some mentorship, around being out in this world. But she shared nothing. But at my second tournament, this athlete invited me—and not the other two rookies—to join her at a birthday party for someone on the other team. And the birthday girl was holding hands all night with her female partner with all the other athletes around, like it was nothing. And I still don't know what her intentions were, but I feel like this was my teammate's way of saying: I can't be out, but you can be. It was the first time in almost 20 years of playing sport that I'd ever had anyone attempt in some way to affirm me or create space for me around queerness.

STEPHANIE What a beautiful story of affirmation and safety from a teammate.

DANIELLE Yes, it was totally life changing. So now much of my work in sport is about creating those micro-affirmations even before (we know) there are marginalized people in the room.

My research and my work with (para)sport and recreation practitioners seek to create preemptively inclusive and explicitly affirming sport spaces. I try to identify things practitioners can do so that those who don't find home in sport (like me) can not only excel, but flourish. For example, it is important that coaches and researchers read about knowledges created within disability communities; if they did this, they would understand the violence of both pity and supercripping, and the immense internal diversity of our communities (Peers, 2018a). It is also important that we don't assume parasport is inclusive and empowering. Parasport was originally designed to be exclusive: our sport is embedded in colonial, racist, classist, (hetero)sexist, and very ableist hierarchies and exclusions (Peers, 2018b). We need practitioners and athletes to bring a critical lens, a transformational approach, and a commitment to both intersectionality and disability leadership if we want to help parasport become an enactment of its stated values. It has honestly been so healing to learn more about your praxis as a coach, and the ways you are creating and enacting the worlds I have only theorized or prescribed. I can only imagine what it would have been like to come of age as one of your athletes: to play the game I loved, and to feel like it loved (all of) me back. It gives me so much hope that you are supporting a generation of athletes who get to be more than athletes. And I have to believe they, in turn, will have the knowledge and confidence to build future sporting worlds that our younger selves, on those monkey bars, could have only dreamed possible.

STEPHANIE I'm filled with gratitude to have had the opportunity to tell our stories together. Through your vulnerability, research, storytelling, and activism, you teach me how to create belonging and affirmation in spaces where you and I longed for it to exist. As a young coach and growing doctoral scholar, I was feeling the weight of social issues in my sport; how hegemonic socially constructed ideals that have served to marginalize those who don't fit the status quo are reproduced through sport and how I reproduced those ideals as an athlete and as a coach.

In my doctoral research, I found your article "Interrogating Disability: the (De)composition of a Recovering Paralympian" (Peers, 2012). I've never connected with an article in the way that I did with your evocative writing and storytelling. It was the first time I've known of a fellow Paralympian expressing what I've been feeling and thinking about parasport; that we have a choice in the role we play in the reproduction of disabling cultures.

You challenged and inspired me to change. I became aware of the ways I perpetuated and reproduced hegemonic ideals in my coaching practice and committed to disrupting those ideals.

Karen DePauw (1997) challenges us to become change agents in the social transformation of sporting culture; to create a sporting culture where all bodies belong and are valued as sporting bodies. I participated in sport to find belonging. One of the most impactful aspects of coaching for me has been learning from my athletes how sport makes them feel; at times devalued, unwanted, needing to change to belong, an outsider. Through coaching, I aspire to create a space of wholehearted belonging for my athletes, transforming their sport experience. That's why I have come to think of my coaching practice as a practice in social justice. Through bringing all parts of who I am (queer, female, disabled, activist), showing and teaching vulnerability, valuing who my athletes are as disabled people, and affirming that they don't have to fit the sexist, heteronormative, ableist ideals of sport to have value in our world. I dream that through practitioners' and coaches' research and coaching praxis, we can help to create spaces where our athletes don't feel like they have to choose the supercrip mountain to escape pity and isolation of the nursing home. They don't have to perfectly fit the script of athlete just to escape the pageant. I dream of a parasport in which they all know they belong. In order to do this, practitioners and coaches should do their best to not contribute to a reproduction of hegemonic ideas in disability sport. This is often seen when researchers focus on stories of athletes and coaches overcoming disability through their participation in sport or when coaches reduce their athletes to only what they can produce on court. We must realize and teach that our athletes, their self-worth, doesn't lie in overcoming their disability or in how many points they can score; they are worthy because they bring their whole, full, multidimensional selves into our gym.

Notes

1 We acknowledge the wide range of terminology used to refer to disability. In this chapter we self-identify with 'disabled person' as a political identity, which characterizes disability not as a problem in our bodies, but a problem of ableist social structures that marginalize us, exclude us, and devalue our lives. (see Peers, Spencer-Cavaliere & Eales, 2014).
2 "AB," short for able-bodied athlete, is a term used within wheelchair basketball communities to refer primarily to any athlete who is not "classifiable" and thus eligible to compete at international levels. Within Canada and some other jurisdictions, such athletes can compete at most local and international competitions (see Brasile, 1990; Spencer-Cavaliere & Peers 2011).

References

Anderson, L. (2006). Analytic autoethnography. *Journal of Contemporary Ethnography*, 35(4), 373–395.

Avner, Z., Bridel, W., Eales, L., Glenn, N., Loewen Walker, R., & Peers, D. (2014). Moved to messiness: Physical activity, feelings, and transdisciplinarity. *Emotion, Space and Society*, 12, 55–62. doi:10.1016/j.emospa.2013.11.002

Brasile, F.M. (1990). Wheelchair sports: A new perspective on integration. *Adapted Physical Activity Quarterly*, 7(1), 3–11.

Braun, V., & Clarke, V. (2006). Using thematic analysis in psychology. *Qualitative Research in Psychology*, 3(2), 77–101. doi:10.1191/1478088706qp063oa

Brown, B. (2017). *Braving the wilderness: The quest for true belonging and the courage to stand alone*. New York: Random House.

DiFranco, A. (1993). My IQ. *Puddle dive*. Righteous Babe Records.

Clare, E. (2009). *Exile & pride: Disability, queerness, and liberation* (2nd ed.). Cambridge, MA: South End Press.

Denzin, N. (2006). Analytic autoethnography, or déjà vu all over again. *Journal of Contemporary Ethnography*, 35(4), 419–428.

DePauw, K.P. (1997). The (in)visibility of disability: Cultural contexts and "sporting bodies." *Quest*, 49, 416–430. doi:10.1080/00336297.1997.10484258

Eales, L., & Goodwin, D. (forthcoming). Addressing trauma in adaptive physical activity: A call to reflexion and action. *Adapted Physical Activity Quarterly*

Ellis, C., Adams, T.E., & Bochner, A.P. (2010). Autoethnography: An overview. *Forum: Qualitative Social Research*, 12, n. 1, ISSN 1438-5627. https://www.qualitative-research.net/index.php/fqs/article/view/1589/3095

Gearity, B.T., & Metzger, L.H. (2017). Intersectionality, microaggressions, and microaffirmations: Toward a cultural praxis of sport coaching. *Sociology of Sport Journal*, 34(2), 160–175. doi:10.1123/ssj.2016-0113

Hardin, M. (2007). "I consider myself an empowered woman". The interaction of sport, gender, and disability in the lives of wheelchair basketball players. *Women in Sport and Physical Activity Journal*, 16(1), 39–52.

McRuer, R. (2006). *Crip theory: Cultural signs of queerness and disability*. New York: New York University Press.

Musgraves, K. (2015). *Pageant material*. Mercury Nashville.

Ngunjiri, F.W., Hernandez, K.C., & Chang, H. (2010). Living autoethnography: Connecting life and research [Editorial]. *Journal of Research Practice*, 6(1), Article E1. Retrieved, from http://jrp.icaap.org/index.php/jrp/article/view/241/186stories!!

Peers, D. (2018a). Engaging axiology: Enabling meaningful transdisciplinary collaboration in adapted physical activity. *Adapted Physical Activity Quarterly*, 35(3), 267–285. DOI: 10.1123/apaq.2017-0095.

Peers, D. (2018b). Sport and social movements by and for disability and deaf communities: Important differences in self-determination, politicisation, and activism. In I. Brittain & A. Beacom (Eds.) *Palgrave Handbook of Paralympic Studies* (pp. 71–97). Basingstoke: Palgrave Macmillan.

Peers, D. (2012). Interrogating disability: The (de)composition of a recovering Paralympian. *Qualitative Research in Sport, Exercise and Health*, 4(2), 175–188.

Peers, D., Spencer-Cavaliere, N., & Eales, L. (2014). Say what you mean: Rethinking disability language in *Adapted Physical Activity Quarterly*. *Adapted Physical Activity Quarterly*, 31, 265–282.

Spencer-Cavaliere, N., & Peers, D. (2011). "What's the difference?" Wheelchair basketball, reverse integration and the question(ing) of disability. *Adapted Physical Activity Quarterly*, 28, 291–309.

St. Pierre, J., & Peers, D. (2016). Introduction: Telling ourselves sideways, crooked and crip. *Canadian Journal of Disability Studies*, 5(3), 1–11. doi:10.15353/cjds.v5i3.293

Rowe, M. (2008). Micro-affirmations & Micro-inequities. *Journal of the International Ombudsman Association*, 1(1), 45–48.

Wing Sue, D., Capodilupa, C.M., Torina, G.C., Bucceri, J.M., Holder, A.M.B., Nadal, K.L., & Esquilin, M. (2007). Racial microaggressions in everyday life: Implications for clinical practice. *American Psychologist*, 62, 271–286. doi:10.1037/0003-066X.62.4.271

Chapter 8

Race, Disability and Sport
The Experience of Black Deaf Individuals

Thomas Irish, Katrina McDonald and Francesca Cavallerio

Introduction

Researching the intersection of race, disability and sport raises many issues for those who wish to foster an inclusive sporting environment. To date, scholars have tended to focus on race and sport, race and disability, or disability and sport, rather than addressing the complexity of their interrelationships (Flintoff, Fitzgerald, and Scraton, 2008). Since this chapter is part of a wider book researching disability sport, we aim to build on the conceptualisation of disability by focusing on the intersection of disability, race, and sport. We would be remiss if we did not mention the current times we live in, with a pandemic, growing calls to challenge police brutality, and systemic racism (Evans, et al., 2020). Therefore, it is paramount that we begin to examine the intersecting social categories – especially within the growing sector which is sport (Dagkas, 2016) – specifically as disability, race, and sport operate simultaneously in social situations and in the wider society. Intersectionality discusses how marginalised identities act to generate different aspects of uniqueness and social status. Chapple (2019, p. 1) states, "Intersectionality is used to conceptualize how intersecting identities such as race, gender, class, sexuality, and disability coexist simultaneously in the lives of marginalized groups". Currently there has been substantial, but separate work on racism in sport, and disability and sport. These two fields have been running in parallel and although they may share characteristics of exclusion, societal barriers, and marginalisation, they have mainly been looked at in co-existing spaces, rather than intersecting ones. Acknowledging the perspective of Berghs and Dyson (2020), we see intersectionality not as a theory, but rather as a tool (Crenshaw, 1991) to be used to examine this dynamic relationship between race, disability, and sport. Specifically, in this chapter we will explore the experiences of those who are Black and Deaf within their involvement in sport.

Following Rankin-Wright and Hylton (2020), in this chapter we will be utilising the term 'Black'. Our rationale for this is twofold: firstly, as all the authors are based in the UK – and acknowledging critiques of the term – the participants who helped contribute to the chapter felt this term was the most inclusive of them as it covered all bases of their experience. Secondly, similar to Berghs and Dyson (2020, p. 3), "we use the term 'Black' politically to describe people of

DOI: 10.4324/9781003153696-10

African, Arab, Asian and Caribbean heritage. This is also in keeping with Black disabled people's self-identification". Similarly, we chose to use the term Deaf, with a capital "D". The literature on D/deafness use this to differentiate the two dominant discourses on D/deafness, which relate to the views of the medical and social models of disability (Corker, 2001). By choosing the word Deaf, we highlight how we are referring to a cultural community, which does not accept Deafness as an impairment (Skelton and Valentine, 2003).

Seal (2012) argues that those with a disability or from a non-dominant ethnicity often experience a disadvantage of some kind in the sporting domain, highlighting how intersectionality first and foremost reflects the reality of daily lives. Our intention for this chapter is to offer a space, an opportunity, to give a voice to those who are Black and Deaf and how they experience sport participation in the UK. Even in simply writing this sentence, a choice is made as to whether to write the word Deaf first, or Black; this is exactly one of the many challenges faced when working in this area. The chapter begins with the focus on a small, preliminary study, to bring the experiences of Black Deaf individuals in sport on centre stage. Results from this study are presented through the use of creative nonfiction (CNF), in an attempt to take the reader into the lived world of these individuals. Our CNF aims to be a tool to raise awareness, and provoke thought and discussion, encouraging change in behaviour (e.g., provocative generalisability; Fine, 2006) and inspiring further research to expand our understanding and knowledge.

The Study

In order to illuminate the experiences of individuals at the intersection of race, disability, and sport, we decided to conduct a small study to begin exploring the stories of those inhabiting this yet-to-be-studied space. Recognising the sensitivity of the territory we aimed to explore and the 'outsider perspective' of Francesca and Katrina as white, hearing females, Thomas, as a Black and Deaf individual, was the one tasked with collecting data. We chose to use interactive interviews, which is a method of narrative inquiry in which those participating are invited to act as both researchers and research participants (Ellis, 2004). This method was deemed appropriate for two reasons: firstly, it recognises the voice of the researcher and invites it in as a co-author (Binns-Terrill, 2012). Secondly, it is considered particularly appropriate when discussing sensitive issues (e.g., race, disability), as both interviewer and interviewee have experience in the area discussed, and the conversation develops between two 'experts', avoiding feelings of judgement and power relations (Ellis, 2004).

Three interviews were conducted, two in English, and one in British Sign Language, and they were all transcribed and analysed using narrative thematic analysis (Riessman, 2008). This analytical method is underpinned by an interpretivist epistemology of social constructivism, which highlights how the stories we tell are grounded in narrative social and cultural resources (Smith and Sparkes, 2009). Firstly, we operated as story analyst, familiarising ourselves with the stories in the interviews (both Thomas' and the participants') and identified two narrative themes: '*People see disability first, skin colour after*' and '*Sport is freedom*'. According to the former theme, deaf people – in sport and elsewhere – are often singled out and marginalised more based on their being Deaf, rather than based on their colour. What is openly in place to provide support for their disability (e.g., note-taker/interpreter at school, or cochlear implant in every day/sport) tends to highlight their difference and often becomes a barrier in their interaction. In sport, this barrier is only brought down when coaches are more aware and inclusive in their practice. The second narrative theme explains how playing sport allows people to forget everything and simply bask in the pleasure of the game. One sub-theme was also identified here (i.e., '*the colour of sport*'), which related to the existence of 'Black sports' and 'White sports', with inclusivity in White sports being challenging, also due to a lack of role models for Black athletes to inspire them.

Once the analysis was concluded, we moved into the role of *storytellers*, using writing as a further layer of analysis (Richardson, 2000) and presenting the results of the study in the form of a creative nonfiction (CNF). As storytellers, we focused on developing a story that carefully reflected the stories participants shared with us. Gutkind (1996) refers to the importance of gathering information – the data – as a fundamental aspect to develop a CNF, and we paid attention to this process by ensuring that our participants' voices were present in the words and dialogues of our story. Therefore, the nonfiction part of the work can be found in what the characters say and think, as their words reflect quotes from the interviews. Nonetheless, we also needed to address the creative aspect of this practice. In order to do so, we worked on the different aspects highlighted by Cavallerio (2021a) to craft a story that would "show rather than tell", by grabbing the reader's attention and evocatively encouraging reflection. Specifically, we paid attention to building scenes for the story to develop, in a way that allowed us to represent our themes. We also worked on the number of characters to be included in the story. Choosing the characters allowed us to represent different voices and perspectives around our themes, which is an effective way of bringing to life the complexity of the area our study aimed to explore. An important aspect for us to develop the realistic quality of the story was the characters' way of speaking and choice of words. While Francesca initially developed the CNF, as she is a non-English native speaker, it was important to discuss within the research team expressions and wording of sentences, to ensure the reader would find the characters credible.

There are numerous reasons to adopt CNF as a way to represent research's findings (see Cavallerio, 2021b), but the rationale for choosing this approach in the present study was mainly due to the complexity in representing a space where so many different aspects, so many different identities, intersect. Stories present complexity in a way that is easier for the human brain to engage with (Zak, 2015) and because of this, they also encourage reflection and engagement with topics that otherwise we could think too difficult or too far away from us. According to Frank (2010), 'stories work *with* people, *for* people, and always stories work *on* people' (p. 3), and with this in mind, the aim of representing our study through a story is to allow it to work on the readers and encourage them to discuss, reflect, research, and engage with the complex space we explored in this chapter.

Kyra's Story

Hands in her pocket, Kyra kicks the can that someone crumpled and threw on the pavement. *Why do people have to be such assholes?* she angrily thinks, without realising the noise the can makes rolling away.

"Kyra, stop! KYRAAA"

Kyra keeps walking.

Suddenly her brother's face appears in front of her.

"What the ..."

"Sorry, you kept walking, but Rob is going to his grandad, so he's going that way. Thought you wanted to say bye".

Of course. That's why she never walks in front when with friends ...

"Hey Rob, sorry. Mate, it's been good to see you. Keep practicing with those hoops, I tell you, you got style".

"Thanks, Kyra. Have a good trip back tomorrow. I'll see you next weekend you come down, yes?". Rob's smiling, expressive face is looking straight at her, lips moving clearly. They've known each other forever, and she knows she can relax in his company, he is always careful to look at her when he speaks, and he even managed to get George to teach him some sign language, surprising her when she came home for the summer holidays.

He is actually cute and thoughtful. If only he wasn't White, she would probably consider him as more than a friend. But she has enough of her situation as it is. 'Oreo' is not a nickname she needs to be added to her list. 'Black on the outside, white on the inside'... what is that supposed to mean, anyway?

Kyra turns away from Rob, head lightly shaking, trying to push all those thoughts away.

She notices Isaac staring at her, a frown on his young face.

"I'm okay, Ise. It's ok"

"If you are okay, then I'm not hungry after shooting hoops for hours..."

Her brother knows her like the back of his hand. Only eighteen months separate them, and yet sometimes their lives seem to happen on different planets.

"I just don't wanna go back there. I know I'm lucky, I know it's a great school and I should be grateful that mum and dad can afford to send me there, but it's just ... it's in the middle of nowhere, Ise! And everyone is so White! There is only another Black person in my year, and that's a boy. Remember when I had my hair braided and had that cool caramel colour on after Easter? You should have seen the look on their faces! The head girl told me off, said it was inappropriate for school. They don't have a clue! Hair is our thing; hair is our culture. I've never seen her say anything to all those brunettes-turned-blondes".

Isaac looks at me, waits until I'm done with my rant, until I turn my eyes to him again, then speaks. "I thought you were looking forward to going back so you could show everyone at the athletics club how much your times improved over summer. I thought you were looking forward to the competition in October ..."

"Yeah, a little ... but to be honest, I don't want to go back to that club. No one pays any attention to me. The coaches barely look at me, and my 'teammates' – Kyra's hands draw inverted commas in the air – never bothered even asking me anything beyond my name".

"Wow ... is that because you are black? Are they really so racist, up there?"

"Ha, sometimes I wish it was. Maybe it'd be easier. With me, people see my disability first, and my skin colour after. As soon as they clock my cochlear implant, that's it. I'm the weirdo, too much too different, all in once. I never stood a chance with that bunch'".

"...but with the track club here in London, you seemed to be okay ..."

"Yes, this summer has been really good. But you see, everyone else is Black there. So at least I have one thing in common, at least with that I fit in. And then the coach ... I don't know, he's just nice. He just pays attention to me, to my needs. He makes sure he explains the exercise before we get started, makes sure I can see him when he speaks, so lip reading is easier. We even worked out a few signals, so I can pick them up even if I'm running, without having to stop what I'm doing, turn around, get closer. With the coach back there, it's like I'm always late to the party. Whatever he explains, I need to stop and ask him to repeat, because he always shouts instructions after we start practicing. So, then he gets bored and stops paying attention to me".

Kyra's shoulders sag even simply recalling how he makes her feel.

"I don't get it. If it's so bad, why do you keep training?"

"Because I love it. I love running. I just love how it makes me feel, it's magic. When I'm running, nothing else matters. I'm free from thoughts, free from anger, free from everything. And I know I'm good. One day I'll show them! There's a reason why all the great runners are Black. Think of Mo, Usain, Dina, Christine. Running is a black sport. I might be a minority, over and over again: Woman, Black, Deaf ... one of the craziest minority situations. But I can run. And one day I'll show them".

Isaac keeps walking, they can see the building where they live, at the top of the hill. He looks down, shoulders hunched forward.

"What's up, Ise?"

"Nothing. I'll miss you. I like it when you are back, I have fun playing ball, and doing stuff together".

"You and Rob should keep practicing; you are both good. I'm sure you can find a team around here, so you guys can keep training this autumn".

"Actually, I thought I'd join Rob's swimming club. I met a few of his mates when we went to the cinema a few weeks ago. Thought I might give it a shot, try something different".

"Aw. Swimming. It's a White sport, are you sure you'd be okay?"

"Why d'you keep putting colours in front of sports' names? Why are you so obsessed with it?"

"I'm not obsessed, it's just how it is. Basketball is a Black sport. What are the names of great athletes there? Jordan, Pippin, Lebron James… the best athletes are Black, and they are inspiring. Running is Black. But can you think of a Black swimmer? It's a White sport. I hope there'll be space for you, but … I just don't want you to get hurt. Disappointed. Just that".

Isaac remains silent. Or maybe he is mumbling, which means whatever he is saying, he does not want to include her in the conversation.

Come on, Ise. Don't worry about it now! Let's go home, mum promised to braid my hair before I leave tomorrow, and that took her six hours, last time. I need to look at my best once I go back, this year I'll show them!

What Does the CNF Tell Us about Intersectionality?

From the story, two distinct themes can be noted, *'People see disability first, skin colour after'* and *'Sport is freedom'*. Examining the literature with these themes at the forefront of our minds permitted an insight into three intersecting areas that we feel deserve greater attention. A point to note here is that predominantly much of the literature that addresses race and disability orginates in the United States (US) and centres on the situations of African Americans with disabilities (Stienstra, 2012). Whilst this is not an issue per se, it does make the authors reiterate their point that they are all based in the UK and, as such, their experience and understanding stems from here.

To examine race, disability and sport through an intersectional lens aims to highlight the lived experience of people who identify in these spheres. Frederick and Shifrer's (2019) work offers a great depth of intersectional analysis in sociology, especially starting at the pretext that racism and ableism are powerful interacting forces that intertwine and interact to create unique forms of inequality and resistance. Wolbring (2012, p. 78) stated that "ableism describes prejudicial and discriminatory behaviours toward person with disability". This definition of ableism is based on a single understanding of normal ability, as well as the rights and benefits afforded to people who are deemed normal.

In general, sport has historically been a space where success and winning often overshadowed participating, with the leading motto of "faster, higher, stronger" perpetuating this opinion, focusing on performance measurements and on pushing the boundaries of human capability. Acknowledging this highlights how the domain of sport can be viewed as a non-inclusive area (Kiuppis, 2018). Seal (2012, p. 5) stated that, "Historically, sport as an institution has been reflective of dominant norms, standards and ideologies prevailing within society. Arguably, this has not always been the case for people with disabilities".

Data gathered by Sport England (2021) on physical activity and disability highlighted how physical inactivity is twice as likely in disabled individuals

(41%), compared with those without a disability (20%). In order to understand why most individuals with physical disabilities are not involved in sports, it is important to understand what prevents them from doing so and how they can be encouraged and inspired to become interested in sports. Sport activity has a physiological and psycho-social advantage for disabled people and reduces hospitalisation risk, as well as secondary health problems such as cardiovascular disease, diabetes, obesity and mental health problems (Jaarsma et al., 2014; Shapiro and Malone, 2016; Stephens et al., 2012). Research has shown that health benefits, fun, and social integration are major facilitators for people with disabilities to participate in sport, whereas obstacles to involvement include environmental inaccessibility, poor resources, and negative societal attitudes (Grandisson et al., 2012; Jaarsma et al., 2015; Shields and Synnot, 2016).

Annamma, Ferri and Connor (2018) raise the visibility of disability critical race theory by acknowledging work that has been undertaken across both areas of disability studies and race. Their work was driven by a desire to give a voice, specifically in literature, to those defined in a unidimensional way, recognising that racism and ableism are interconnected, so they started to utilise disability critical race theory. These authors recognise that one of the criticisms of disability studies is that it has traditionally been limited to a focus on White, middle-class individuals, whereas a criticism of racial studies is that issues of dis/ability remain largely underexplored. Berghs and Dyson (2020) concurred with this viewpoint, suggesting that some argued the predominant control of the disability movement by disabled white men was racist and disregarded Black people's experience.

Within the story, the view that people see Kyra's disability first and skin colour after illuminates a general lack of awareness of the intersecting nature of race and disability. Within the literature, it is suggested this is due to the different models that are utilised to represent disability and how the medical model of disability is seen to fragment the individual and focus either on race or on disability, never examining the interplay (Artiles, 2013). Liasidou (2013) suggests that the modern monopoly of biomedicine on the notion of disability has limited disabled individuals to unequal and discriminatory treatment, rationalising this on perceived deficits and inferior identities. Erevelles (2011) infers that many scholars who examine race, distance themselves from nurturing any alliance with disability as they mistakenly conceive disability as a biological category. Evidently, as suggested by Frederick and Shifrer (2019), there is still work to be done in developing intersectional scholarship and activism at the nexus of race and disability.

An important distinction to make between race and disability is that it is impossible to change one's race; however, it is highly possible for every human being to have the potential to develop an impairment or disability (Liasidou, 2013). The last distinction to make, which can be found in the literature – while in the story the opposite is experienced by Kyra – is that it may be possible to not disclose one's disability or impairment if one chooses to, whereas race is available for everyone to see. 'Passing' was defined by Goffman as being considered a member of a social group, even when one does not qualify for it (1963), like homosexuals passing for heterosexuals. Depending on their disability, individuals might be able to pass as able-bodied, and might want to reject their disabled identity (Watson, 2002). Not surprisingly, sport can be seen as a potential tool to 'feel normal', therefore encouraging passing behaviours (Powis, 2018). Nonetheless, like in Kyra's experience, at times passing might become impossible due to the nature of the sport and the need for support (Irish et al., 2018). The work of John Howard Griffin, author of *'Black like me'* (1961) is an interesting example of the merging of intersectionality and passing, highlighting how the writer hid his blindness both in his life and in his writing, while discussing his passing as a black man and experiencing racism (Brune, 2013). It might be that, in line with our subtheme, *'The colour of sport'*, passing race-wise might be easier than disability-wise due to the skin colour normalised in the sporting context. Stienstra (2012) suggested that those people who have these multiple identities, often feel constrained or restrained and experience situations of disadvantage, marginalisation, and oppression. This is clearly observed throughout Kyra's narrative.

The intersectionality of race and disability in sport is complex, as captured in the CNF, with Liasidou (2013) suggesting that this interaction needs to be utilised to assist in informing policies and their implementation. Her review subscribes to the view that race and disability studies have developed in parallel yet distinctive ways. The lack of synergy between the two damages their potential political strength to challenge the dynamics that form the oppression that is experienced by both sets of people alike. The compounding effects of multiple identities result in various experiences of disadvantage or advantage (Moodley and Graham, 2015). As a consequence, both race and disability are viewed as the result of hegemonic conceptions of normality, which is one of the most powerful likenesses for human exclusion (Liasidou, 2013).

In sport, the discourses of 'whiteness' and 'ableism' (Liasidou, 2013) are significantly entwined where the hierarchical supremacy of certain individuals is not only represented as the ideal, but they are also celebrated as role models in society. In the story, the theme *'Sport is freedom'* and its subtheme *'The colour of sport'* help to highlight conflicting views related to Liasidou's (2013) work. The former theme helps strengthening the message that sport offers an opportunity to engage with individuals as whole people, rather than dividing them into subcategories of their identity, invoking thoughts around inclusion and breaking of barriers. Whereas the latter reiterates the point that sport actually reinforces harmful views instead, seeing sport as a space of inequality, discrimination, exploitation and ultimately inherently racism (Carrington, 2013).

Initial works into race and sport can be traced back to the early 1960's and there has been considerable growth in the area. Over the past decades, sport sociologists focused on the interweaving of race and sport from a variety of perspectives, for example, the lived experiences of migrants in sport (e.g., Michelini, 2020), or discrimination experiences (e.g., Evans & Piggott, 2016; Maguire, 1988). Hylton (2005) called out the systematic neglect of 'race' as a research area in sport, and the subsequent marginalisation of individuals. Where race was discussed, it was more often than not as a statistical variable with a lack of theorisation or discussion of racism (Carrington, 2013). Scholars replied to the call, and over the past decade research in this area increased.

Within the CNF, the role of sport and race is portrayed by Kyra's experiences, both in a freeing and restrictive way. It is too simplistic to say that there is a unidimensional relationship between race and sport, both are complex, but they do cross, merge and collide. It is this relationship that simultaneously can both challenge and confirm racial ideologies (Carrington and McDonald, 2001), and because of this, there has been a repeated call to critically engage in this area and debate the changing meaning and significance of race and sport (Carrington, 2013). Currently, the role that sport can play in highlighting racial issues has been seen more widely with sport stars using their status as athletes to advocate for the need for racial equality (e.g., Colin Kaepernick, Megan Rapinoe, Lewis Hamilton, Naomi Osaka), encouraging this to occur not only in sport but in society as well (Evans et al., 2020). Such awareness raising and positive outcomes inspire some hope in the role that sport can play as a microcosm of society (Hylton, 2020).

Conclusion

Despite recent growth in the areas of race and disability research (e.g., underrepresentation of Black coaches, racism amongst fans and media; Kilvington and Price, 2019; Rankin-Wright et al., 2016), too little research exists to-date focusing on D/deaf athletes and their experiences participating in sport. When one also wants to explore how two identities, such as those related to race and disability, integrate and interact in the context of sport, no research at all appears to be available. Atherton (2007) suggested that one of the biggest barriers to deaf people participating in sport is the attitudes of the hearing majority. Too often examples of inequality and discrimination are not taken into account by policymakers or stakeholders who have the power to make a difference (Evans et al., 2020). Therefore, acknowledging this power and the dominant role that sport has within popular culture and the mass media (Carrington, 2013) could help to bring about change and could create a significant impact to people with intersecting identities.

Questions therefore need to be asked in relation to the point to which sport is being used as an effective platform in leading towards systematic change (Hylton, 2020). The second point to note is that one of the most challenging aspects of approaching the intersectionality of sport, race and disability is that of nationality, culture and history. Therefore, as Carrington (2015) questions, is it possible to build a coherent field with these varying factors? While the challenges for researchers are easy to see – even if simply based on our brief review – so are the possibilities and understanding that work conducted at the intersection of these three areas can provide to society.

References

Annamma, S., Ferri, B., and Connor, D., 2018. Disability critical race theory: Exploring the intersectional lineage, emergence, and potential futures of DisCrit in education. *Review of Research in Education*, 42, pp. 46–71.

Artiles, A. J. (2013). Untangling the racialization of disabilities: An intersectionality critique across disability models. *Du Bois Review: Social Science Research on Race*, 10, pp. 329–347.

Atherton, M., 2007. Sport in the British deaf community. *Sport in History*, 27(2), pp. 276–292.

Berghs, M., and Dyson, S. M., 2020. Intersectionality and employment in the United Kingdom: Where are all the Black disabled people? *Disability & Society*, DOI:10.1080/09687599.2020.1829556

Binns-Terrill, R.A. 2012. *Inside NFL marriages: A seven-year ethnographic study of love and marriage in professional football*. Doctoral dissertation.

Brune, J.A., 2013. The multiple layers of disability passing in life, literature, and public discourse. In J. A. Brune and D. J. Wilson (eds.), *Disability and passing: Blurring the lines of identity* (pp. 33–57). Philadelphia: Temple University Press.

Carrington, B., 2013. The critical sociology of race and sport: The first fifty years. *Annual Review Sociology*, 39, pp. 379–398

Carrington, B., 2015 Assessing the sociology of sport: On race and diaspora. *International Review for the Sociology of Sport*, 50(4–5), pp. 391–396

Carrington, B., and McDonald, I., 2001. *'Race', sport and British society*. London: Routledge.

Cavallerio, F., 2021a. "Where do I start?": Getting to grips with creative nonfiction. In F. Cavallerio (ed.), *Creative nonfiction in sport and exercise research* (pp. 13–31). London: Routledge.

Cavallerio, F. (ed.), 2021b. *Creative nonfiction in sport and exercise research*. London: Routledge.

Chapple, R.L., 2019. Toward a theory of black deaf feminism: The quiet invisibility of a population. *Affilia*, 34(2), pp.186–198.

Corker, M., 2001. Sensing disability. *Hypatia*, 16(4), pp. 34–52.

Crenshaw, K., 1991. "Mapping the margins: Identity politics, intersectionality, and violence against women." *Stanford Law Review*, 43 (6), pp. 1241–1299.

Dagkas, S., 2016. Problematizing social justice in health pedagogy and youth sport: Intersectionality of race, ethnicity, and class. *Research Quarterly for Exercise and Sport*, 87(3), pp. 221–229.

Ellis, C., 2004. *The ethnographic I: A methodological novel about autoethnography*. Lanham, MD: Rowman Altamira.

Erevelles, N., 2011. *Disability and difference in global contexts*. New York: Palgrave Macmillan.

Evans, A.B., Agergaard, S., Campbell, P.I., Hylton, K., and Lenneis, V., 2020. 'Black Lives Matter:' Sport, race and ethnicity in challenging times. *Journal for Sport and Society*, 17(4), pp. 289–300.

Evans, A.B. and Piggott, D., 2016. Shooting for Lithuania: Migration, national identity and men's basketball in the East of England. *Sociology of Sport Journal*, 33(1), pp. 26–38.

Fine, M., 2006. Bearing witness: Methods for researching oppression and resistance—A textbook for critical research. *Social Justice Research*, 19(1), pp. 83–108.

Flintoff, A., Fitzgerald, H. and Scraton, S., 2008. The challenges of intersectionality: Researching difference in physical education. *International Studies in Sociology of Education*, 18(2), pp. 73–85.

Frank, A.W., 2010. *Letting stories breathe: A socio-narratology*. Chicago: University of Chicago Press.

Frederick, A., and Shifrer, D., 2019. Race and disability: From analogy to intersectionality. *Sociology of Race and Ethnicity*, 5(2), pp. 200–214.

Goffman, E., 1963. *Stigma: Notes on the management of spoiled identity*. New York: Simon and Schuster.

Grandisson, M., Tétreault, S., and Freeman, A.R., 2012. Enabling integration in sports for adolescents with intellectual disabilities. *Journal of Applied Research in Intellectual Disabilities*, 25(3), pp. 217–230.

Griffin, J.H. 1961. *Black like me*. New York: Signet.

Gutkind, L. (1996). From the editor: The 5 Rs of creative nonfiction. *Creative Nonfiction*, 1–14.

Hylton, K., 2005. 'Race', sport and leisure: Lessons from critical race theory. *Leisure Studies*, 24(1), pp. 81–98.

Hylton, K., 2020. Black Lives Matter in sport…? *Equality, Diversity and Inclusion: An International Journal*.

Irish, T., Cavallerio, F., and McDonald, K., 2018. "Sport saved my life" but "I am tired of being an alien!": Stories from the life of a deaf athlete. *Psychology of Sport and Exercise*, 37, pp. 179–187.

Jaarsma, E.A., Dekker, R., Koopmans, S.A., Dijkstra, P.U. and Geertzen, J.H., 2014. Barriers to and facilitators of sports participation in people with visual impairments. *Adapted Physical Activity Quarterly*, 31(3), pp. 240–264.

Jaarsma, E.A., Dijkstra, P.U., de Blécourt, A.C., Geertzen, J.H., and Dekker, R., 2015.

Kilvington, D., and Price, J., 2019. Tackling social media abuse? Critically assessing English football's response to online racism. *Communication & Sport*, 7(1), pp. 64–79.

Kiuppis, F., 2018. Inclusion in sport: Disability and participation. *Sport in Society*, 21(1), pp. 4–21.

Liasidou, A., 2013. The cross-fertilization of critical race theory and disability studies: Points of convergence/divergence and some education policy implications, *Disability & Society*, 29(5), pp. 1–14.

Maguire, J.A., 1988. Race and position assignment in English soccer: A preliminary analysis of ethnicity and sport in Britain. *Sociology of Sport Journal*, 5(3), pp. 257–269.

Michelini, E., 2020. Coping with sport ambitions after forced migration: strategies of refugee athletes. *European Journal for Sport and Society*, pp. 1–17.

Moodley, J. and Graham, L., 2015. The importance of intersectionality indisability and gender studies. *Agenda: Empowering Women for Gender Equity*, 29(2), pp. 1–10.

Powis, B. 2018. Transformation, advocacy and voice in disability sport research. In T. F. Carter, D. Burdsey, and M. Doidge (eds.), *Transforming sport: Knowledges, practices, structures* (pp. 248–259). London: Routledge.

Rankin-Wright, A., and Hylton, K., 2020. Black women, intersectionality and sport coaching. In S. Bradbury, J. Lusted, and J. van Sterkenburg (eds.), *'Race', ethnicity and racism in sports coaching* (pp. 128–142). London: Routledge.

Rankin-Wright, A. J., Hylton, K., and Norman, L., 2016. Off-colour landscape: Framing race equality in sport coaching. *Sociology of Sport Journal*, 33(4), pp. 357–368.

Richardson, L., 2000. New writing practices in qualitative research. *Sociology of Sport Journal*, 17(1), pp. 5–20.

Riessman, C.K., 2008. *Narrative methods for the human sciences*. London: Sage.

Seal, E., 2012. Understanding complexity in disability sport: The potential of feminist philosophies and intersectionality. *Psychology of Women Section Review*, 14(2), pp. 34–40.

Shapiro, D.R., and Malone, L.A., 2016. Quality of life and psychological affect related to sport participation in children and youth athletes with physical disabilities: A parent and athlete perspective. *Disability and Health Journal*, 9(3), pp. 385–391.

Shields, N. and Synnot, A., 2016. Perceived barriers and facilitators to participation in physical activity for children with disability: A qualitative study. *BMC Pediatrics*, 16(1), pp. 1–10.

Skelton, T., and Valentine, G., 2003. 'It feels like being Deaf is normal': An exploration into the complexities of defining D/deafness and young D/deaf people's identities. *Canadian Geographer/Le Géographe Canadien*, 47(4), pp. 451–466.

Smith, B. and Sparkes, A.C., 2009. Narrative analysis and sport and exercise psychology: Understanding lives in diverse ways. *Psychology of Sport and Exercise*, 10(2), pp. 279–288.

Sport England (2021) Disability – mapping disability. Available at: https://www.sportengland.org/campaigns-and-our-work/disability (Accessed: 10th April 2021).

Stephens, C., Neil, R., and Smith, P., 2012. The perceived benefits and barriers of sport in spinal cord injured individuals: A qualitative study. *Disability and Rehabilitation*, 34(24), pp. 2061–2070.

Stienstra, D., 2012. 'Race/ethnicity and disability studies: Towards an explicitly intersectional approach', in N. Watson, A. Roulstone, and C. Thomas, (eds.) *Routledge handbook of disability studies* (pp. 376–381), Lancaster: MTP.

Watson, N., 2002. "Well, I Know this is Going to Sound Very Strange to You, but I Don't See Myself as a Disabled Person": Identity and disability. *Disability & Society*, 17(5), pp. 509–527.

Wolbring, G., 2012. Expanding on ableism: Taking down the ghettoization of impact of disability studies scholars. *Societies*, 2(3), pp. 75–83.

Zak, P.J., 2015, January. Why inspiring stories make us react: The neuroscience of narrative. In *Cerebrum: The Dana forum on brain science* (Vol. 2015). Dana Foundation.

Chapter 9

Disability and Ageing
Dads, Sons, Sport and Impairment

James Brighton

Introduction

Walking into hospital for the birth of my baby brother, Andrew, I vividly remember asking my Dad why he walked "differently" to everyone else. An unassuming question for an inquisitive 4-year-old to ask perhaps, but one which I now realise was laden with stigma. "I didn't realise!" he jokingly replied, and then forced his feet together in an attempt to walk like 'normal' people do. My Dad's use of humour to detract from a potentially sensitive interchange was, as I was to learn, to become a central feature in our relationship. What I did not know back then was that my father has polio, short for poliomyelitis, or also known as 'infantile paralysis'. A small percentage of people who contracted polio at the time of his birth died. He survived, but his right leg remained permanently paralysed from the knee down resulting in among other things, a non-normative gait, which even a 4 year old noticed demarked him as different.

I didn't really think much about his impairment for a long time after that, he was just my Dad. The only other occasions that I was ever conscious of it in my childhood was when in the depths of winter he would remove the family Labrador from her usual recumbent position in front of the log fire, peel down his thick woollen socks and prop his lifeless limb as close to the open flames as he could in an attempt to warm it up. His impaired leg had not only lost functionality but suffered from poor circulation and became cold quickly. I'd often see him vigorously rub his big hands over his ankle in an attempt to create further heat from the friction. This was often accompanied by sipping a caramel coloured whisky from a crystal cut glass as if further attempting to warm his leg from the inside. As I got older and more capable of empathy and understanding of difference, I would often gaze at his leg as he undertook this ritual. I'd look at the deep scars crisscrossing over his ankle and foot from multiple infantile surgeries, the atrophied calf muscle, the dry loose skin from the abrasion of the aggressive rubbing. Contrastingly, I would look at his other leg, strong, powerful, calf bulging from years of taking the sole responsibility for propelling his body through a lifetime of work and sport.

Having always been so captivated by physical movement myself, whether that be the pure freedom of running, the joy of kicking a football or hitting a

DOI: 10.4324/9781003153696-11

cricket ball, I have increasingly wondered how my Dad's experiences of sport and physical activity, which are so central in both of our lives and understandings of self, differed to mine. Now 40 and not capable of physical feats that I once was, I have also become more reflective of a previous youthful sporting body. Consequently, I find myself wanting to explore my Dad's relationships with his body and sport over time as he aged and how these embodied experiences offer valuable critique of the social and cultural structures of sport and ableist society. Resultantly, this chapter engages with a plurality of autoethnographic methodologies through which experiences that have been lived as father and son are told in the form of personal stories as both of our bodies have aged.

Telling Stories in Disability Studies

Although I have previously written about who I am and my interest in researching disability (Brighton, 2015), I have been wary of writing autoethnographically directly about experiences of impairment and disability. Identifying as able-bodied, it is not only a methodological necessity but a moral and ideological responsibility for me to position myself in relation to the disabled people I engage with and be reflexive of the way I listen to stories and interpret and write about the lives I study. I have not experienced the insidious forms of oppression, stigma, prejudice and exclusion that many disabled people face at an individual and structural level, nor do I claim to ever be able to fully understand what this feels like. I am also very conscious that presenting individual stories of disability have been critiqued by some disability studies scholars who feel that such an approach risks evoking medicalised interpretations of disability experience, draws attention away from the collective struggle for equality and makes little material difference to disabled people's lives (e.g. Finkelstein, 1996). In presenting the stories of my Dad in this chapter therefore, I am acutely aware that I am entering a contested methodological and political terrain which requires acknowledgment. Equally, like others before me (e.g. Sparkes, 2000), I do not feel the need to be drawn into an over apologetic justification for the stories presented.

In response to acerbic academic criticism (e.g. Atkinson, 1997[1]) over the last three decades, autoethnographers have fought hard to legitimise their craft as a form of scientific inquiry and create a caring community through which stories can be told, shared and experienced together (e.g. Ellis & Bochner, 1996; Muncey, 2010; Holman Jones et al., 2013; Sparkes, 2018). As Adams et al. (2022) outline, this autoethnographic movement has acted as an enlightenment, helping i) foreground particular and subjective knowledge; ii) illustrate sense-making processes; iii) make contributions to existing research; iv) challenge norms of research practice and representation; and, v) engage and compel responses from audiences. Rather than detract from the collective struggle of disabled people therefore, personal stories reveal and communicate unique experiences of disability, expose and challenge oppressive societal and cultural structures, imaginatively diversify the methods of researching disability, broaden the audiences that receive our work and inspire them into action and change. This can be demonstrated through briefly attending to each advantage highlighted. *Firstly*, foregrounding subjective knowledge of disability provides thick, powerful, sentient and valid insight into different experiences of impairment, ways of being and phenomena that are often unobtainable to able-bodied others through revealing:

> ...the complexity, messiness, serendipity of social life; the personal often-hidden nuances of challenging, thrilling, traumatic, joyful, and taboo encounters; patterns of experience that shift and change with time; the ways a past occurrence informs present and future acts; and the emotional, sensory and material effects of experience that escape observation of even conscious awareness.
> (Adams et al., 2022, p. 4)

The power of autoethnography lies not just in illuminating subjective knowledge, but also in allowing for observations of events as they occur whilst more deeply appreciating how they are lived (Adams et al., 2022). My Dad's experiences of ableism for example are tied up in the relational dynamics of able-bodied privilege, the times in which he lived and the able-bodied sporting subcultures in which he resided. These experiences are also inseparable from other intersecting identity characteristics which locate him as otherwise privileged (white, male, 'straight', hegemonically masculine, middle class, normalcy of his impairment). It is also important to recognise here that prioritising stories and subjective knowledge from disabled people themselves is particularly significant given that disabled people are often Othered in research (turned form being a person into an object) and reduced to the status of their "malfunctioning bodies" (McDougall, 2006, p. 395). As a result, disabled voices have historically been silenced and oppressed (e.g. Yoshida & Shanouda, 2015) and subjected to being researched by others who themselves have not experienced disability (e.g. see Wigginton & Setchell, 2016).

Secondly, through constructing stories we nurture alternative ways of knowing and ways of making sense of our experiences through attending to "some of the most challenging, confusing and formative events, relationships, and social and political experiences we encounter throughout life" (Adams et al., 2022, p. 4). This is important when experiences are uncomfortable and do not make sense, such as becoming ill or navigating everyday life being demarked as disabled within the tyrannical structures of ableism. *Thirdly*, autoethnographies of disability and sport add important contributions to existing research and critique ableist social and cultural perceptions, beliefs, values, identities and actions. Since ex-Paralympian Danielle Peers' (2012) seminal autoethnography (de)constructing their Paralympic identity, we have only recently begun to witness the emergence of autoethnographies of disability sport emerge and their value to field (e.g. Irish et al., 2018; McMahon et al., 2020; Lowry et al., 2022; Bundon & Manella; Wheeler & Peers, both this volume)[2]. Such stories demonstrate how we can learn from individual disability experience from the inside.

Fourthly, autoethnography challenges the norms of disability research practice and representation by contesting researcher objectivity and neutrality instead assuming relativist ontological (there are multiple meanings of reality) and subjective epistemological (knowledge is subjective and socially constructed) positions. This is not to say that disabled people do not succumb to writing about themselves in objectified and over simplified ways as a result of being relentlessly subjected to being Othered in social interaction (Richards, 2016) or are free from the social and cultural dynamics that place restrictions on what stories can be told and how they are told (e.g. Smith, 2013, 2017). Importantly, the way that personal stories are represented offers a contrast to dry and abstract theoretical debate about how to challenge structural inequality found in much disability studies research. Instead, experiences of disability are presented in evocative and compelling ways that explicitly or implicitly critique the forms of structural oppression. I would also argue that this form of representation is more accessible to wider audiences, encouraging both disabled and able-bodied audiences to engage with them.

Fifthly, through engaging and compelling responses from audiences and providing alternative views of reality, autoethnographies of disability sport can further inspire resistance, action and activism (e.g. Smith et al., 2016; Choi et al., 2021) leading to social change (e.g. Wigginton & Setchell, 2016). As Owton and Sparkes (2017) highlight, from a social constructionist perspective, the audience that receives the story and engages with experiences of another's' life cannot claim that they have not heard it, and so it becomes inseparable from their own world view. Stories themselves therefore have agentic power. Indeed, presenting stories that are emancipatory deepen the cultural repertoire of narrative resources available for others to tell their own stories differently (e.g. Frank, 2000). Taking the above into consideration, I now outline the collaborative autoethnographic methodological plurality through which Dad and I construct and tell our stories of impairment and ageing.

Telling Stories Together

Collaborative autoethnography is an umbrella term that can be best understood as one person writing stories about their own lived experiences in collaboration with another within given social and cultural contexts (e.g. Chang et al., 2016). The approach I take in this chapter borrows from multiple collaborative autoethnographic methods. Some stories represent affective moments that are experienced together between my Dad and I which might be seen as a lived form of 'collective witnessing' which focuses on and tells "the lives of others in shared storytelling and conversation" (Ellis & Rawicki, 2013, p. 366). Having shared experience of some of the same events but told through different perspectives (James identifying as able-bodied; Dad positioned as disabled), other stories bear hallmarks of a 'duo-autoethnography' which are characterised by the juxtaposition of life stories in order to generate multiple understandings of the world (Norris et al., 2012). In creating a space for Dad and I to work together across these differences, reflect on our relationship over time and develop stories that are openly ideological in their intention, stories also borrow from critical co-constructed autoethnography (see Cann & DeMeulenaere, 2012). Together, the plurality of the approach employed allowed for personally lived and shared stories to be collectively remembered (Haug et al., 1983/1987) and intertwined, offering critique of social and cultural ableism (and other isms) through different embodied and interpretative lenses, language and storytelling apparatus.

Clearly, my Dad existed before I was born or had a conscious awareness of him. He has many stories to tell of his body before my own body entered the world. To collect these earlier stories as well as later stories as his body aged, a series of short[3] life history interviews (Atkinson, 1998) were conducted face to face and transcribed. These mediated interviews supplemented a lifetime of casual conversations and focused on experiences of impairment and ageing that I wanted to find out about in more depth for the purposes of this chapter. As his son, these recollections were at times joyous, and other times were challenging and difficult to listen to. Doing so however provided further context of stories located in time, space, place and circumstance (Adams et al., 2022), and shed further embodied and emotional insight on 'epiphanal moments' (Denzin, 1989) as well are more mundane everyday experiences. Interviews were not formally analysed but were used as resources in the construction of individual stories and in informing decisions on what stories should be told. For example, what sticks as important in my memory may not be as important to my Dad, and these experiences will be interpreted and remembered differently, so joint decisions were made on what stories were included and how they were told. The stories of my Dad are his own stories, told in his own words, but now by necessity due to fatigue and difficulties in articulating through language, I have crafted them into storied extracts from his life. They are represented through taking an evocative stance. That is, I have resisted the "methodological impulse" (Sparkes, 2018) to analyse the story through theory, but simply show the reader our stories with social and cultural understandings of disability and impairment implicitly implied and embedded within the narrative. It is hoped that this approach allows readers to experience with the story by not detracting from its emotional richness (Ellis et al., 2011), provides counter narratives that resist and challenge ableism (see Sparkes, 2018) and inspires the reader to consider, care, feel, empathise, take action and effect change (Ellis & Bochner 2006; Holman Jones 2011; Sparkes, 2020). In presenting the stories below, we hope to advance collaborative autoethnography as a method to imaginatively explore experiences of impairment, sport and shared human existence.

The Boy with the Brace

> **SON**: A couple of years ago my Dad's Mum (my Gran) died and we were faced with the poignant task of clearing out the belongings from her house so it could be sold. Amongst the boxes of books, clothes and collectables I came

across a crude looking contraption. About 8 inches long, two now rusted metal rods were joined together by four circular dark brown leather buckles with a hinge in the middle. "What's this, Dad?" I inquired. He reached over, took it in his bear like hands and bought it closer to his face. His green eyes glazed over as if being flooded with memories from a previous time, a previous body and a previous self. Gently running his fingers over the worn leather, he said wistfully "That's the brace I wore as a kid for my leg". I was shocked by its size and its antiquity. I struggled to imagine my Dad, who I had always known as so big and strong, being so small and so fragile. The brace itself seemed so primitive and raw, hardly fit to wrap around a child's delicate limb. Unable to get the brace out of mind for the rest of the day, I tried to imagine what life would have been like for Dad growing up with an impairment and how different it was to my own privileged able-bodied childhood memories. The youngest of four brothers born towards the twilight stages of the World War Two baby boom, he rarely spoke about his childhood memories. Not that he wouldn't tell me if I asked, he is an emotional man who speaks from his heart. It was more a case that the English stoicism and resilience that was so necessary at the time of his childhood had been staunchly embedded in his character. Or, maybe he had repressed experiences of trauma, burying them deep in his psyche without seeing the need to revisit or articulate them. Perhaps it was simply a requirement to be tough in order to survive. Later that evening after sharing a glass (or three) of red wine, I tactfully asked "What was it like wearing that brace Dad, did people take the piss out of you even more than they do now?".

DAD: I had to wear it from when I was nine months old to when I was ten, so I knew no different. It provided stability from surgery and helped me to walk, yet it also was a marker of my disability. When we went to the beach in the summer as a family, I'd always be more conscious of it, sand would get stuck underneath it and I couldn't go into the sea with everyone else as the salt water would corrode it. Others noticed it more too, looked at me differently. Even though it helped me walk, I didn't really like walking. I couldn't keep up with the other boys and they would run off and leave me behind. Instead, I got a bike. I'd cycle everywhere. I'd go further and faster than anyone else as proof that my mobility and independence were not restricted. I'd climb to the highest branches in trees and when it snowed, sledge down the steepest hills. I didn't really think about hurting myself, I had the fearlessness of youth and I loved physical challenge and trying new things. Mum never mollycoddled me, she just used to say, "If he wants to do that, he can do it", which is perhaps why I did not see myself as fragile or get treated differently to others. I just loved being outside and I loved sport. I'd spend every day in the garden playing with my older brothers, experimenting with what I was capable of doing. Because I could not do all sports, I concentrated on mastering new skills in sports that I could compete, like cricket or archery which were either stationary or required only a few steps. Perhaps compensating for my leg, my upper body grew strong. I was able to use a longbow before any other kids, which helped me become Worcestershire Junior Archery Champion. I even became an accomplished boxer at school. Other boys quickly learned that if they insulted me, I had the physical size to hit them hard, as the boy who once threw stones at me shouting "You'll never catch me you cripple" will testify. Because I loved sport so much, I hated it when I had to go back to hospital for more surgeries or was confined to a bed due to the severe pain, sickness and fatigue. I was often too unwell to go to school. Instead, I'd spend the days at home with Mrs Sampson, a domestic support worker who I grew close to. We used to pass the time by playing board games and picking red currants in the garden whilst everyone else was at school or work living their lives. On the whole however, relationships with other children was positive and everything was done to try and make me feel included. I even remember having a party where my parents moved my bed out into the garden so that friends could join me.

Ability, Masculinity and the (In)visibility of Impairment

DAD: Shards of early evening summer sun hazily illuminate the English country pub garden I'm sitting in. With the scent of grass and lilac in my nostrils, I look to the sky, close my eyes and absorb the remaining warmth into my face. I grip my glass tankard and take another long swig of a smooth, nutty, hazel-brown beer, letting it quench my throat. After a long hard-fought day in the field playing cricket, I think to myself that moments like these are some of the great pleasures in life and how thankful I am for them. "Well played, Rich" the captain says, siding his portly frame up next to me. "The way you bowled today was clever, not only were you metronomically accurate with your line and length, but you were quick and moved the ball through the air and off the seam. You deserved more than five wickets". "Thanks Mike, you did okay yourself for someone so corpulent!" I joke back. Long have I developed ways to beat the batsman in these ways, making the ball swing and move laterally off the pitch, changing my pace and the angle of delivery and using the weather conditions to my advantage. I liked making it a cerebral as well as a physical battle, drawing the batsman in my mind games and then executing my skills. When I was 16 and practised bowling in the nets, I was fast. So fast that a group of builders once stopped and applauded as I slung the ball down, peppering the helpless batsman at the other end covering him in bruises. Unfortunately, I could never get as much grip and purchase in my delivery stride on the grass field as I could on the concrete floor that the nets were on, so the speed I generated never translated into a real game. I was however able to use my strong upper body and shoulders to propel the ball with some velocity. Indeed, I often used to this to my advantage, shocking the batsman by bowling more quickly than they expected coming off such a short run up of a couple of paces. When I was invited to join the local team, other blokes were from the same village and knew who I was. Although, my leg very visibly gave away my disability, they were encouraging. I couldn't run between the wickets very well and needed to be 'hidden' in the field by being put in the slips because of my immobility. I also felt I had to bat aggressively, to hit boundaries so I didn't have to do any running. But I was good, and in sporting terms that's all that mattered. And because I was good, even relative to able-bodied standards of performance, I was accepted. All I had to do was to buy two pairs of spikes, one size 11 and one size 8. I'd use the bigger size on my left foot and get an orthopaedic platform fitted to the smaller size on my right foot and secure it with a sport specific brace. It allowed me to take the couple of steps that I needed. Cricket, like the other sports I have played throughout my lifetime, provided a sense of belonging, allowed me to compete against others deemed more able than me and made me feel included. I loved the camaraderie too, the jocularity, the banter in the changing room. I learned how to be self-deprecating, to take the piss out of myself for being disabled. It didn't matter, I really enjoyed it all. Upon reflection, in many ways, the way I viewed my body when I was younger in different situations was paradoxical. In some contexts, I was hyper conscious of my body, like when I refused to walk across a dance floor at a party because people would notice my limp. I was afraid that my difference would be highlighted, and this would put girls off fancying me. Yet I didn't care about such surveillance in sport, I was happy showing off what my body was capable of. Perhaps there was no expectation for me to be good, which took the pressure off and allowed me to focus on enjoying it more.

SON: Fucks sake. Another forehand sails long over the baseline. Aged 18 I am approaching the peak of my physicality and still can't beat my 48 year old Dad, who is pretty much playing on one leg. I can feel the frustration build inside me, get stuck in my throat, I just want to scream. He's 5-1 up in the set and I don't want him to start feeling sorry for me, or even worse go lightly on me. He has a notoriously good serve and a dangerous backhand helping him become a doubles specialist at the club. Even so, he can't get around court as well as he'd like, and I should be able to beat him at singles. *Boom.* Another bomb of a serve whistles past me, and that's it, it's over. Having had my emerging sense of masculinity utterly alpha'd, I walk to the net and begrudgingly shake Dad's hand. In spite of the loss, I value the time together. Anything sporting has become our world, whether that be playing tennis, watching the test match at Lord's on television or talking about Gloucester Rugby over dinner. Like so many other Dads and sons, sport and the rituals around it has facilitated communication between us and provided a platform through which we could construct positive senses of identity and assert a culturally valued form of masculinity. Of course, our sporting selves and perceptions of masculinity fundamentally depended on, among other things, the functionality of our bodies. Although Dad never took this for granted, I had never encountered trauma to my body.

Ageing and Breaking Bodies

SON: It's the middle of winter, a far cry from the balmy late summer evening where my body broke. Still in a post-anaesthetic haze, I look up to see my Dad in a long black winter coat and business attire walking purposefully down the hospital corridor. His limp is instantly recognisable to me. Over time this has created a unique familiarity which has become synonymous with love, security and happiness. As he gets closer, he looks into my eyes knowingly and sits his still large muscular frame on top of the blood covered sheets. Without saying a word, he leans over my forlorn body, wraps his big arms around me and pulls me tight into his chest. In the comfort of the embrace and the familiarity of his scent I let go. Tears pour out of my eyes saturating his shirt until it clings to his skin. After the 6th successive surgery to my chronically degenerative knee, any dreams I had of playing sport at a high level are now over. I feel ashamed that my broken body has let us both down. Sensing what I'm thinking, he pulls me in closer. "C'mon son, let's get out of here". Before I leave, I am fitted with a leg brace which I am required to wear for the next 6 months. "Hurry up hop along" quips Dad ironically, as I struggle to keep up with him back down the corridor on my crutches.

DAD: *Thwack.* That felt good. Just from the sensation cursing through my body I can feel that my iron club has made a good connection with the little dimply white ball sending it high into the air towards the green. Now 65, my body is too old to play tennis effectively, so I took up golf a few years ago. I know I will never be great at it; I can't put my weight on my front foot when I swing, but I'm really enjoying it. It's good exercise, I still get to see my mates, and, on the longer courses where I struggle to get around, I hire a buggy. I've also been walking more in the Herefordshire countryside around our house and escape to the Yorkshire Dales with Lin for walking holidays. Now that all of the kids have grown up and left the family home and I have retired from teaching cookery, I have more time again for longer lasting activities. Today, I am playing with James, my eldest son. We try and get out on the course when we can, it's a good opportunity to have a chat and catch up with him and hear about his busy life. He now has a family of his own and does not have much time for sport along with the responsibility of work. Watching him take a swing next to me reminds me of when I used to watch him play football and cricket in his younger days. When he ran, his body was so fast, so fluid, something I could never do. When he swings the club next to me, I notice how his body is more flexible, more snappy and agile than my ageing rigid body. The scores between us are always pretty close though as I am more consistent and have more experience in reading the course. My putting is better than his. Almost sensing my thoughts, James says nostalgically "You know I wanted to use my body to do what your body had prevented you from doing Dad, by competing in high level sport I wanted to make you proud of me". "I know son, you did, you do everyday" I reply offering comfort. Although neither of us say it, our broken bodies have united us, made us closer and helped us understand impairment and experiences of life in different ways as we have both aged.

SON: I couldn't listen to all the answerphone messages. I just sensed something was gravely wrong. I just read the first line of the text, made an excuse to finish my lecture early, hurriedly jumped in my car and drove across the country as fast as I could. When I finally got to the hospital four hours later, the first person I saw was Mum running towards me, tears streaming uncontrollably down her cheeks. "I just want my husband back" she managed to whisper between the cries. Still holding my mother, I looked up at my older sister, Laura, who shook her head as if to confirm that things were not good. Making my way back down those familiar hospital corridors to the specialist stroke ward, I walked through the door to see Dad lying on his back in bed, unable to move a muscle, unable to say a word. Rushing over to him, I gripped his lifeless hand and hugged his motionless body. I could tell in his eyes that he knew that I was there. "Unfortunately, your father has experienced a severe stroke. Partly due to his having Polio and complications with circulation, he was at a high risk. We don't know how he will recover yet, if at all" the consultant informs me. My mind races out of control. What must he and Mum have gone through in the last few hours. Flashbacks of a lifetime of memories coalesce into an incomprehensible blur. Teaching me to play cricket, taking me to buy my first bat, sharing our first beer together, shaping me from being a little shy boy into a man I hope he is proud of. Life without him is unimaginable.

Three Strikes Not Out

SON: Having temporarily moved back into the family home to help my Mum, I get up and undertake the same routine: shower, make breakfast, send work e-mails, collect my things and head off to see Dad. The consultants are hopeful that with the aid of speech therapist, he will be able to talk again. They also tell us that his physical rehabilitation will take much longer, warning that he is unlikely to recover movement in the effected side of his body. It is likely that he will require the use of a wheelchair for the rest of his life. Luckily, however the stroke paralysed the right side of his body, the same side that is already impaired by polio. So, there is hope that he might be able to walk in some capacity again with the aid of a stick. "Morning big guy" I say as bright and breezily as I can. Still non-linguistic, he is desperate trying to say something. "Gurrr … gurrr … gurr". I try to guess what he means. Using his facial expression, he tries to emphasise. "Girl?" I finally figure out of a few moments, "She's fine Dad, she sends her love". A look of panic suddenly spreads across his face. Unsure again what he is trying to say, I notice him faintly nod towards the toilet door. "Ok Dad, hold on". I side up to the bed, pull him up to a seated position, and lean his body over my shoulder. Like a couple entangled in a strange rhumba, we shuffle over and make it into the bathroom. I can tell from his face that being vertical so abruptly after so long lying down has made him feel sick, but this feeling would pale in comparison to the social embarrassment I know he would feel of pissing on the floor. Ensuring I take his body weight on his paralysed side, I reach into his striped pyjama bottoms and help him urinate. Later, when he was able to say a few words he jokes that this was getting his own back for all the times he changed my nappies.

DAD: "It is going in now Richard, you will feel some discomfort" the nurse says sliding a small tube into my urethra so that the immunotherapy can be administered directly into my cancerous bladder. I wince at the feeling, but I must endure it. I've had two surgeries to remove tumours, and this is the next stage of my treatment. A couple of minutes later, the tube is pulled out from the depths of my body and that is it, done. "You need to rest here for a couple of hours so we can keep you under surveillance" the nurse instructs before leaving me alone in an isolated room off the main oncology ward. It hasn't been three years since I was here after suffering a stroke. Sitting still, letting my ravaged body absorb the substance that has just been pumped into me, I look out of the window into the grey February sky. My mind wonders. I start to nostalgically reminisce about previous bodies I have inhabited throughout my life. I miss those summer days playing cricket and tennis, those leisurely rounds of golf and going on long walks in the winter countryside with my wife. Those bodies seem like distance memories. After this 'third strike' after polio and the stroke, only thoughts of survival and existence occupy my mind now. My body doesn't feel the same anymore. Food doesn't taste the same anymore. Beer doesn't hold the same flavour anymore.

Most of Europe has Seen My Penis

DAD: For a long time after the stroke, I couldn't talk very well and I couldn't move. I felt like I was locked inside my own internal world. Looking down over my body, I didn't recognise what I saw. I have lost over two stones of weight, most of which is muscle mass from one side of my body. Coupled with the cancer, I am feeling weak, not just physically but mentally. At least I am learning to communicate with my family again, even if I do slur my speech and forget my words. I have never valued my family more, we have always been close, but the stroke bought us all even closer. They have always been the most important thing to me. Of course, James still takes the piss out of me relentlessly, "C'mon Dad, spit it out" he will say when I fail to remember a word or use the incorrect vocabulary. Although I can manoeuvre around the house a little bit now with the aid of a wheelchair and my walking sticks, I can't help Lin much with the domestic duties. She has become a full-time carer. I often feel like a burden. I fell off the toilet the other day and she couldn't help me back up, she had to go and get the neighbour to help me off the bathroom floor. Sometimes I make things worse by getting frustrated when I can't articulate myself or move my body in the ways I used to. I get angry. I get upset. With Lin's help however, I have been meticulous with my physiotherapy. The discipline helps with my daily routine and gives me a sense of achievement. I am still seeing improvements, more than the doctors and 'physio-terrorists' as I call them, expected. There are some community activities I was beginning to try, like mobility schemes where you can hire all terrain scooters and wheel over the Malvern Hills. I've been to a few stroke groups too. Surprisingly, I have quite enjoyed going to these and sharing and empathising with others' stories. Because they have been through similar experiences, we seem to understand each other and are able to learn off each other. Just before my cancer diagnosis, I had also joined the local gym and swimming pool. I liked the feeling of weightlessness I get when my body submerges into the water. The door swings open again "Once I've seen you pee, you are free to go". I feel that no nurse in this place has not seen me in a state of undress; it's so hard to maintain any sense of dignity. "Most of Europe has seen my penis now", I joke to Lin when she visits, which is every day. She says that I speak with "no filter now", like my words are emotional expressions direct from my heart without being subject to processing. Perhaps that is a good thing, strips away the bullshit. Looking back at my life and at all of my sporting bodies now, I exceeded what I thought I was capable of, what I thought someone who is disabled is capable of. Other than the polio, until recently my body held up pretty well. I wouldn't change anything about my life or my sporting career; I just wish it lasted longer.

Notes

1 Atkinson critiques autoethnography as inappropriately emotional, individualised, and therapeutic, rather than being an authentic academic practice (Atkinson, 1997).
2 For example, Irish et al. (2018) reflect on experiences of being a deaf athlete; McMahon et al. (2020) present a collaborative autoethnography of parents of children with autism in sport and physical activity; and Lowry et al. (2022) use personal stories in 'cripping' the care experienced by disabled athletes. Further autoethnographies in disability sport have addressed the experiences of coaching disabled swimmers (Cronin et al., 2018), volunteers experiences of a para-sports event (Lachance & Parent, 2020) and reflect on a career researching disabled athletes (Berger, 2016). With specific interest to this chapter, Lindemann (2010) brings the corporeality of his disabled father's story to life through autoethnography.
3 These were kept to a duration of 30 minutes or less due to Dad's current capacity to verbalise thoughts and feelings and that he quickly fatigues.

References

Adams, T.E., Holman Jones, S. & Ellis, C. (2022) Making sense and taking action: Creating a caring community of autoethnographers. In T.E. Adams, S. Holman Jones, & C. Ellis (eds.) *Handbook of Autoethnography* (2nd Edition, pp. 1–19). New York: Taylor & Francis.

Atkinson, P. (1997) Narrative turn or blind alley? *Qualitative Health Research*, 7(3), pp. 325–344.

Atkinson, R. (1998) *The Life Story Interview*. London: Sage.

Berger, R.J. (2016) Disability and life history research: An autoethnography of qualitative inquiry. *International Review of Qualitative Research*, 9(4), pp. 472–488.

Brighton, J. (2015) Researching disabled sporting bodies: Reflections from an 'able'-bodied ethnographer. In I. Wellard (ed.) *Researching Embodied Sport* (pp. 163–177). London: Routledge.

Cann, C.N. & DeMeulenaere, E.J. (2012) Critical co-constructed autoethnography. *Cultural Studies? Critical Methodologies*, 12(2), pp. 146–158.

Chang, H., Ngunjiri, F. & Hernandez, K.A.C. (2016) *Collaborative Autoethnography*. London & New York: Routledge.

Choi, I., Haslett, D. & Smith, B. (2021) Disabled athlete activism in South Korea: A mixed-method study. *International Journal of Sport and Exercise Psychology*, 19(4), pp. 473–487.

Cronin, C., Ryrie, A., Huntley, T. & Hayton, J. (2018) 'Sinking and swimming in disability coaching': An autoethnographic account of coaching in a new context. *Qualitative Research in Sport, Exercise and Health*, 10(3), pp. 362–377.

Denzin, N. (1989) *Interpretive Biography*. London: Sage.

Ellis, C., Adams, T.E. & Bochner, A.P. (2011) Autoethnography: An overview. *Historical Social research/Historische sozialforschung*, 36(4) pp. 273–290.

Ellis, C. & Bochner, A.P. (eds.) (1996) *Composing Ethnography: Alternative Forms of Qualitative Writing* (Vol. 1). Walnut Creek, CA: Rowman Altamira.

Ellis, C. & Rawicki, J. (2013) Collaborative witnessing of survival during the Holocaust: An exemplar of relational autoethnography. *Qualitative Inquiry*, 19(5), pp. 366–380.

Ellis, C.S. & Bochner, A.P. (2006) Analyzing analytic autoethnography: An autopsy. *Journal of Contemporary Ethnography*, 35(4), pp. 429–449.

Finkelstein, V. (1996) Outside, 'Inside Out'. *Coalition*, April, pp. 30–36.

Frank, A.W. (2000) The standpoint of storyteller. *Qualitative Health Research*, 10(3), pp. 354–365.

Haug, F., Andresen, S., Brunz-Elfferding, A., Hauser, K., Lang, U. & Laudan, M. (1983) *Female Sexualisation: A Collective Work of Memory* (trans. E. Carter, 1987). London: Virago.

Holman Jones, S. (2011) Lost and found. *Text and Performance Quarterly*, 31, pp. 322–341.

Holman Jones, S, Adams, T.E. & Ellis, C. (2013) *Handbook of Autoethnography*. Walnut Creek, CA: Left Coast Pess.

Irish, T., Cavallerio, F. & McDonald, K. (2018) "Sport saved my life" but "I am tired of being an alien!": Stories from the life of a deaf athlete. *Psychology of Sport and Exercise*, 37, pp. 179–187.

Lachance, E.L. & Parent, M.M. (2020) The volunteer experience in a para-sport event: An autoethnography. *Journal of Sport Management*, 34(2), pp. 93–102.

Lindemann (2010) Cleaning up my (father's) mess: Narrative containments of "leaky" masculinities. *Qualitative Inquiry*, 16(1), pp. 29–38.

Lowry, A., Townsend, R.C., Petrie, K. & Johnston, L. (2022) 'Cripping' care in disability sport: An autoethnographic study of a highly impaired high-performance athlete. *Qualitative Research in Sport, Exercise and Health*, pp. 1–13. https://doi.org/10.1080/2159676X.2022.2037695

McDougall, K. (2006) "Ag shame" and superheroes: Stereotype and the signification of disability. In B. Watermeyer, L. Swartz, T. Lorenzo, M. Schneider & M. Priestly (eds.) *Disability and Social Change: A South African Agenda* (pp. 387–400). Cape Town, South Africa: HSRC Press.

McMahon, J., Wiltshire, G.-E., McGannon, K.R. & Rayner, C. (2020) Children with autism in a sport and physical activity context: A collaborative autoethnography by two parents outlining their experiences. *Sport, Education and Society*, 25(9), pp. 1002–1014.

Muncey, T. (2010) *Creating Autoethnographies*. London: Sage Publications.

Norris, J., Sawyer, R.D. & Lund, D. (2012) *Duoethnography: Dialogic Methods for Social, Health, and Educational Research* (Vol. 7). Walnut Creek, CA: Left Coast Press.

Owton, H. & Sparkes, A.C. (2017) Sexual abuse and the grooming process in sport: Learning from Bella's story. *Sport, Education and Society*, 22(6), pp. 732–743.

Peers, D. (2012) Interrogating disability: The (de) composition of a recovering Paralympian. *Qualitative Research in Sport, Exercise and Health*, 4(2), pp. 175–188.

Richards, R. (2016) Saying the word: Voice and silence in an autoethnography about chronic illness. *Stellenbosch Papers in Linguistics Plus*, 49(1), pp. 233–247.

Smith, B. (2013) Disability, sport and men's narratives of health: A qualitative study. *Health Psychology*, 32(1), p. 110.

Smith, B. (2017) Narrative inquiry and autoethnography. In M. Silk, D. Andrews & H. Thorpe (eds.) *Handbook of Physical Cultural Studies* (pp. 505–514). London: Routledge.

Smith, B., Bundon, A. & Best, M. (2016) Disability sport and activist identities: A qualitative study of narratives of activism among elite athletes' with impairment. *Psychology of Sport and Exercise*, 26, pp. 139–148.

Sparkes, A.C. (2000) Autoethnography and narratives of self: Reflections on criteria in action. *Sociology of Sport Journal*, 17(1), pp. 21–43.

Sparkes, A.C. (2018) Autoethnography comes of age: Consequences, comforts, and concerns. In D. Beach, C. Bagley & S.M. da Silva (eds.) *The Wiley Handbook of Ethnography of Education* (pp. 479–499). Oxford: Wiley.

Sparkes, A.C. (2020) Autoethnography: Accept, revise, reject? An evaluative self reflects. *Qualitative Research in Sport, Exercise and Health*, 12(2), pp. 289–302.

Wigginton, B. & Setchell, J. (2016) Researching stigma as an outsider: Considerations for qualitative outsider research. *Qualitative Research in Psychology*, 13(3), pp. 246–263.

Yoshida, K.K. & Shanouda, F. (2015) A culture of silence: Modes of objectification and the silencing of disabled bodies. *Disability & Society*, 30(3), pp. 432–444.

Part III

From Theory to Practice
Contemporary Issues in Disability Sport

Chapter 10

Seeing without Sight

The Athlete/Guide Partnership in Disability Sport

Andrea Bundon and Staci Mannella

Introduction

The Paralympic Games are described as an elite competition for athletes with disabilities. Yet what if we told you that at every Games, dozens of athletes compete without any impairment at all? We are not talking about athletes engaging in 'intentional misrepresentation', whereby individuals present as more severely impaired in order to gain a competitive advantage or entry into the Games (Deuble et al., 2016). We are talking about the sighted guides who race as the 'performance partners' of athletes with visual impairments.

At the Paralympics, individuals with low vision or no vision compete in athletics, alpine skiing, cycling, nordic skiing, and triathlon with the assistance of sighted guides.[1] The guides run or swim alongside, ski in front of or pilot tandem bikes for their visually impaired (VI) partners.[2] These partnerships transform many sports traditionally understood to be individual events into team events dependent on communication, trust, and rapport. Despite the central role these partnerships have in enabling the participation and performance of VI athletes, they are not acknowledged in the academic literature beyond a few brief mentions of guides alongside 'equipment' and 'supports' used by VI athletes, or in relation to the classification system where VI athletes qualify to participate with a guide in the first place (see Mann & Ravensbergen, 2018; Patatas et al., 2018; Slocum et al., 2018).

The omission of research on athlete–guide partnerships[3] has several implications. First, not acknowledging these partnerships contributes to the ongoing erasure of athletes with disabilities by obscuring *how* they engage in sports and making their performances invisible. Second, it represents a failed opportunity to interrogate how these partnerships might challenge binary divides of able and disabled and normative notions of ability and athleticism. Our intent is to make visible these often overlooked and poorly understood partnerships and to prompt others to critically engage with the topic. To accomplish this, we reflect upon our own experiences as a VI athlete (in alpine skiing) and a sighted guide (in nordic skiing), and discuss with reference to critical disability and disability sport scholarship. We take up the challenge issued by DePauw in her seminal text, The (In)visibility of Disability: Cultural Contexts and "Sporting Bodies" (1997), to

DOI: 10.4324/9781003153696-13

"use the perspective of disability to reflect on sport as a social institution, and therefore, a site of and for cultural transformation" (p. 418).

The cultural narrative surrounding Paralympic sport over the past two or three decades has been one of growth and 'progress'. Paralympians are setting new records and there has been increased commercial investment and media interest in the Games. However, critical scholars of sport and disability have pointed to the more problematic aspects of how progress has been conceptualized: specifically, that there has been an overwhelming trend towards associating progress with 'integrating' people with disabilities into sport in ways that do not fundamentally change the existing structures of sport (Howe, 2007). Concerns have been raised about the 'Olympification' of Paralympic sport (Gérard, 2020) – the taken-for-granted assumption that non-disabled, Olympic sport is the normative, ideal form of elite sport. The Olympics are used as a model that the Paralympics should strive to emulate rather than advancing a parallel sport system and culture that is disability-centered. Fully addressing all of these issues is beyond the scope of this chapter. Instead, we aim to use the athlete–guide partnership as an example to explore "some of the basic and underlying tenets of sport, including primarily our socially constructed views of the body, ability, athletic performance, and sport" (DePauw, 1997, p. 427). Specifically, we provide insights into how we personally experienced the athlete–guide partnership and the ways in which our relationships with our respective partners impacted our own engagement with sport and our understanding of ourselves as athletes. We explore how these partnerships disrupt the progress narrative of parasport by demonstrating that the failure to account for guides continues to marginalize VI athletes even when they are included in predominately non-disabled sport systems. It is our desire that this work contributes to advancing a transformative vision for disability sport that is disability-centered and views difference as a strength rather than an obstacle to be overcome.

'Para'llel Auto-Ethnographic Accounts of Paralympic Sport

This chapter is informed by the authors own experiences with Paralympic sport. Staci is a woman with a visual impairment and a two-time member of the US Paralympic Alpine Ski Team. Andrea is sighted and competed at two Paralympic Games as the guide for VI athletes on the Canadian Para-Nordic Ski Team. She is an Assistant Professor in the School of Kinesiology at the University of British Columbia (UBC). Our paths crossed when Staci applied to conduct graduate studies at UBC. Over two years, together and separately, we pursued programs of research that included projects on and about parasport and the experiences of Paralympic athletes. As part of Staci's degree, we also engaged in a 'directed study' and met bi-weekly to read and discuss literature on parasport and particularly research informed by ethnographic methodologies.

Although the findings of our research projects are detailed in other manuscripts, what we felt missing was the opportunity to share some of the conversations between us and how these conversations had challenged us to interrogate our own involvement in parasport. In so doing, we were given an opportunity to reflect on how our personal experiences were tied up within broader cultural narratives about sport, disability and athletic identities. With that in mind, we set out to write an auto-ethnographic account of VI athletes and guides. We were inspired by the work of sport scholars including Dean (2019) who describes auto-ethnography as exploring personal stories through the lens of culture. We weave non-linear, first-person accounts into our text alongside traditional academic citations to demonstrate how our own embodied experiences enabled us to engage with the literature on disability sport in a way that our academic training alone could not. We are not the first to do so – Howe (2008) and Peers (2012) use auto-ethnographic methodologies and 'vignettes' describing their experiences as disabled athletes and Paralympians to write deeply evocative accounts of disability sport. Where our work departs from theirs is that our tale is a 'collaborative' auto-ethnography (Allen-Collinson & Hockey, 2017) – or a '*para*'llel auto-ethnography of separate yet parallel experiences in parasport. Our vignettes are derived from conversations over two years of reading and researching together. Below is the first of the vignettes where we describe our own entry into parasport and trajectory of our careers.

> [Staci]: I started skiing when I was four years old, and by the time I was a teenager I had begun to ski faster than all of the ski instructors at my local mountain's adaptive sport program. I have been legally blind my whole life, but in spite of that, learning to ski at an early age made me fearless on the mountain. I didn't know much about Paralympic sport, but one coach in the adaptive race program saw potential in me and, in 2009, with minimal understanding of the adventures, opportunities, and adversities we would encounter together, I officially asked Kim to be my guide. At that point, I needed a parent-like figure to travel with, a coach to teach me what it meant to be a high-performance athlete and, of course, a guide to be my eyes on the mountain. Kim stepped up into all of those roles and, in return, I gave her an opportunity to be a ski racer in a completely new way. There was a big age difference between us, which sometimes made it challenging to see eye to eye, but I had the opportunity to travel with Kim all over the world; I grew up alongside of her, learned what it meant to be an elite athlete, and navigated my place in the world as a person with a disability. We set lofty goals as a team, and six years later competed together at the Sochi 2014 Paralympic Games. At 17 years old I had been working towards the Sochi Paralympics for over a third of my life. Kim and I finished with two sixth place results.
>
> It was just the start of my career but the end of Kim's. In 2015, I started skiing with Sadie, a retired ski racer from Park City. We began our career together as strangers, but in our first season we quickly became friends and experienced almost immediate success. We won all three races in our debut series on the world cup circuit, settled into a routine of living out of suitcases, and learned to enjoy each other's company. My dreams became hers and

over the next three years we learned to navigate our partnership through the wins and losses both on and off the slopes. We complemented each other with unwavering loyalty, brutal honesty, and the occasional tough love when necessary. By the end of our career together, we had successfully competed in several world cups, world championships, and the PyeongChang 2018 Paralympic Games, but we also developed a friendship that I still value deeply. Reflecting on my athletic career, I recognize that my success as an athlete was made possible because of the dedication and sacrifices of the guides I have had the privilege of following.

[Andrea]: I was first 'hailed' to Paralympic sport in 2008. Although I had competed as a cross country skier on a provincial team, my own ski career was unremarkable and I was never on track to race internationally. In 2008, I was living and studying in Vancouver and I had recently made the decision to retire from the sport. Then a chance encounter with a local VI skier changed my trajectory.

Courtney was a four-time summer Paralympian with several medals in athletics. She had recently transferred to nordic skiing and was attempting to make the selection standards for the 2010 Paralympic Games. She couldn't do it alone. She was in the market for a new guide, someone to ski in front of her and call out directions and course information over a two-way radio. Her coach thought we might be a good match. Courtney and I trained together for four years and competed at number of national and international events including the 2010 Vancouver Paralympic Games. Not only did we spend extended periods of time travelling, training and competing together, we also volunteered together to run a local para-nordic program, we supported each other in our studies, and we spent time with each other's family.

When Courtney made the decision to retire from racing after the 2011 season, another VI athlete asked if I would guide her 'just until she found someone permanent'. Margarita and I skied together from 2012 to 2014 and our final race was at the Sochi Paralympics. This relationship was different – we were living in different cities and at different stages in our lives – but it was no less close. We worked towards a common goal and shared the triumphs and challenges of an athletic career – one career – though there were two of us. This time when Margarita decided to retire, I did as well – having had an extra six years of racing in a sport I thought I was done with.

Dyadic Relationships and the Athlete–Guide Partnership

As seen in the vignettes above, there was a specific moment in our lives when we entered into what is referred to in the literature as 'dyadic relationships' which are characterized as situations in which two people's behaviors, emotions, and thoughts are mutually and causally interdependent (Jowett & Cockerill, 2003; Kelley & Thibaut, 1978). Interdependence itself can further be defined as the coordination needed to work with others in order to achieve a desired outcome

(Bandura, 1999) – in both or our accounts this was the pursuit of a spot on the Paralympic team. There are many examples of dyadic relationships in sport including the athlete–coach relationship and the athlete–athlete relationships found, for example, in pairs figure skating, beach volleyball, and two-person bobsled. Sport psychologists have studied these dyads (both athlete–coach and athlete–athlete), and developed a number of models to illustrate and understand how partners work together (Jowett, 2007), how the actions of one partner impact the other partner (Kenny & Cook, 1999), and how perceptions of and beliefs about one partner's competency and commitment shape the relationship (Jackson et al., 2010).

While the existing literature does have relevance to the athlete–guide partnership, we would argue there are also important differences. Other athlete–athlete partnerships are understood to be the coming together of two independent athletes who combine their efforts and compete as equal partners. Although athlete–athlete partnerships may be longstanding, there is an underlying assumption that each athlete also has a sport career independent of the other and has the agency to leave the partnership, find a new partner or (depending on the sport) compete solo in another event. Athlete–coach partnerships are characterized as two individuals each with fundamentally different functions and an inherently unequal relationship – the coach frequently has considerable power over the conditions in which the athlete trains and competes, but also unequal in that during the competition, the athlete controls the performance. Neither of these situations accurately represents the athlete–guide partnership because the VI athlete is dependent on the guide in order to participate in sport, and the guide competes with the athlete rather than watching from the side. We would argue that the composition of the athlete–guide partnership – neither able to fulfill their role without the other – sets the conditions for a unique type of dyadic relationship not addressed in the sport literature.

The other underlying assumption about these dyadic partnerships has to do with the classification of one partner as disabled and the other as able. Smith and Bundon (2018) outline how the classification system used in parasport draws on a medical model of disability that perpetuates a dangerous normal/abnormal divide that disempowers the disabled athlete and grants non-disabled others authority over those judged to have disabilities. In the section that follows, we attempt to demonstrate how the athlete–guide partnership challenges the able/disabled divide.

Feeling Lost Apart, Invincible Together

> [Andrea]: I'm going crazy. We arrived nearly a week ago for the World Cup and have yet to race. This was supposed to be a big week for us – a key opportunity to get world cup points to qualify for Sochi. But Margarita isn't feeling well. She's decided that rather than suffering through for mediocre results on all of the races, she is going to get some rest and then go all out for the final

> race. A big result in one race will punch our ticket to the Games but a bunch of 'near misses' won't do a thing. It's the right decision but… I'm going crazy! I get that Margarita doesn't want to race – she feels like shit. She just wants to sleep. But I did the training, I did the taper, and I'm ready to go!! I think people forget you can't just turn me on and off. I train for this and right now I'm going out of my skin. To make matters worse, everyone else has something to do – the techs are testing skis, the coaches are in meetings, the other athletes are out pre-skiing the course… one of the standing class skiers joked that I looked so lost he would wear a blindfold just to give me something to do. I'm a guide without an athlete.

Understanding how each individual is reliant on their partner to participate in sport is important because it challenges dominant societal discourses about disability, ability, and high-performance sport. While individuals with disabilities are frequently portrayed in society in ways that highlight their incompetence and dependence (Carvalho-Freitas & Stathi, 2017), elite athletes are commonly described in terms that reinforce notions that they are uniquely responsible for their own destiny (the performance narrative, see Carless & Douglas, 2012). The athlete–guide relationship disrupts these narratives by demonstrating that VI athletes perform ability as athletes by working interdependently with sighted guides. Athletes in these partnerships take on both disabled and athletic identities challenging the assumptions that such identities are mutually exclusive. The guides also perform athletic identities through working with VI athletes – but neither is able to do so alone. Above Andrea describes the feeling of being lost when her athlete partner makes the decision to withdraw from a series of races due to illness. These emotions are amplified by her sense that others around do not understand what she is experiencing. In contrast, below Staci describes the intense emotions that she experiences when competing with her partner.

> [Staci]: When we finished our first run at World Championships, I knew we had not skied well. I could feel the time slipping away, turn for turn – we were out of synchrony. She didn't say it explicitly, but she didn't have to – I knew Sadie was disappointed - we both were. We had trained for months leading up to these races and things did not start off well. Getting into the start for a slalom run we focused on putting our previous results aside and feeling confident – believing in our individual abilities and how each of our strengths would contribute to our success as a team. We pushed out of the start and I felt it all come together. Our communication was clear, our rhythm flowed well, we found synchronicity together as if we were one skier rather than two. Sadie called each of the combinations – hairpin, flush, delay - and even though I couldn't see them coming, I knew nothing would surprise me because I trusted her implicitly and she trusted me too. I was so proud to stand on the podium with her that day. It felt like all of our hard work – the hours of training, weeks of travel, and countless time spent in the gym

together – had culminated into something tangible, a World Championship medal! With her by my side I was capable of anything in spite of the limitations I often encounter as a person with a visual impairment.

The above vignette points to the intense emotions that are experienced when the partners achieve synchrony with respect to movement together, but also in the alignment of goals and intentions. Both authors have had that experience of 'it all coming together' and have heard it when speaking with other VI athletes and guides.

[Andrea]: It's the morning of the 5km classic race at the 2010 Vancouver Games. I'm terrified, I am excited. This race has particular significance for me and Courtney but for different reasons. She's more of a sprinter, I excel at the distance races. The 5km is where we 'meet' – it's the one event where I will be pushing my physical limits to stay ahead of her. There's also the matter of the course itself … when the race maps for the Olympics and Paralympics were released, a few athletes commented these trails were a little 'easy' – I know better. The trails in Callaghan are easy until the snow changes… At the Olympics a few weeks ago several of the top skiers went flying off course on one of the final turns and had rather spectacular crashes (and injuries). I've had a few big wipeouts there myself, and I've spent hours just practicing the final turn through a bridge to overcome the urge to snowplow and dump speed. My anxiety is compounded by the knowledge that if I choose the wrong line Courtney will go down with me. This morning, the conditions are fast, icy… dangerous […]

It's the final kilometre. The race has gone perfectly – or rather imperfectly perfect. Courtney was catching up to me on the downhills and had to 'push' the basket on my pole to avoid passing me. There were a few spots where I had to go wide into the soft snow to give her the space to take the best line and then scramble to get ahead of her again while 'guiding from behind' over the radio. But we had rehearsed those scenarios and executed seamlessly […] 200m, 100m, 50m… I'm yelling a countdown over the radio as we approach the finish line. I can *feel* Courtney behind me, right on my skis. We cross the line and we're already reaching for each other. Hugging. I know even then that I have never experienced this before and probably never will again. A few weeks later a photographer will send me a photo he snapped at this exact moment. We look so happy.

Andrea's emotions at the completion of this race are overwhelming and stem from the realization that she just skied not *her* perfect race but rather that she perfectly set up Courtney to have her best race. The type of results described in the above vignettes also depend on the partners achieving what Jowett and colleagues have called 'closeness, commitment and complementarity' in their 3C model of interdependence used to study dyads in sport psychology research (Jowett, 2007; Jowett & Ntoumanis, 2004). While we agree that there is indeed a need for alignment in these three areas in order for athlete–guide partnerships to perform in sport, there are some underpinning sociological considerations that also need to be addressed to understand the nature of the athlete–guide relationship and the prerequisite conditions for achieving closeness, commitment and complementarity that we discuss in the following section.

The Athlete–Guide Partnership and the Intersectionality of Disability

Disability scholars, particularly those coming from feminist theoretical traditions, remind us that it is not only the able/disabled binary that we need to be attentive to but also the ways that disability intersects with other social identities and positionalities such as age, gender, sexuality, race, ethnicity, education, class and more. It is not just that various social identities 'intersect', it is that these identities and positionalities are shaped and understood in the intersections. As Crenshaw (1989) writes when speaking of race and gender, there is a tendency to think of identities as mutually exclusive categories and distorts the experiences of individuals whose identities are always 'and' and not 'or'. Garland-Thompson (2016) refers to the way that identities are mutually 'interpellated' and in the context of sport this is seen in how dominant assumptions of what constitutes an 'athletic body' is one that is simultaneously masculine, muscular, able, white and heterosexual. This conceptualization of intersectionality is relevant to the athlete–guide partnerships when you consider that disability sport is almost always 'for' athletes with disabilities but delivered 'by' non-disabled others (Howe, 2008). The classification system whereby athletes are deemed eligible for parasport (and eligible to have a guide) is carried out almost exclusively by non-disabled sport practitioners. The team staff are almost exclusively non-disabled as well. Peers (2009, 2012) writes about how the disabled athlete identity is thereby created and recreated through multiple, ongoing interactions with these non-disabled others and these interactions disempower disabled athletes despite the rhetoric of the empowering potential of the Paralympic movement.

When intersectionality is taken into consideration, it opens up the possibility for considering how other relationships beyond disabled/non-disabled also shape the experiences of individuals within the context of sport. We have had many discussions about the intersections of gender, age and (dis)ability and how these might inform the athlete–guide partnership. For example, when Staci was a young athlete, she appreciated having a guide who had experience on the ski circuit – but occasionally, as a teenager, she rebelled or bristled at the advice of her older guide. With her second guide, the relationship was characterized by their friendship, they were two young athletes on a mission. Both athletes that Andrea guided spoke frequently about selecting her because they had a preference for a woman guide and close to their own age. They had had experiences with men as guides (usually older than them) who tried to assert authority over them (for example, speaking directly to the coaches 'on their behalf') in ways they described as paternalistic rather than establishing more collaborative partnerships. The athletes used their agency to select guides that were compatible with them on the race course but that they also – by way of their own identities and social positionalities – perceived to be their 'equals' and thus capable of true partnership.

A Sport System Built for One

We have focused on the interactions between partners. However, the pair also has to negotiate a sport system that is designed for non-disabled (independent) athletes. Issues arise when it comes to team selection, travelling with the team, and negotiating relationships with team members and team staff. These issues can be linked back to the ways in which disability sport has been 'integrated' into mainstream sports systems that are wrought with ableist assumptions (Hammond et al., 2021).

One of the first issues that athlete–guide pairs encounter has to do with the guides' status on the team. While sport organizations responsible for selecting athletes to compete at prestigious competitions such as the Olympic and Paralympic Games have extensive policies to name athletes to teams that include references to the selection standards, selection periods, team composition and appeals processes, these policies tend to be silent on the issues of guides. For example, during Andrea's time as a guide on the Canadian para-nordic team, the selection documents gave very clear criteria for VI athletes attempting to make the Paralympic team but never specified whether the athlete was required to ski with the same guide for all selection races, could use multiple guides during the selection period, or if the guide that they skied with during the qualification competitions needed to be the same guide that travelled with them to the Paralympic Games. The rules (both nationally and internationally) about whether guides were required to have a race license or whether an athlete could purchase a race license that was transferable to anyone who guided them were constantly changing. These issues came to a crux for Andrea when the athlete that she had been guiding during the selection for the 2014 Sochi Paralympics was informed that she was selected to the Paralympic team but Andrea was not – the team staff had another guide that they wanted her to take to the Games. The other guide (a man) was fast enough to serve as a 'spare' guide for all the VI athletes on the team whereas Andrea was fast enough to guide the women on the team. The other guide also had considerable skill as a wax technician and could assist in preparing skis when not racing. Eventually the team secured enough accreditations to bring both Andrea and the other individual to Sochi, but the situation was deeply distressing to the athlete who felt she would not be able to achieve her performance goals at the Paralympics with a guide with whom she had no rapport or race experience with. It was also distressing to Andrea, who, after having committed a number of years to guiding, realized that she had no contract, no official standing as an athlete, no process for appeal. This situation highlights how both athlete and guide were rendered powerless in light of existing ableist and gender discourses.

The situation also illustrated the inconsistencies in the status and treatment of guides across the sport system. At certain moments, they are regarded as athletes and, for example, subject to drug testing. At other moments, guides are seen performing tasks associated with being a member of the 'support staff' and assisting with equipment or dealing with travel logistics. The lack of official status can make both athlete and guide vulnerable – athlete is vulnerable because they do not have agency in determining who will be their guide and the guide is vulnerable because of the precarity of their place on the team. Moreover, the uncertainty serves as an ongoing reminder that VI athletes are training and competing within a system that was never designed with them in mind and that regularly fails to meet their needs. This reinforces what others have observed (Howe, 2007), that when athletes with disabilities are integrated into mainstream sport systems, little change happens within the system to accommodate them. This further marginalizes those disabled athletes whose sport performances are least 'like' those of non-disabled athletes.

Her 'eyes' – on and off the Race Course

The scenario described above also prompted us to consider the personal nature of the relationship between guides and athletes. In requiring that Margarita ski with a guide of their choice, the team management was considering only the function of the guide on the field of play and overlooked the intensely personal nature of the athlete–guide relationship. Guides often assist their athletes to navigate the sighted world. Many individuals who are Blind or VI are very independent when in familiar settings but find themselves much more vulnerable or dependent when navigating new spaces. Athletes and guides typically travel together for training and competition, and in these situations, it is frequently the guide – their partner – that VI athletes turn to for assistance. The type of assistance provided can range from fairly non-intimate (helping to find a suitcase on a conveyor belt) to very intimate (accompanying the athlete to a medical appointment). The pairs often share a hotel room, eat together, and spend their free time together. As described in the vignette by Staci, the nature of the relationship is unique to each partnership, but it is nearly always a 'close' one. The assumption that a coach or sport manager could assign a guide to an athlete is at complete odds with the views of many disability communities who argue that individuals with disabilities must have agency over their personal relationships and over who they ask for support. However, the same assumption completely aligns with the sport system that tasks sport managers with making decisions that they believe will result in the best performance outcomes for the team. It is our position that this lack of clarity regarding the status of the guide, understanding about the nature of the relationship, and engagement with issues surrounding the rights of VI athletes puts VI athletes in vulnerable positions and threatens their ability to participate in sport.

Moreover, the ableist assumption that guides are only relevant on the field of play has different implications for different VI athletes. For example, within

VI sport there are three 'classifications' with B1 being the label given to Blind athletes and B2 and B3 referring to partially sighted athletes. While athletes in all three classes can use and benefit from a guide on the racecourse, B1 athletes are typically more reliant on others for assistance off the field of play (Powis, 2020). Because of their higher support needs, B1 athletes are inequitably harmed by policies and decisions that dictate when they have access to a guide (or if their guide is assigned other tasks) and who they can have as a guide. The varying support needs of VI athletes can also lead to situations such as those described by Powis (2020) in his work with VI cricket players. Powis found that athletes with the least sight (B1) were dependent on their B2/B3 teammates off the field of play which reinforced a "hierarchy of sight" within the team. Similar to the experiences of VI cricket players, controlling who can guide and limiting how and when VI athletes can interact with their partners could also perpetuate exclusion of athletes with the least vision because of the belief that they will be a burden on the team – a burden that would not exist if they were supported by guides of their choosing.

Conclusion and Future Directions

The athlete–guide partnership is premised on the notion that it is by working interdependently with their guide that the VI athlete is able to experience independence. This is unique theoretically as dependence, interdependence and independence are typically thought to be mutually exclusive categories. Notions of dependence are also closely related to issues of agency – the more a person depends on others, the less agency one has. Once again, the athlete–guide partnership disrupts this assumption by demonstrating that it is by working collaboratively that agency is enacted, athletic performance is achieved, and athletic identities performed. Returning to DePauw (1997), this is an example of how thinking from a disability-centered position can be a productive exercise to facilitate critical discussions about what it means to be an athlete and who can claim an athletic identity.

We started this parallel autoethnography frustrated by the lack of recognition of the unique partnership between VI athletes and guides. Our intent was to use our own experiences to interrogate the disabled and non-disabled binaries that continue to be (re)produced in sport contexts. By sharing our stories in the form of short vignettes, we highlight how these experiences might prompt others to reflect on their own sporting identities and the intersection of sport performance and disability. We are cognizant of the limitations of this approach – while our experiences may resonate with other athletes and guides, we do not represent them or speak for them.

As mentioned previously, the omission of literature about the athlete–guide partnership does a disservice to athletes with disabilities and further marginalizes their experiences in sport. Methodologically, further research is needed to more broadly and thoroughly explore the experiences of VI athletes and guides separately and together. We would also propose research that considers the systems, structures and cultures in which these relationships operate. It would be worthwhile to consider the practices within and across various organizations to identify how athlete–guide partnerships might be better supported and integrated. This could take the form of case studies and organizational ethnographies. There is a substantive contribution to be made by more thoroughly exploring how some of the topics we raised could extend both socio-cultural and psychological sport studies. For example, the concept of synchrony in sport that we raise is not new – Allen-Collinson and Hockey (2017) wrote about the intercorporeality of runners training together and the constant "reciprocity of attention and an ongoing adjustment of rhythm and pace" (p. 179) in a way that resonates deeply with our own experiences. How synchrony might disrupt binaries of able/disabled is yet to be explored. The work of sport psychologists into athlete-athlete dyads also resonates but does not entirely capture the intricacies of these pairs. For example, the 3+Cs model of interdependence can be used to operationalize feelings, thoughts, and behaviors relative to interdependence and relationship functioning in athletic dyads (Poczwardowski et al., 2019) but does not address the challenges faced by athletes and guides, how these experiences cultivate mutual support, and the contexts that shape these unique relationships. We touched only briefly upon the work of feminist scholars, but it is clear that theorizing on intersectionality (Crenshaw, 2018) and the (gendered) ideology of dependence (Pape & McLachlan, 2020) will be critical to understanding how these dyads operate within gendered and ableist sport structures. This could also lead to work that explores other relationships unique to disability sport including the use of personal support workers by athletes with high support needs.

While there has been 'progress' in the Paralympic Movement, overwhelmingly the narrative has been to compare parasport with sport for the non-disabled rather than interrogating how parasport might be different and what types of opportunities these differences facilitate. The athlete–guide partnership is a specific example of how disabled athletes cannot simply be integrated into existing ableist sport structures. However, it is also because it does not 'fit' that athlete-guide partnership provides a unique opportunity to reframe the conversation from how sport must be adapted for disabled athletes and to consider instead what is gained when sport is done differently.

Acknowledgements

The authors thank their athlete and guide partners for the incredible experiences shared, the years of friendship and the permission to share their/our stories.

Notes

1 The terms 'visual impairment' and 'visually impaired' have been used throughout to be consistent with the terminology employed within parasport to encompass events for athletes who are Blind or partially sighted.

2 In some sports and classes, VI athlete are 'permitted' but not 'required' to have a guide as is the case for athletes classified as B2 in nordic skiing. In other sports, the use of a guide is mandatory.

3 Throughout the text we will refer to athletes with visual impairments as 'athletes' and their sighted partners as 'guides' – such terminology is not to imply that sighted guides are not *also* athletes but rather a language choice to distinguish between the roles in these partnerships.

References

Allen-Collinson, J., & Hockey, J., 2017. Intercorporeal enaction and synchrony: The case of distance-running together. In: C. Meyer & U. van Wedelstaedt (Eds.), *Moving bodies in interaction – Interacting bodies in motion: Intercorporeality, interkinesthesia, and enaction in sports* (pp. 173–192). Amsterdam: John Benjamins Publishing.

Bandura, A., 1999. Social cognitive theory: An agentic perspective. *Asian Journal of Social Psychology*, 2(1), pp. 21–41.

Carvalho-Freitas, M. N. D., & Stathi, S., 2017. Reducing workplace bias toward people with disabilities with the use of imagined contact. *Journal of Applied Social Psychology*, 47(5), pp. 256–266.

Crenshaw, K., 2018. *Demarginalizing the intersection of race and sex: A Black feminist critique of antidiscrimination doctrine, feminist theory, and antiracist politics [1989]* (pp. 57–80). New York: Routledge.

Dean, N. A., (2019). "Just act normal": Concussion and the (re) negotiation of athletic identity. *Sociology of Sport Journal*, 36(1), pp. 22–31.

DePauw, K.P., 1997. The (in)visibility of disability: Cultural contexts and "sporting bodies". *Quest*, 49(4), pp. 416–430.

Deuble, R.L., Connick, M.J., Beckman, E.M., Abernethy, B., & Tweedy, S.M., 2016. Using Fitts' Law to detect intentional misrepresentation. *Journal of Motor Behavior*, 48(2), pp. 164–171.

Garland-Thompson, R., 2016. Integrating disability, transforming feminist theory. In L. J. Davis (Ed.), *The disability studies reader* (pp. 360–380). New York: Routledge.

Gérard, S., 2020. The best of both worlds? In D. Chatziefstathious, B. García, B. Séguin (Eds.), *Routledge handbook of the Olympic and Paralympic Games* (pp. 84–97). New York: Routledge.

Hammond, A., Bundon, A., Pentifallo-Gadd, C., & Konoval, T., 2021. Enactments of integrated, disability-inclusive sport policy by sporting organizations in British Columbia. Canada. *Sociology of Sport Journal*.

Howe, D., 2008. *The cultural politics of the Paralympic movement: Through an anthropological lens*. Routledge.

Howe, P., 2007. Integration of Paralympic athletes into athletics Canada. *International Journal of Canadian Studies/Revue internationale d'études canadiennes*, (35), pp. 133–150.

Jackson, B., Dimmock, J.A., Gucciardi, D.F., & Grove, J.R., 2010. Relationship commitment in athletic dyads: Actor and partner effects for Big Five self-and other-ratings. *Journal of Research in Personality*, 44(5), pp. 641–648.

Jowett, S., 2007. Interdependence analysis and the 3 + ICs in the coach-athlete relationship. In S. Jowett & D. Lavallee (Eds.), *Social psychology in sport* (pp. 15–27). Champaign, IL: Human Kinetics.

Jowett, S., & Cockerill, I.M., 2003. Olympic medallists' perspective of the althlete–coach relationship. *Psychology of Sport and Exercise*, 4(4), pp. 313–331.

Jowett, S., & Ntoumanis, N. 2004. The Coach–Athlete relationship questionnaire (CART-Q): Development and initial validation. *Scandinavian Journal of Medicine & Science in Sports*, 14(4), pp. 245–257.

Kelley, H.H., & Thibaut, J.W., 1978. *Interpersonal relations: A theory of interdependence.* New York: Wiley.

Kenny, D.A., & Cook, W., 1999. Partner effects in relationship research: Conceptual issues, analytic difficulties, and illustrations. *Personal Relationships*, 6(4), pp. 433–448.

Mann, D.L., & Ravensbergen, H.J.C., 2018. International Paralympic Committee (IPC) and International Blind Sports Federation (IBSA) joint position stand on the sport-specific classification of athletes with vision impairment. *Sports Medicine*, 48(9), pp. 2011–2023.

Pape, M., & McLachlan, F., 2020. Gendering the coronavirus pandemic: Toward a framework of interdependence for sport. *International Journal of Sport Communication*, 13(3), pp. 391–398.

Patatas, J.M., De Bosscher, V., & Legg, D., 2018. Understanding parasport: An analysis of the differences between able-bodied and parasport from a sport policy perspective. *International Journal of Sport Policy and Politics*, 10(2), pp. 235–254.

Peers, D., 2009. (Dis) empowering Paralympic histories: absent athletes and disabling discourses. *Disability & Society*, 24(5), pp. 653–665.

Peers, D., 2012. Interrogating disability: The (de) composition of a recovering Paralympian. *Qualitative Research in Sport, Exercise and Health*, 4(2), pp. 175–188.

Poczwardowski, A., Lamphere, B., Allen, K., Marican, R., & Haberl, P., 2019. The 5c's model of successful partnerships in elite beach volleyball dyads. *Journal of Applied Sport Psychology*, 32(5), pp. 476–494.

Powis, B., 2020. *Embodiment, identity and disability sport: An ethnography of elite visually impaired athletes.* Abingdon: Routledge.

Slocum, C., Kim, S., & Blauwet, C., 2018. Women and athletes with high support needs in Paralympic sport: progress and further opportunities for underrepresented populations. In *The Palgrave handbook of Paralympic studies* (pp. 371–388). London: Palgrave Macmillan.

Smith, B., & Bundon, A., 2018. Disability models: Explaining and understanding disability sport in different ways. In *The Palgrave handbook of paralympic studies* (pp. 15–34). London: Palgrave Macmillan.

Chapter 11

Confronting Ableism from within
Reflections on Anti-Ableism Research in Disability Sport

Carla Filomena Silva

Introduction

Dear reader, allow me the impertinence of describing you:

- You love sport;
- You believe sport is a tool for social good;
- Social justice matters to you;
- You are sensitive to the systemic oppression of people experiencing disability;
- You are not ableist, but you want to educate others on Ableism …

I am sure you are much more complex than I suggest here. Yet, the more you identify yourself with the affirmations above, the more relevant you will find this chapter.[1]

I love sport myself. For as long as I can remember, I have loved moving. And I love that we have a kaleidoscope of movement cultures to marvel ourselves with, as participants, spectators, supporters, and consumers. Yet, I found myself often conflicted between my love for sport[2] and my repulse for its dark side. Throughout my life, first as a volleyball player, coach, physical education teacher, and as a student and academic, the ugly stains of sport have become increasingly harder to ignore. My personal and professional relationship with sport is now a balancing act requiring me to remain critically vigilant of harmful biases in sport and myself. I encourage you, the reader, to do the same. You see, just as you, I am also deeply committed to social justice, and I have often found difficult to conciliate these two passions.

When we start reading and exploring social justice endeavours, one of the fundamental lessons we are taught that our inaction is sufficient to cause harm, since most systems of oppression, such as racism and ableism, are so naturally and invisibly embedded in our social and cultural structures. This is why this chapter focuses on anti-ableism work. Anti-ableism suggests that, in order to progress towards a world that is more equitable for individuals experiencing disability, we must intentionally and consistently fight ableism and actively implement actionable change (Kaundinya & Schroth, 2022).

DOI: 10.4324/9781003153696-14

The goal of this chapter is to navigate the challenges of anti-ableist research together with our eyes on the prize: the promise of more inclusive, empowering, ableism-free sporting cultures. As groundwork, we will attempt to understand what ableism is and how it operates. After identifying the invisibility of ableism as our main barrier, we will reflect on key challenges within disability sport research: 1) sport is a main cultural and social agent in the perpetuation of ableism and 2) the impact of a politics of ableism on the research context. To illustrate key struggles, I draw upon my own research experience in disability sport.

Ableism: the most invisible of all -isms

The core assumption of ableism— that life without disability is more desirable and better than life with disability— is deeply buried "into the very heart of our ontological souls" (Goodley, 2014, p. 32). That life with disability is unquestionably worse than a life without disability is epitomized in the way expecting parents often declare: 'I don't care if it's a boy or a girl, as long as it's healthy.' As Davio points out "…we, who are sick understand intuitively that we are, in these people's minds, the worst possible outcome. We are the spooky unknown. We embody others' darkest fears. Sometimes, we are less, in their eyes, than full people." (2017, p. 18). Yet, both individually and socially, we fail to recognize how this deep-rooted and compulsory desire for ableness undermines the humanity of those perceived as 'unhealthy' and/or 'disabled'.

Ableism is so deeply interwoven into our ways of perceiving and being that it remains, for the most part, invisible. It asserts the able-bodied norm as the *natural* and *right* way to be, legitimizing a constitutional divide, an essential separation between the 'able' and the 'disabled' (Campbell, 2009). Despite its pervasiveness, it is only when someone looks, thinks and/or acts *abnormally* that able-bodied normalcy surfaces. Thus, as a signifier of a marginal, inherently negative, inferior existence, disability is essential to validate ableness: "the unruly, uncivil disabled body is necessary for the reiteration of the 'truth' of the 'real/essential' human self who is endowed with masculinist attributes of certainty, mastery and autonomy" (Campbell, 2009: 11).

The dominant norm of the *able citizen* is consistently projected by authorities (e.g. the State, the Church, the School, the Media, the Sciences and Sport) as the *species- typical* existence through rhetorical "ways of knowing, valuing and seeing the so-called abnormal body as inferior" (Cherney, 2019, p. 8). To highlight the socially constructed nature of ableism, in this chapter, I use Cherney's definition of ableism as a "system of discrimination that rhetorically invents and employs the idea of a 'normal body' and treats physical deviance from that norm as lacking something that all nondisabled people share" (2019, p. 8).

The totalizing harmful power of ableism lies precisely in its capacity for self-erasure, its invisibility. And the closer we are to its normative centre (the more *able* we are), the more likely we are to remain oblivious to its rhetorical operations. Arguably, it is hard to notice the lack of obstacles. Instead, we believe our privilege to be a legitimate reward for our merit within a fair, level-playing field; rather than the outcome of complex intersecting systems of privilege and disadvantage (Sandel, 2020). We tend to interpret inequity, discrimination, and oppression against people experiencing disability as *natural*. And what is perceived as *natural* is neither noticed, nor fought against. It is that something that 'goes without saying'. Ableism's silent pervasiveness eludes its harmful nature because "it becomes part of the generalized and commonsensical orientations that a culture encourages people to adopt as conventions" (Cherney, 2019, p. 18). It compels all of us, to emulate and desire ableness, ignoring precariousness (we are only temporarily able) as a universal quality of human lives (Scuro, 2017). When we emulate ablebodiedness without realizing it, the disciplinary power of ableism is fully enacted as we survey, discipline, and subjugate ourselves and each other into ableist docility (Campbell, 2009; McRuer, 2006; Siebers, 2008). Even those individuals who experience disability and have felt vividly the harmful impact of the able-bodied norm are likely to have accepted ableism as valid and internalized their difference as *inadequate* and *wrong*: a process Campbell (2009, p. 16) calls "Internalised Ableism: The Tyranny Within".

In short, the invisibility of ableism constitutes our most significant barrier to anti-ableism informed work in all contexts, including sport. The starting point is to expose ableism, to notice its expressions buried under what is taken for granted. This is an arduous process. We must confront conscious and unconscious ableism, whilst recognising that doing so "…requires a new way of seeing, and we must develop that orientation while examining things that we can only fully recognize as ableist once that view is developed" (Cherney, 2019, p. 7). To break this cognitive loop, we must bravely drill through thick layers of internalized conditioning, to uncover ugly truths about ourselves and our valued institutions. This process of 'unlearning' biases is emotionally taxing, but necessary (Choudhury, 2021). We will realize we are not as 'good' as we thought. Yet, only then can we expose our's and sport's active responsibility as a cultural agent in the construction and reproduction of ableism and start working on its transformation.

Anti-ableism research

Although some authors conflate ableism and disablism, I understand these concepts as different. Disablism denotes the harmful outcomes of ableism, whereas ableism targets the genesis of disability oppression. Anti-ableism research, therefore, focuses on the larger, ingrained, and unrecognized "ideological problem behind a multitude of ways that society discriminates against, and disadvantages disabled people." (Cherney, 2019, p. 4). Once the 'cause of the causes', the primordial source of oppression has been recognized, we can then investigate the "production, operation and maintenance of ableism" (Campbell, 2009, p. 4). Anti-ableism research is inherently emancipatory, as it aims to expose and invalidate the ideological assumptions legitimizing the multiple inequities, deprivation, and discrimination endured by people experiencing disability, by relocating the disability 'problem' from the individual into its ideological foundations.

For instance, a research project adopting a disablism-informed lens would illuminate unequal opportunities or discriminatory practices against people experiencing disability in physical activity and sport contexts. Conversely, an anti-ableist study would scrutinize sports' responsibility in creating and reinforcing ableism, and its potential to challenge it. While both standpoints are useful, if we are to maximize sport's potential to advance social justice for people who experience disability, we must target ableism, the primal cause of disability oppression. Reflecting on my own trajectory as an able-bodied, aspiring anti-ableist warrior, I have identified two fundamental reflections to engage in when developing disability sport research. The first reflection entails recognising sport as a social cultural institution implicated in the perpetuation of ableism and the second reflection invites us to consider the ways in which ableism politics shapes and impacts our research. In the following sections, I explain each of these, and propose ways to navigate them, illustrating these considerations with examples and vignettes from my own experience. Strategies to navigate these challenges are also suggested.

Sport as an ableist agent

When I decided to invest considerable time and energy studying something I was passionate about, I thought my first big research project would explore the multitude of ways in which the Paralympic Games could positively affect societal perceptions not only of Paralympians, but of disability, more generally. I was still, at the time, a sport disciple, a firm believer in the inherently good qualities of sport and their power to magically fix the world.

Through extensive immersion into disability studies literature, critically informed conversations with scholars, athletes, and people with disabilities and many hours of self-reflection, my initial standpoint substantially changed. I have realized that sport cannot be a naturally empowering ally for people who experience disability simply because sport was, and continues to be, a key agent in the creation and perpetuation of ableism. I am not alone in my epiphany. Some sports scholars, using a Foucaldian lens, have exposed sport as a tool to normalize and discipline the bodies of citizens in order to satisfy cultural, economic and political imperatives (e.g. Markula-Denison & Pringle, 2007; Shogan, 2020). Unsurprisingly, former Paralympic athletes, such as Anne Mette Bredhal, Danielle Peers, David Howe, have also started to expose the ways in which the Paralympics and disability sport have been reinforcing ableism, exploring issues of cultural representation of the 'dis-abled' moving bodies (Peers et al., 2020; Pullen et al., 2020; Silva & Howe, 2012); power imbalance between the able and disabled within these contexts (Howe, 2008; Peers, 2009, 2012); practices of biopower through practices such as categorization and classification (Howe, 2008;

Howe & Jones, 2006; Jones & Howe, 2005; Shogan, 1998); problematic research ethics, axioms and practices (Bredahl, 2008; Peers, 2018); and the overall cultural politics of the Paralympic movement and disability sport (Howe, 2008; Peers, 2012; Silva & Howe, 2018). These are only a few of the most significant issues evidencing disability sport ableist tendencies.

Adopting a disability studies lens, Cherney (2019) examined how the ableist premise that ability lies in the body (*the body is able*) has been a rhetoric warrant largely disseminated by sporting cultures. Rhetoric warrants are interpretative frameworks that have become so naturalized they are accepted as truths, guiding practical reasoning, and shaping everyday interactions, especially in contexts marked by ambiguity and complexity. In Cherney's words:

> Everyone seeking to comprehend something- such as an audience watching a performance, students reading a book, or people seeking to understand a perplexing encounter- constructs an interpretive framework from previous existing opinions, values, and views and applies these as warrants to determine what that thing means.
>
> (2019, p. 13)

Reflecting on my own experiences in sport, I recognize this as a valid point. For the short time I was a physical education (PE) teacher working in public high schools in Lisbon, Portugal I remember the naturalness with which I accepted that a few of my students, whose mobility function had been impacted by polio, were excused from participating actively in class. That is, doing something else other than refereeing, taking attendance or 'assisting' the teacher. I had accepted this exclusion as natural, not only because in my years as a student I had never witnessed a classmate with a visible impairment participating in PE, but more importantly, because during the five years of my sports and PE degree, the possibility of teaching or coaching 'dis-abled' students was never entertained. At my institution, there was an undergraduate degree dedicated to 'special' populations, which further reinforced the idea that these students would be someone else's 'issue'. My experience as a PE student and sports professional had taught me that these were spaces reserved to ablebodiedness, and that the absence of bodily impairment was a minimal prerequisite to enter these spaces.

The body is able warrant crystalizes the core ableist assumption that disability equates to impairment and that both can be located within the individual bodies, therefore "obscuring the rhetorical construction of social institutions, cultural systems, popular assumptions, and the ways these shape our world" (Cherney, 2019, p. 90). As a high school student, I had learned that my classmate Christiana would not be able to do the class because *she* had an impairment, and therefore *she* was unable to play sport. Even later, as a PE teacher, it had not occurred to me that perhaps the problem was not located within the student, but in the design and cultural parameters of the discipline (essentially a sports-based curriculum), the environment, and myself, the teacher. I perceived sport as a 'neutral', non-exclusionary space, its cultural ableist premises buried in my subconscious as 'natural'.

Sport assumes "an ideal of the stable and controllable body as the foundation of ability" (Cherney, 2019, p. 100) and consistently reinforces it through its technological and scientific apparatus (biomechanics, physiology, medicine, nutrition, training methodology (Shogan, 2020)). These assumptions and technological apparatus provided the impetus and rationale for sport to be used as a rehabilitation tool, most notably exemplified by the efforts of Doctor Ludwig Guttmann in Stoke Mandeville, largely credited as the founder of the Paralympic Games (Anderson, 2003). But, if this was the case, if sport can help 'broken' bodies return to a state of ablebodieness, why do we need separate sport provision? Why is disability sport and athletes who experience disabilities still seen as inferior to their able-bodied counterparts? The answer to these questions lies in the recognition that sport constitutes a cultural space where *normal ablebodieness* is defined and reinforced. Deviance may be accepted, insofar as it is perceived as super ability, the case of athletes considered super talented (Cherney, 2019). Athletes whose deviant embodiment is perceived as *de-efficient*, as *dis-abled*, are ineligible to denote athleticism, more so if there is not a previous state of ablebodieness to return to, if impairments are congenital (Purdue & Howe, 2013). As Purdue and Howe (2012) remark, the "social appraisal of an individual with an impairment and that of an athlete is seen as contradictory, incompatible within the same body at the same time" (p. 192). Disability and sport are largely perceived as a paradox because neither are value 'neutral'. Sport, as an ablebodieness preserve, performs the cultural work of rhetorically affirming not only that '*the body is able*' but also that '*normal is natural*' Cherney (2019).

The '*normal is natural*' warrant is instrumental to the validation of a constitutional divide between the able and the disabled, as proposed by Campbell (2009). This warrant enacts the essentialization of disability as a quality residing within the person. It "refers to the practice of naturalizing normal behavior, viewing the normal body as a natural construct, and regarding any deviation from the norm as 'freaks of nature' or violations of 'natural law'." (Cherney, 2019, p. 20). It constructs disability as 'otherness' (Clapton & Fitzgerald, 1997). This warrant is enacted in the need for two separate contexts for able and disabled athletes: the Olympic and the Paralympic movements. This distinctive arrangement is a societal "solution" to manage such essential difference because it is the difference itself and not sport that is seen as 'wrong'. While some athletes have been allowed to compete in mainstream sport competitions, therefore challenging the need for such division, the practical challenges surmount. Scholarly discussion centres on issues of competitive fairness, especially when technology is thought to expand one's ability and challenges the ideal of biologically bound humanness (Swartz & Watermeyer, 2008; Wolbring, 2008, 2012). These are nuanced discussions revealing a deep disability phobia, manifested in the need to preserve the ideal of able-bodiedness as a baseline for normal humanness. The participation of athletes with atypical bodies in the Olympic movement will always receive pushback because they significantly disturb this ableist order. While practically, the existence of separate sport movements for the 'able' and for the 'disabled' appears positive, as they provide opportunities of competitive fairness for athletes previously excluded, culturally, this separation reinforces the perception of the *normal as natural* and the perception of essential difference between the able and the disabled, what Campbell names a "constitutional divide" (2009, p. 7).

A case in point is the sport of sitting volleyball (SV). As I started my own ethnographic research as an apparently abled bodied player attempting to earn my legitimacy as a member of the SV community, the perception that SV was for 'broken' bodies was apparent. My participation in the first tournaments was marked by many requests to explain 'what was wrong with me'. The question could have been framed as 'Why are you interested in SV?' or 'What is your impairment?', but the expectation that membership required something to be 'wrong' with me reveals the circulating assumption that impairment and/or disability signified 'inappropriate for sport' and that SV, as a space marked by such 'wrongness' would be undesirable to someone whose body was not broken.

As I got more involved in the SV community, always painfully managing my liminal position as an abled bodied player in a disability sport context and my dual role as both a researcher and a community member, I began to revise my previous assumption of sport as inherently positive. The fractures on the ground were too many and significant to miss: the power imbalance towards ablebodieness, with most institutional managers and coaching staff being able-bodied individuals; a visible social hierarchy, within which the intersections between gender, volleyball expertise, class and embodiment determined one's status; the unproblematic validation of expert knowledge (doctors, classifiers -often medical doctors or physiotherapists, nutritionists and coaches) and the often subtle but visible dismissal of knowledge derived from the lived experience of athletes who experience disability (Silva, 2013).

Had I persisted firmly committed to the view of sport as a neutral, value-free space, ignoring its role in reinforcing ableism, my work would continue to disseminate those same assumptions and reinforce the status quo. I would have continued to investigate how disability sport 'helped' athletes who experienced disability 'overcome' their disability, while remaining oblivious to how disability sport reinforced systemic and structural ableism. And a valuable opportunity to explore the transformative potential of the disability sport paradox for anti-ableism work (see Silva & Howe, 2019) would have been missed.

As Shogan (2020) suggests, "Diversity and hybridity are antidotes for the potential totalizing effects of discipline." (p. 100). As disability sport researchers, we have an ethical responsibility to question and disrupt the normalizing processes of sport. And we can only do so by identifying our own allegiance to normalizing biases, seriously reflecting upon the ways we may be reinforcing those processes. An excellent starting point is to seriously scrutinize our own compliance to the myth of sport as a naturally empowering context (Coakley, 2015), and the perception of disability as wrong. From this position of intellectual humility, we can then hold space for the once thought radical: that we may not be as good as we thought we were (and this is ok, as long as we acknowledge it and better ourselves), that sport is not harmless, and that disability may indeed add richness and value to our human lives and societies. By recognizing and consciously suspending our ableist judgements, by truly listening and validating the experiences of participants who experience disability, we may nurture anti-ableist understandings of ability and disability.

The following are my proposed starting points to ignite reflection on the role of sport and sport researchers as agents of ableism:

- How do you articulate the cultural and social value of sport and disability sport, in particular? Does your view reflect a critical positioning of sport as a potential keeper of the status quo, not only at the service of ableism, but serving other dominant systems of privilege and oppression? Do your views express a balanced understanding of sport, as both a positive agent for social justice, but also acknowledging challenges?
- Do you follow disability sport? What motives sustain or obstruct your interest? What immediate thoughts and judgments surface when you 'consume' disability sport? Pay close attention to potential ableist warrants you may be enacting as an interpretative framework.
- Prepare for your disability sport research by investigating the genesis of the specific sporting culture you are focusing upon. Has the sport been designed to help participants 'overcome' their impairment or for 'rehabilitative' purposes? Has the sport been created anew to align more closely with the specific qualities of diversely embodied participants (goalball is a good example) or does it emulate an able-bodied version? What are the goals embraced by this sport's institutions? Look out for both ableist and anti-ableist undertones in institutional discourses.
- Try your best to suspend your own ableist judgments during the research process. Start by accepting they are inevitable. We are all ableist – remember this. As the research progresses, engage in continuous critical reflection scrutinizing the different ways in which your own positionality as a researcher may reinforce or challenge ableist tendencies. Embrace the emotional discomfort as essential to the process.

The next section expands on this last point, exploring issues related to researcher's positionally, triggered by my own naivety on issues of an ableist researcher's authority and legitimacy.

Fighting ableism from within an ableist world

Very early on in my career as a disability sport researcher, my naïve impetus to play my small part in making the world a better place suffered painful blows. Recently graduated from an Adapted Physical Activity master's degree, I had identified an area I was truly passionate about, a purposeful endeavour in which I could marry my love for sport with my deep commitment to social justice. As a working-class female Portuguese woman, I had experienced a host of avoidable barriers to sports participation I was just starting to recognize as expressions of systemic oppression. In many regards, I thought, my struggles for sport's participation and validation would be similar to those of many athletes who experience disabilities. To me, there was no essential separation between myself, an able-bodied person, and someone who experienced disability. I was confident that my 'good' intentions and my non-ableist nature would naturally show and grant me access to the rich world of disability sport. I wanted to join people who experienced disability in their quest for empowerment and I was exhilarated by the sense of purpose deriving from fighting a good cause. Until … I wasn't!

Witnessing an academic discussion on the legitimacy of non-disabled allies in the disability movement (Branfield, 1998; Drake, 1997; Duckett, 1998), I learned that "'non-disabled' people, no matter how 'sincere', 'sympathetic' or whatever, are always in the position of being 'non-disabled' people and all that this carries with it: domination, oppression and appropriation." (Branfield, 1998, p. 143). The same system responsible for ableist oppression positioned me, because of my visible able embodiment and against my will, on the culprit side of the divide, because "'non-disabled' people are not where we are and can never be." (Branfield, 1998, p. 143) for "… them, their experience, their history, their culture is our oppression" (Branfield, 1998, p. 143).

It was heartbreaking and deeply unsettling to realize my fight for social justice in relation to disability was perceived as illegitimate, at best; at worst, as academic parasitism - as a way to benefit personally from the oppression and vulnerability of another group. Such uneasiness was further intensified by a personal conversation with another ('disabled') disability sport researcher at an academic event. After sharing my genuine drive for social justice, but also the insecurities due my perceived illegitimacy as an ablebodied researcher, his response compounded my feelings of inadequacy: "Would you like me to hit you in the head with a hammer, so that you know what it is like to be disabled?" (Silva, 2013, pp. 4, 5).

When the emotional hurt and shock subsided, I realized I had completely overlooked the political power of the able/disable constitutional divide, which would, by virtue of my ablebodieness position me as a disability 'outsider' (Macbeth, 2010), if not oppressor. I realized that, insofar as ableism persists, my ablebodieness will always be perceived as problematic. That, regardless of my intentions and personal awareness, I have benefitted from ableism. I have internalized ableism and that I too have played and will, unwittingly, continue to play my role in its perpetuation. Such realization triggered the need to deeply scrutinize my assumptions, my goals and how my work should be framed. How could I make sure my research represented the interests, experiences, and voices of a group I could not fully understand? If such reductive dichotomy mattered to highly educated academics such as Branfield (1998), how would it matter in terms of my positionality in the field? How would 'disabled' participants perceive me? How would my research be received in both academic and non-academic circles? If I wanted to do some anti-ableism work, I would have to navigate the artificial dichotomies imposed by ableism and be prepared to counteract legitimate suspicion. Rather than just a theoretical abstraction, the able/disable, outsider/insider dichotomy mattered. As researchers, being aware of this impact must lead to careful examination of the ways in which our personal positioning within that divide affects all aspects of the research process and how we can navigate its complexities. Of significant usefulness is for instance, Peers (2018) identification of "axiological gaps": mismatches between the assumptions guiding the researcher's judgments on what qualifies as meaningful and valid research and the perspectives of the ones whom the research proclaims to serve.

That my dis/ability status mattered to be accepted in the SV community was explicit in the numerous requests to explain what was 'wrong' with me. I did not have to lie. Although I was ineligible to be classified as an SV player, I had suffered a serious injury that limited my ability to jump and therefore to compete in mainstream volleyball. SV offered me an outlet to continue playing the sport I loved, but also convincingly justified my personal drive to develop academic research in SV. Everyone should have a chance to play, should they wish to do so, and I wanted to play my part in making that possible. But my intellectual dialogue with disability sport scholars (Fitzgerald, 2009; Macbeth, 2010; Stone & Priestley, 1996) made me also acutely aware of my outsider/oppressor status and thus preoccupied with how my every behaviour would be interpreted. No matter how hard I tried to avoid doing anything that could be interpreted as ableist, there would always be moments when my efforts fell short:

> *Gerard, the new guy (....) struggles to carry his bag and walk with the crutches. "Do you need some help?"- I ask immediately, giving little thought to my offer. His look hits me hard, even before the harshness of his words: "Why, DO YOU?" Oops ... I understand immediately.... his anger, resentment.... I feel embarrassed and ashamed. Did I deserve that? Wait a moment.... I would probably say the same to any other person struggling with bags, with or without crutches... Should I feel bad for offering help? What is it about help that it generates such a strong reaction?*
>
> (Silva, 2013, p. 168)

In the interaction represented in this vignette, Gerard's interpretated my offer within the context of everyday systemic ableism, within which individuals who appear disabled are often assumed to be in constant need of help and incapable of taking care of themselves. Rather than teammate offering a helping hand, I was an able-bodied oppressor perpetrating yet another micro aggression. This event led me to pay more attention to how the able/disabled constitutional divide was reinforced or otherwise challenged within the SV community. For instance, by determining who was and was not eligible to be a full-fledged member of the SV community, classification verdicts often triggered a difficult conciliation between public and private identities. Eligible participants who had never identified themselves as disabled, either because their impairment was minor or because they hid their impairment, were forced to "come out" as disabled, if they were truly committed to their new athletic identity as potential Paralympians (Silva, 2013). Despite having their classification sanctioned by experts, some players classified as 'minimally disabled' (MD's) felt they were cheating the system, as they did not self-identify as disabled in any other context of their lives; while some players classified as 'disabled' (D's) felt that the minimally disabled athletes were hindering opportunities for 'disabled' players who had limited opportunities to engage in sport. To complicate matters further, anyone, able or disabled could participate in national competition, and so there were many other participants, who, like me, were labelled as ablebodied (AB's) (Silva, 2013).

Leg amputee athletes, classified as disabled, were usually more proficient players than able bodied participants whose legs restricted the movement on the small space of the court, subverting the usual able/disabled hierarchy. Also, competitive success depended on the team's ability to function as one unit, which demanded a profound knowledge of each player's embodiment potential and the strategic ability to symbiotically perform as one unit, one body. Playing SV emphasized the inter-relational, complementary nature of ability and disability, completely denying the validity of essential difference between abled and disabled bodies (Silva & Howe, 2019). In order words, the constitutional divide simply does not hold practical value, because it is based upon artificial distinctions that are contradicted by the lived experience of athletes. At a practical level, the constitutional divide between ability and disability simply did not make sense and such dissonance was explicit to anyone involved in playing the game of SV.

Summary

With insights from my position as an ableist ablebodied researcher, who has a desire for social justice for those who experience disability, I believe we must pursue a robust anti-ableist agenda. To do so it becomes essential not only to expose ableism but, more constructively, to highlight and explore moments of transformative disruption (Silva and Howe, 2019), when playing and representing disability sport challenges ableist foundations. Triggered by such disruptions, can we dare to imagine ability/disability not as a divide, but as a continuum? Can we, as disability sport researchers, advocate for the creation of more universal sporting cultures where the individual specificity of different embodiments can be respected? When we finally recognize that the problem of exclusion in sport is in the sporting contexts and not in the participants' embodiments, can we dare to break the old mould and create anew? Yes, we can … if in doing anti-ableism work, we refuse to participate in the grand narratives of ableism and the grand sports myth and instead anchor the validity and legitimacy of our research efforts on the unacceptable failure of sporting cultures to live up to its idealized vision of equitable access for all citizens. Our goal must be *fixing* sport, not to *help* or *fix* the individuals oppressed by it.

Notes

1 Reading this chapter will probably make you uncomfortable. Please, persevere. Discomfort is not only an ally, but inevitable when it comes to learning and transformation, especially regarding personal and social biases (Linker, 2014) and becoming an anti-oppression warrior (Choudhury, 2021).
2 In this chapter, sport will be used in its broader sense to encompass all culturally relevant movement practices, to include physical activities not formally recognized as sports, such as dancing, walking, etc.

References

Anderson, J. (2003). Turned into taxpayers': Paraplegia, rehabilitation and sport at Stoke Mandeville, 1944-56. *Journal of Contemporary History*, 38(3), 461–475.
Branfield, F. (1998). What are you doing here? 'Non-disabled' people and the disability movement: A response to Robert F. Drake. *Disability & Society*, 13(1), 143–144.
Bredahl, A.M. (2008). Ethical aspects in research in adapted physical activity. *Sports Ethics and Philosophy*, 2(2), 257–270, DOI:10.1080/1751132080222388.
Campbell, F. (2009). *Contours of ableism: The production of disability and abledness*. New York: Palgrave Macmillan.
Cherney, J.L. (2019). *Ableist rhetoric: How we know, value, and see disability* (Vol. 11). University Park, Pennsylvania: The Pennsylvania State University Press.
Choudhury, S. (2021). *Deep diversity: A compassionate, scientific approach to achieving racial justice*. Vancouver: Greystone Books Ltd.
Clapton, J., & Fitzgerald, J. (1997). The history of disability: A history of 'otherness'. *New Renaissance Magazine*, 7(1), 1–3.
Coakley, J. (2015). Assessing the sociology of sport: On cultural sensibilities and the great sport myth. *International Review for the Sociology of Sport*, 50(4–5), 402–406.
Davio, K. (2017). *It's just nerves: Notes on a disability*. Minneapolis, Minnesota: Squares and Rebels.
Drake, R.F. (1997). What am I doing here? 'Non-disabled' people and the disability movement. *Disability & Society*, 12(4), 643–645.
Duckett, P.S. (1998). What are you doing here? 'Non-disabled' people and the disability movement: A response to Fran Branfield. *Disability & Society*, 13(4), 625–628.
Fitzgerald, H. (2009). Are you a 'parasite researcher'? Researching with young disabled people. In H. Fitzgerald (Ed.), *Disability and youth sport* (pp. 145–159). London: Routledge.
Goodley, D. (2014). *Dis/ability studies: Theorising disablism and ableism*. New York: Routledge.
Howe, D. (2008). *The cultural politics of the Paralympic movement: Through an anthropological lens*. London and New York: Routledge.
Howe, P.D., & Jones, C. (2006). Classification of disabled athletes: (Dis)empowering the Paralympic practice community. *Sociology of Sport Journal*, 23(1), 29–46.
Jones, C., & Howe, P.D. (2005). The conceptual boundaries of sport for the disabled: Classification and athletic performance. *Journal of the Philosophy of Sport*, 32(2), 133–146.
Kaundinya, T., & Schroth, S. (2022). Dismantle ableism, accept disability: Making the case for anti-ableism in medical education. *Journal of Medical Education and Curricular Development*, 9, 23821205221076660.

Linker, M. (2014). *Intellectual empathy: Critical thinking for social justice*. Ann Arbor: University of Michigan Press.

Macbeth, J.L. (2010). Reflecting on disability research in sport and leisure settings. *Leisure Studies*, 29(4), 477–485.

Markula-Denison, P., & Pringle, R. (2007). *Foucault, sport and exercise: Power, knowledge and transforming the self*. New York: Routledge.

McRuer, R. (2006). *Crip theory: Cultural signs of queerness and disability* (Vol. 9). New York and London: New York University Press.

Peers, D. (2009). (Dis)empowering Paralympic histories: Absent athletes and disabling discourses. *Disability & Society*, 24(5), 653–665.

Peers, D. (2012). Patients, athletes, freaks: Paralympism and the reproduction of disability. *Journal of Sport and Social Issues*, 36(3), 295–316.

Peers, D. (2018). Engaging axiology: Enabling meaningful transdisciplinary collaboration in adapted physical activity. *Adapted Physical Activity Quarterly*, 35(3), 267–284.

Peers, D., Konoval, T., & Naturkach, R. M. (2020). (Un)imaginable (para-) athletes: A discourse analysis of athletics websites in Canada. *Adapted Physical Activity Quarterly*, 37(1), 112–128.

Pullen, E., Jackson, D., Silk, M., Howe, D., & Silva, C. (2020). Extraordinary normalcy, ableist rehabilitation, and sporting Ablenationalism: The cultural (re)production of Paralympic disability narratives. *Sociology of Sport Journal*, 38(3), 209–217.

Purdue, D.E., & Howe, P.D. (2012). See the sport, not the disability: Exploring the Paralympic paradox. *Qualitative Research in Sport, Exercise and Health*, 4(2), 189–205.

Purdue, D.E., & Howe, P.D. (2013). Who's in and who is out? Legitimate bodies within the Paralympic Games. *Sociology of Sport Journal*, 30(1), 24–40.

Sandel, M.J. (2020). *The tyranny of merit: What's become of the common good?* New York: Farrar, Straus and Giroux.

Scuro, J. (2017). *Addressing ableism: Philosophical questions via disability studies*. Lanham, MD: Lexington Books.

Shogan, D. (1998). The social construction of disability: The impact of statistics and technology. *Adapted Physical Activity Quarterly*, 15(3), 269–277.

Shogan, D. (2020). *The making of high-performance athletes*. Toronto: University of Toronto Press.

Siebers, T. (2008). *Disability theory*. Ann Arbor: University of Michigan Press.

Silva, C. (2013). *The impact of sitting volleyball participation on the lives of players with impairments* [Doctoral dissertation, Loughborough University].

Silva, C.F., & Howe, P.D. (2012). The (in)validity of supercrip representation of Paralympian athletes. *Journal of Sport and Social Issues*, 36(2), 174–194.

Silva, C.F., & Howe, P.D. (2018). The social empowerment of difference: The potential influence of para sport. *Physical Medicine and Rehabilitation Clinics of North America*, 29(2), 397–408.

Silva, C.F., & Howe, P.D. (2019). Sliding to reverse Ableism: An ethnographic exploration of (dis)ability in sitting volleyball. *Societies*, 9(2), 41.

Stone, E., & Priestley, M. (1996). Parasites, pawns and partners: Disability research and the role of non-disabled researchers. *British Journal of Sociology*, 47(4), 699–716.

Swartz, L., & Watermeyer, B. (2008). Cyborg anxiety: Oscar Pistorius and the boundaries of what it means to be human. *Disability & Society*, 23(2), 187–190.

United Nations. (2006). *International convention for people with disabilities.* https://www.un.org/development/desa/disabilities/convention-on-the-rights-of-persons-with-disabilities/article-30-participation-in-cultural-life-recreation-leisure-and-sport.html (accessed 25th August 2021).

Wolbring, G. (2008). Oscar Pistorius and the future nature of Olympic, Paralympic and other sports. *SCRIPTed: Journal of Law, Technology and Society,* 5(1), 139–160.

Wolbring, G. (2012). Paralympians outperforming Olympians: An increasing challenge for Olympism and the Paralympic and Olympic movement. *Sport, Ethics and Philosophy,* 6(2), 251–266.

Chapter 12

Exercise, Rehabilitation and Posthuman Disability Studies

Four Responses

Javier Monforte, Barbara E. Gibson, Brett Smith and Dan Goodley

Posthuman disability studies (PDS) is a field of ideas, theories and debates that emerged from the intersection between Critical Disability Studies and posthumanist thinking (Goodley et al., 2014, 2020). This merging of an interdisciplinary field with a distinct theoretical approach reflects a number of overlapping concerns, including the importance of non/human interrelations in the lives of disabled people and the need to develop a more affirmative reading of the complex non-human entanglements experienced by many disabled individuals. This chapter looks at exercise and rehabilitation through PDS, and vice versa. It asks: what can exercise and rehabilitation and PDS do to and for each other? It offers four independent responses to this question. Drawing on these responses, it provides some further thoughts. The purpose of the chapter is to show that PDS can be a valuable thinking tool for researchers and professionals working in the field of exercise and rehabilitation.

Javier's Response

It is often assumed that disability is an individual problem in need of rehabilitation, and that the end goal of rehabilitation for disabled people is to restore themselves back to normality. We might disagree with such assumptions and feel the need to challenge them, as well as to provide creative alternatives. But how? One possibility is through engaging with PDS.

Briefly, PDS is an approach to the analysis of disability distinguished from other disability approaches by a critical but constructive stance towards humanism and its associated conception of the human being. To explain, PDS scholars argue that the humanist human is premised on an unacknowledged white, male, heterosexual and of course able-bodied subject that dances to the rhythm of ableism. Goodley et al. (2020, p. 139) defined ableism as the 'discriminatory processes that idealize a narrow version of humanness and reject more diverse forms of humanity'. He elaborated: 'being abled is akin to being fully human. And being able marks what it means to be a typical or normal human being ... Being able is what we presume human beings to be' (Goodley, 2021, p. 79). Under this conception, disability evokes an otherness to humanity. Disabled

DOI: 10.4324/9781003153696-15

people cannot claim full human status. They have a less human status. For example, wheelchair users are understood as less human because they do not embody the idealised mobility of the autonomous walker. Here, walking is understood as an essential ability of humans. To be proper human beings, then, wheelchair users need to fight against impairment and recuperate the capacity to walk. Paraphrasing Straus (1952, p. 534), 'each individual has to struggle in order to make it really his own. Man has to become what he is'.

According to Monforte, Smith and Pérez-Samaniego (2019), humanist, ableist rehabilitation represents the struggle through which disabled people try to become what they 'are'. Exercise is an important part of this struggle. It takes the role of restitution: it is, in the words of Papathomas, Williams and Smith (2015), 'the chief means by which a person can return to their former, able body' (p. 4). Exercise-is-restitution has shaped the rehabilitation of many disabled people. One example is Patrick, the former participant of my PhD -and now a good friend. Patrick had a tumour located in the spine that resulted in a spinal cord injury (SCI). During his rehabilitation process, Patrick used to believe that with "patience, time, and hard work in the gym", he would be able to "reverse the situation", that is, to return to 'normal' states of functioning that existed before the SCI onset. He was especially adamant in walking again or, at least, escaping the wheelchair. Once, he told me:

> I used a walker, dragging my legs! The ambulance left me at the threshold of the hospital door, well, in, let's say where the hospital gym was, and I went inside, thud, thud, thud, dragging my legs as I could, uh, dude. Anyway, trying my best to be able to walk again, that was my goal.

While notions of exercise-is-restitution were useful for Patrick early on post-SCI and during rehabilitation, they became increasingly less useful and more constraining as time went on. Following several surgeries, the possibility of walking became impossible for him. Once he realised this, Patrick dropped out of exercise. This shows how exercise and rehabilitation were defined or enslaved by a particular outcome: becoming independent from the wheelchair. For Patrick, rehabilitation had no other purpose.

But rehabilitation can move beyond that. This is possible once we think outside the classical conception of the human. Once we make the turn, then the ableist principles and notions that organise rehabilitation change radically. To keep with this example, exercise goes from being a means to fight against the wheelchair to being a way of connecting with it (Papadimitriou, 2008; Winance, 2019; Monforte, Pérez-Samaniego & Smith, 2022). Thinking with PDS, the person connecting with a wheelchair means more than making the most of a passive instrument. From a posthuman perspective, we do not say that a person uses a wheelchair, but rather that a person becomes one with it. The boundaries between object and subject are blurred. The human is still there, but now inextricably entangled with the nonhuman. Importantly, to be entangled does not simply mean to be intertwined with another, as in the joining of separate entities. It means to lack an independent, self-contained existence. Existence ceases to be an individual affair. To insist, the human is no longer understood as a binary between human versus nonhumans. There are no hierarchies.

Humanist thinking is hierarchical. The humanist human is superior to other beings and just needs 'him'self. Whereas the humanist subject resists his multiple dependencies with human and nonhuman others and desires to achieve self-sufficient independence, the posthuman subject abandons human exceptionalism to embrace dependencies, being open to new connections. Of course, this reorganisation of desire does not emerge overnight. Being at ease with the posthuman condition of disability is often a slow, progressive process.

As much as rehabilitation and exercise can reproduce narrow and ableist forms of humanity, they can in contrast play a key role in the process of becoming posthuman. As I envision it, a posthuman rehabilitation would use exercise as a means for a slow 'transformation of negative into positive passions' (Braidotti, 2013, p. 134). In the case example, exercise would be a means of transforming the negation of a wheelchair into a supportive and meaningful part of one's body and selfhood. The words of Naira (a woman I interviewed as part of a research project in Spain) illustrate this:

> To me, the prostheses are my legs. I have various prostheses, and for me it's not a material that I use. I mean, you end up growing a connection with the prosthesis, a kind of affect (…) I see them as part of my body. I strive to ensure that my prostheses are well, that the materials are adequate, in taking care of the skin, in doing exercise (…) in working on my quadriceps so it fits with the prosthesis … I didn't use to exercise, but now it's part of my life.

When I think about PDS, rehabilitation and exercise, I cannot but think about Naira and how she stood up in the middle of our interview to lend me three legs. I think about the idea that, when she handed the prosthetic legs to me and I held them, I was holding her. She was talking to me from another sofa and I was holding *her*. I was holding *Naira*, and now that I revisit that moment once again, I feel the paradox: that moment comprised one of the most human connections I have ever had.

Dan's Response

Exercise. What problem could anyone have with exercise? Health, fitness—being sound of mind and body—are human attributes that we aspire to. Moreover, when exercise is demonstrated to have some rehabilitative or socialising impacts then the value of exercise is further realised. It is fair to say that many of us have an ambivalent relationship with exercise. We know that exercise is good for us but will often find the most menial of tasks to avoid exercising. Or perhaps that's just me. Exercise's relationship with health ensures that many of us disavow exercise. That is to say, to get psychoanalytic for a second, we are attracted to exercise at the same time as we are repulsed by it. When exercise becomes taken up by health and medical professionals in the service of rehabilitation then this might lead to a further disavowal of exercise. On one hand we would want to emphasise the potential of exercise to increase the functioning and health of those accessing rehabilitation services. After all, many people (especially with an acquired impairment) will value the physical and mental benefits of rehabilitation that draw upon exercise. Here, then, exercise is desired. On the other hand we might worry about exercise's appropriation by rehabilitation or rehab's uses of exercise. For a start one might argue that we are taking the fun out of exercise and transforming it into a methodology of rehabilitation. And, in another sense, to pull exercise into rehabilitation will subject exercise to some of the same critiques that have been made about rehabilitation. Perhaps exercise in this sense is undesirable.

Critical disability studies have had an uneasy relationship with rehabilitation. For a start, scholars and researchers in this area of interdisciplinary work share concerns about any practice that medicalises or individualises disability. This is not to say that critical disability studies rejects rehabilitation. On the contrary, rehabilitation and other forms of medical and social care have literally saved the lives of many people with impairments for many years. This is an observation made by Mike Oliver in 1996 in his seminal work on stories of disability. Oliver was an ardent proponent of the social model of disability: an approach that was developed in response to the medical model of disability. The social model posited that disability was a social, political and economic phenomenon and that disabled people were politicised subjects capable of identifying their own modes of emancipation. Too often, disability activists argued, the medical model dominated the lives of disabled people and dominant representations of disability in society.

The problem was not medicine necessarily but medicalisation. So the practice of rehabilitation offered by many practitioners associated with medicine has many enabling impacts. However when the medical model becomes the only framing through which to view disability then this leads to the medicalisation of disabled people. Hence, in the arena of critical disability studies, rehabilitation is disavowed: it is desired for its recuperative and enabling effects on disabled people and, at the same time, is rejected when it becomes part of a wider medicalisation of disabled people. From a critical disability studies perspective we should be at least wary of rehabilitation and its associated practices. When exercise becomes part of the project of rehabilitation then it will also be subjected to this disavowing analysis.

PDS is an emerging branch of critical disability studies scholarship. Disability might be considered the quintessential post-human phenomenon. If the posthuman refers to the blurring of bodies and culture, the organic and the inorganic, the given and the technological, the actual and the virtual, the human and the non-human then disabled people can claim a rich posthuman history. Disabled people have always lived lives that fuse human and nonhuman elements (Shildrick, 2015). Consider the wheelchair, the guide dog, the prosthetic, Braille, hearing aids, personal assistance, the centrality of family, importance of community: these are but some examples of the extended humanities lived by disabled people. So posthuman disability studies seek to celebrate the human and nonhuman entanglements that are often common elements of the lives of disabled people while also critically analysing the costs and benefits of these non-human and human interrelations. While we might argue that disability is the quintessential posthuman condition this should not lead us to develop some kind of technophilia nor uncritical acceptance of the postanthropocentric moment. Yes, disability does embrace many human and nonhuman entanglements but we should also be mindful that many disabled people still continue to lead excluded lives. Hence posthuman disability studies encourage us to explore, say, bodily and technological fusions in ways that are sensitive to questions of power and structure, voice and choice and place and context. When we consider exercise-based rehabilitation we should not only be critical about both exercise and rehabilitation but, following a post-human perspective, attend to questions of power that are raised by the very practices and interventions that target the bodies and minds of disabled people.

So let us consider one example, echoing Javier's response: a wheelchair user with a spinal injury who is utilising exercise-based rehabilitation. First, we can acknowledge the complexity of the disabled body and its associations with human and nonhuman phenomena. These will include health professionals, supporters and allies as well as non-human technologies associated with the wheelchair and other devices. A post-human perspective would want to interrogate the ways in which the disabled person becomes increasingly entangled in an assemblage of various human and nonhuman into relations. This could lead to some rather productive understandings of disability. But, it could also engender some of more negative events in the lives of disabled people.

Second, we would want to ask questions about the aims of exercise and the aspirations of rehabilitation. We would want to consider questions of health, well-being and empowerment that might be raised by these practices. These seem like desirable questions to ask. However, remembering that we often disavow exercise and rehabilitation, we would also want to pose questions associated with autonomy, self-sufficiency and independence. These phenomena are often more problematic in the lives of disabled people. While we might think of autonomy as a very desirable destination point of rehabilitation, we also need to recognise that autonomy is key to a neoliberal society in which disability services and support mechanisms are erased and self-sufficiency is emphasised as the only way to be a valued citizen. Exercise and rehabilitation therefore take place in social and political moments. And one of the benefits of a posthuman disability studies perspective is that it recognises the inequality that persists in the lies of disabled people even when those same disabled people are complex fusions of human and nonhuman elements. Is it possible to desire exercise and rehabilitation when we live in a society that devalues interdependence mutuality and support? Can we find examples of exercise that escape these ideological pincers?

Third, a posthuman perspective would seek to understand in equities, differences, and diversity that are always at play in any human and non-human interrelationship. Braidotti (2019) argues that a key device of posthuman scholarship, arts and activism relates to illuminating and responding to what she terms the Missing People's Humanities. If modernist humanist perspectives (against which posthuman thinking responds) centralised white, male, able-bodied, western, heterosexual, living-in-towns-speaking-a-standard-language-kinda-people then a posthumanist perspective starts from an alliance with those who have marginalised, erased or ignored. Disabled people constitute but one example of the missing people and we would therefore want to work from out the outset with their desires. Therefore, we would ask what do disabled people want to get from exercise and rehabilitation? And, as importantly, are the end goals of exercise-based rehabilitation in line with the perceived end goals of disabled people?

Barbara's Response

An acquaintance of mine, Vera, with cerebral palsy, tells the story of how her childhood free time was dominated by two activities: doing homework and going to physiotherapy. She had asked some other children want they did on the weekends and discovered that they went swimming 'for fun'. She was incredulous! She viewed swimming as rehabilitation with the purpose of 'building core strength and coordination'. Swimming for her WAS physiotherapy. She had not conceived it as fun, pleasurable, or something anyone chose to do. From her first moment in the pool, she had learned that swimming was part of all the other exercises and interventions that were aimed at *fixing* her impaired body.

A posthuman accounting of swimming-as-therapy considers the enactment of a swimming body and the implications for rehabilitation. The subject position of 'rehabilitation patient' emerges in the extension of clinical imperatives into daily life. Disability as a problem that inheres in bodies is produced through the coming together of body materialities inscribed with biomedical logics. But things [are and] could be otherwise: swimming bodies as pleasure-able emerge when rehabilitation shifts towards enabling a posthuman appreciation of disability in terms of bodily *potentials rather than deficits*.

What does a posthuman appreciation of bodily potentials entail? Posthumanism addresses the humanist privileging of stable human subjects and asks how people of a certain type are made and unmade in/with time and place. Pleasure is not only an emergent experience but an affective force of production. Said differently, pleasure is not free-floating joy that is or is not experienced by an essentialised subject, but political, affective and precarious. Pleasures are produced and productive. They can be accessed or not, experienced or not. They can be thought or unthinkable, depending on how activities are enacted and formed through the intermingling of material and semiotic forces. Fun is doing and undoing. How pleasures are made and experienced is specific to the microphysics of encounter that play out in clinical spacings and their extension into home and community life. For Vera, swimming-as-fun could not be experienced because it was not complicit in the assemblage of swimming-as-therapy and its affective algebra: therapy = not fun = swimming = therapy = not fun =... This loop is not a trap. It has no permanence. Lines of flight are inevitable as the loop bumps up against other forces and configurations (Deleuze & Guattari, 1987). Swimming can be fun? Let's give it a go! Moreover 'swimming' can be enacted differentially, in other modes of body-water couplings. What does that do?

Consider another story about swimming-bodies—this time from Mark Mossman (2001). Mossman refers to his body as 'a postmodern text ... a constant physical tooling and re-tooling, a life marked by long swings into and out of "health" and "illness," "ability" and "disability."' Mossman recounts an experience of walking to the ocean for a swim. He was using crutches and notes that he 'had to leave my (leg) limb upstairs' and in so doing had to endure the 'stares of roughly forty sunbathing, vacationing people' on the way to the ocean. He then describes the experience of swimming:

> When I did get to the water, however, I was free again, my disability hidden beneath the waves. And at that point, typically, I felt a rush of emotions. I was thankful and pleased to be in the water swimming. I was embarrassed by my body's power to cause discomfort. I was anxious about the return passage back to the condo. I was ashamed of my profound inability to resist becoming what those stares had made me into: disabled, a person who needs help—the gates opened for him, the pathways cleared—a person who needs kindness and smiles to offset the uncomfortable stares and questions.

Swimming-body in Mossman's account is enacted through geotemporal interactions or 'spacings' (Horton & Kraftl, 2006). It is driven by and toward affective forces, productive of emotive states and sensations—freedom, gratitude, pleasure, shame, anxiety—that intersect with multi-variants of disability. He notes that stares and water 'make him into' something: respectively an object of scrutiny and a pleasure-able swimming- body. Swimming is not oriented to fixing the body, like it was in Vera's story, but rather enacts a freedom from and to, a line of flight into pleasures and an alternative engagement with the forces of stigma and shame that had dis-abled his impaired body. Disability temporarily and precariously dissolves into water, making pleasure-time. The stigmatised body has not disappeared. It exists in the same moment and place, but as accompaniment rather than melody until the next movement -emergence from (breaking with) the waves.

A posthuman account of pleasure-able swimming bodies has implications for rehabilitation. As noted above, rehabilitation has been critiqued for its association with the medicalisation of disabled people and veneration of neoliberal imperatives of independence and self-sufficiency. Rehabilitation has traditionally been a project of restoration and/or approximation to a state of normalcy that disavows the possibility of living well with non-normative morphologies (Gibson, 2016). Putatively "therapeutic" assemblages emerge from and express neoliberal logics of autonomy, productivity, and self-management that are implicated in the history of stigmatisation and exclusion of disabled people despite a commitment to addressing these forces (Fadyl et al., 2020). Rehabilitation is always and necessarily about return to something that was lost (Stiker, 2019), implicitly to the unitary wholeness of an independent and upright (male) citizen. These logics extend to bodies with congenital differences wherein a re-turn to evolutionary norms persist within enactments of so-called 'normal development' and its unidirectional progression to productive adulthood. Such rehabilitation imperatives act on and produce material bodily practices that pervade both clinic and community/home spaces. But things [are and] could be otherwise.

We return to the question of what a posthuman appreciation of bodily potentials entails. Post-critical rehabilitation studies (e.g., Abrams et al., 2019; Edwards et al., 2014; Gerlach et al., 2018; Gibson, 2016; Nicholls, 2017) entangle with physical culture studies and posthuman disability studies in bringing into relation posthuman readings of rehabilitation, disability, movement, and exercise. Enacting pleasure is not typically central to the aims of rehabilitation. Rather the slogans of rehabilitation ('Today It Hurts Tomorrow It Works'), and jibes levelled at its practitioners ('My Physical Therapist is a Physical Terrorist'), reveal an underlying disposition and reputation for a neoliberal reification of hard work, commitment, compliance and self-management towards normalisation. Contra these tendencies, a posthuman rehabilitation is one that embraces pleasure, not as goal or method but as enacted affect. Bodies enter water to become pleasure, joy, sensation. Exercise is exorcised, or rather transformed. Rehabilitation instead of moulding and manipulating seeks to enact connectivities between bodies, things, and forces to explore what is possible. The experiencing body knows itself in multiple sensual ways through movement and in these moments resists the territorialising forces of disability. Such a project is one of micro-activism (Dokumaci, 2016) that conspires to enable through doing differently. Pleasure is productive and produced within posthuman rehabilitation: Pleasure-able exercise can also work to improve bodily functions and processes ('building core strength and coordination') but the impetus to normalise difference for its own sake is radically re-moved. Posthuman rehabilitation may be 'therapeutic' but in what ways must always remain open to scrutiny and multiple possibilities. These opportunities arise when bodies labelled as disabled are reconfigured as *potentials rather than deficits*.

Brett's Response

The following 'A letter to my younger self' is a creative non-fiction. It is based on interviews with people who have acquired SCI and observations within a SCI rehabilitation unit

'A letter to my younger self'

Matt: when you wake up in the hospital and are told you've broken your neck you will be scared. The darkest images will fill and spin in your head. You will think incessantly about taking your life. In the bed that will be your temporary home but will feel like a prison, you will peer at the wheelchair the person opposite uses with dread and pity. You will imagine what it will be like to sit in it for your life, to be defined by it, to be restricted by it, and be stared at by others as you push its mental rims to get through town. What you won't realise Matt is that you are ambulatory. Your spinal cord injury will mean you can walk with the aid of crutches. The crutches will be like friends. You will decorate your new companions and over time learn to love them. That won't be easy. You go through rehabilitation with a deep desire to walk alone. You will spend hours in the gym building your strength and core stability. Your physiotherapists (sadly your favourite one will leave due to budget cuts) will set you goals, give you visualisation exercises where you imagine walking straight, and tick off the outcomes you will measure your success by. Your core strength and coordination' outcomes will become an obsession in order to gain a high level of independent walking. You will later make herculean efforts to master walking symmetry. You will read on the internet that walking symmetry is an important variable for the ability of well-controlled walking. You will exercise like you've never exercised before to do all this. Exercise in rehabilitation, and later on for a year, you will spend hours exercising and lifting weights to keep you out of a wheelchair and to walk independently as well as symmetrically. You won't enjoy exercise. It will be a means to these ends. The ancient metal weights, tattered walking gait frames, well-worn exercise machines, and inner self determination will be your hope to return to normal.

But Matt, life won't turn out like you hope. Don't worry though. You will have a good life. You will be happy, smile, do crazy things, have amazing sex, marry an amazing woman, and travel. There will be some bad times too. Those won't be due to your injury though. Life is complicated. Exercising won't bring what you desire so badly now. I am not saying don't exercise in rehab Matt. Keep lifting weights and practicing walking. But look up. Look through the big open patio door on a hot summer and say hello to the birds. Take time to feel the sun on your cheeks and listen to the birds talk to you. They have been watching you for some time. I think a few of them would like to share time with you. Don't look at the crutches as another thing to beat through exercise and leave behind.

You will always be a wobbly walker and need your crutches. That's fine too. Your son will later take the piss out of your walk and you will both share your special jokes about your walking. Your wobbly walking will create a bond that you will cherish. And enjoy your wobbly walking. Don't look at rehab as exercise. Throw that word out. Walk wobbly for pleasure. Part of that pleasure will be walking in the countryside with your friends and family. They will thank you for the fact that your slow walking will make them enjoy even more the nature they are part of. You slow down their clocks and they come to appreciate the walks differently. The walks not become exercise for exercise sake but physical activity for fun, pleasure, being with friends, and rich connection with the woods, fields, wind, sun, drizzle, and animals.

And one last thing Matt. Your obsession with exercise in rehab will also limit what you can do. Your crutches will become your friends but you need another friend. You will do everything to stay out of a wheelchair, to be bound to it and less human. But Matt becoming independent from the wheelchair will only harm you. Don't tell your occupational therapist you don't want to learn how to use a wheelchair. You will leave rehab with no wheelchair skills. You will regret this. Don't exercise to stay out of a wheelchair. That will later impede your opportunities to do things with your wife and son. It will leave you with thinking that wheelchair sports are not for you. Your lack of wheelchair skills will cause you pain too. Mostly Matt you will walk wobbly with crutches. You will even mourn the loss of a crutch when it breaks. But you will at times need to use a wheelchair. Your wheelchair will open things up for you too. You will enjoy playing sport in your chair and as a result meet new people who will become your pals. It can be fun too doing wheelies in your chair and chasing your son around the tennis courts in your new chariot.

All this might be difficult to imagine Matt. You may not even believe it is you writing this with the fountain pen your mum gave you. So, let me say this. Remember what you dreamed about becoming as a 10 year old. You never told anyone. You would imagine yourself as an astronaut, travelling in a spaceship to the moon, walking on it, and then firing off again to a distant planet where you'd meet new alien friends. You'll be ok Matt.

Responding to the Responses: Some Messy Notes

Four differently crafted responses have been offered. As a whole, they constitute an elusive and fragmentary 'big picture' of posthumanism in exercise-rehabilitation. This is the first paper to draw such a picture. It is messy. It shows that PDS means different things for different authors. It also shows diverse ways of communicating theory into practice. Despite the differences, the four responses belong together and help capturing the essence of PDS in action. This 'essence', however, is not easy to grasp at, not least because it is made of tensions, connections, and paradoxes. There is, in short, no essence to be captured; PDS is neither one thing nor an end in itself. It 'never exists, it never is. It must be invented, created differently each time' (St. Pierre, 2020, p. 4).

Bearing the above in mind, when we decided that each of us would write a separate response we also agreed to save some space to read them altogether and distil the emerging ideas that our responses, in relation to one another, might contain. In what follows below, we offer a product of such 'diffractive reading' (Geerts & Van der Tuin, 2016). Before proceeding, a caveat: readers will be disappointed if they expect to find conclusive statements and reach major epiphanies in relation to what is and how to do PDS. We invite them to think about the text as if it were a colleague who, after reading the four responses, shrugs her shoulders and says: "Ok, these are my notes. They are a bit messy, but I hope you find them useful".

In conventional rehabilitation, the posthuman potentials of exercise are rarely considered. Rehabilitation pushes exercise towards humanism, where life speaks in dualist terms and the human body is separated from the non-human world. This separation, often expressed as 'independence', is seen as desirable. It is casted as a compelling human attribute. Accordingly, exercise is used to claim back the humanity lost as a result of disability. Ironically, though, doing exercise in rehabilitation might help disabled people imagine new forms of doing humanity, which do not demonise disability. When people discover potential in disability, their purpose and experience in doing rehabilitative exercise unplugs from the conventional goals of normalisation inherent in rehabilitation practices.

Take: I swim. I sustained an injury, and I have been told to swim in order to fix my impaired body. However, I feel good when I swim. I do not feel good because I am repairing my body. Simply, I enjoy in the water. Even though my body is being subjected to medicalisation, I am come back to the pool because I enjoy it. The water makes sense of my disability. Swimmers became friends. The rubber ring became an ally. When I think about it, it is as if I discovered a glitch in the system. The normative rehabilitation system will try to correct this and drive me to its own expectations. I am always reminded why I am coming here (to return my life to 'normal'). At the beginning, I wanted to restore, preserve and maximise my functional ability. This would make my life easier. But now, I do exercise to live meaningfully with my impairment, which is now a feature of my reality of life. Why not? As Buetow, Martínez-Martín and McCormack (2019) noted, 'although it would still be wrong to presume that every person who is disabled wants to flourish, it may be just as wrong to assume that all persons with disabilities want to recover or normalise their lives' (p. 744).

Against this backdrop, PDS shifts rehabilitation from 'exercise as physiotherapy or medicine or restitution' to exercise as physiotherapy, medicine, restitution, but also pleasure. We find in 'pleasure' a key provocation for rehabilitation. Certainly, the calls to move towards pleasure are not new or specific to PDS. These have been made from narrative (Phoenix & Orr, 2014), psychobiology (Ekkekakis, 2017) and public health (Smith & Wightman, 2019) perspectives. PDS links with these but presents another way of theorising pleasure (see Goodley et al., 2018), where pleasure is not to be found inside disabled people but rather in their connections.

Together with pleasure, PDS injects a desire of connecting with disability. By connecting with disability, we mean affirming a disability identity and becoming with (as opposed to against) disability artefacts. Wheelchairs, prostheses and crutches are examples mentioned above. PDS is about learning to appreciate them and see them as friends, rather than enemies. Or as part of us. Or, *as us*.

There is a new subject, the posthuman subject that knocks on the door of our imagination. This subject *is* itself a connection. It is still human (even *more* human, as the ending of Javier's response suggests), but it is different from the humanist human. It is always already connected with others: humans, objects, fluids '*and ... and ... and*' (Deleuze and Guattari (1987, p. 25). Existence is not a self-centred, individual matter. It has never been, but now the subject knows it. As Bojack Horseman understood in an episode of the TV show he stars in, 'in this terrifying world, all we have are the connections we make'. So, why resist connections? Would not it be better to go in the other direction, to connect with others (human and non-human), together exploring new ways of being and doing? Shouldn't we include, as part of the goal of rehabilitation, learning how to find, expand and enjoy connections? What if we emphasise in the relational dimension of pleasure to promote exercise. Can rehabilitation programs use exercise to enable connections, to 'be with' rather than 'independent of' others? PDS suggests so. Its purpose is not to condemn rehabilitation that cares about independence, which is desired and claimed by many disabled people. Rather, the point is to broaden the discourse and consider creative directions for exploration. As Gibson, Carnevale and King (2012) pointed out,

> the task of rehabilitation shifts to facilitating creative assemblages rather than (only) independence. The goal becomes helping persons to live well through making and breaking connections. We do not mean to suggest that rehabilitation does not already do this in a number of creative ways. However, we are suggesting that reflecting on current practices and the tacit assumptions that underpin our work may help to liberate new and creative rehabilitation approaches.
>
> (p. 1897)

We must not be naïve, though. The possibilities to engage in life-enhancing connections are limited. For example, many disabled people simply cannot afford to purchase proper prosthesis to feel good with. Importantly, PDS does not perpetuate the individualistic ideology of the positivity myth, which insists that will and a positive attitude overcomes all barriers and is the certain pathway to achievement (Clifton, Llewellyn & Shakespeare, 2018). Enabling (as opposed to disabling) connections are not infinitely accessible. Austerity cuts connections. Neoliberal-ableism cuts connections. Many disabled people lead limited lives. Affirming different forms of being human through disability is made difficult for them. Their process of becoming at ease with the posthuman condition is rarely, if ever, a bed of roses. But exercise, sometimes, finds a way to help.

References

Abrams, T, Setchell, J, Thille, P, Mistry, B & Gibson, BE 2019, 'Affect, intensity, and moral assemblage in rehabilitation practice', *BioSocieties*, vol. 14, no. 1, pp. 23–45.
Braidotti, R 2013, *The Posthuman*, Cambridge, Polity Press.
Braidotti, R 2019, *Posthuman Knowledge*, Cambridge, Polity Press.
Buetow, SA, Martínez-Martín, P & McCormack, B 2019, 'Ultrabilitation: Beyond recovery-oriented rehabilitation', *Disability and Rehabilitation*, vol. 41, no. 6, pp. 740–745.
Clifton, S, Llewellyn, G & Shakespeare, T 2018, 'Quadriplegia, virtue theory, and flourishing: A qualitative study drawing on self-narratives', *Disability & Society*, vol. 33, no. 1, pp. 20–38.
Deleuze G & Guattari F 1987, *A Thousand Plateaus: Capitalism and Schizophrenia*, Minesota, University of Minnesota Press.

Dokumaci, A 2016, 'Micro-activist affordances of disability', in M Denecke, A Ganzert, I Otto & R Stock (eds), *Reclaiming Participation: Technology – Mediation – Collectivity*, Bielefeld, Transcript Verlag, pp. 67–83.

Edwards, G, Noreau, L, Boucher, N, Fougeyrollas, P, Grenier, Y, McFadyen, BJ & Vincent, C 2014, Disability, rehabilitation research and post-cartesian embodied ontologies– has the research paradigm changed, in *Research in Social Science and Disability*, Bingley, Emerald Group Publishing, pp. 73–102.

Ekkekakis, P. 2017, 'People have feelings! Exercise psychology in paradigmatic transition', *Current Opinion in Psychology*, vol. 16, pp. 84–88.

Fadyl, JK, Teachman, G & Hamdani, Y 2020, 'Problematizing 'productive citizenship' within rehabilitation services: Insights from three studies', *Disability and Rehabilitation*, vol. 42, no. 20, pp. 2959–2966.

Geerts, E & van der Tuin, I 2016, *Diffraction and Reading Diffractively*. Retrieved from http://newmaterialism.eu/almanac/d/diffraction.html

Gerlach, AJ, Teachman, G, Laliberte-Rudman, D, Aldrich, RM & Huot S 2018, 'Expanding beyond individualism: Engaging critical perspectives on occupation', *Scandinavian Journal of Occupational Therapy*, vol. 25, no. 1, pp. 35–43.

Gibson, BE. 2016, *Rehabilitation: A Post-critical Approach*. Boca Raton, CRC Press.

Gibson, BE, Carnevale, FA & King, G 2012, '"This is my way": Reimagining disability, in/dependence and interconnectedness of persons and assistive technologies', *Disability and Rehabilitation*, vol. 34, no. 22, pp. 1894–1899.

Goodley, D. 2021. *Disability and Other Human Questions*. Bingley (UK), Emerald Group Publishing.

Goodley, D, Lawthom, R & Runswick-Cole, K 2014, 'Posthuman disability studies', *Subjectivity*, vol. 7, no. 4, pp. 342–361.

Goodley, D, Lawthom, R, Liddiard, K & Runswick-Cole-Cole, K 2020, 'The desire for new humanisms', *Journal of Disability Studies in Education*, vol. 1, no. aop, pp. 1–20.

Goodley, D, Liddiard, K & Runswick-Cole, K 2018, 'Feeling disability: Theories of affect and critical disability studies', *Disability & Society*, vol. 33, no. 2, pp. 197–217.

Horton, J & Kraftl, P 2006, 'Not just growing up, but going on: Materials, spacings, bodies, situations', *Children's Geographies*, vol. 4, no. 3, pp. 259–276.

Monforte, J, Smith, B & Pérez-Samaniego V 2019, "It's not a part of me, but it is what it is': the struggle of becoming en-wheeled after spinal cord injury', *Disability and Rehabilitation*. doi: 10.1080/09638288.2019.1702725

Monforte, J, Pérez-Samaniego, V & Smith, B 2022, 'Ethnography and its potential to understand and transform the rehabilitation of spinal cord injury', in CM Hayre, D Muller & P Hackett (eds.), *Rehabilitation in Practice: Ethnographic Perspectives*. Singapore, Springer Nature.

Mossman, M. 2001, 'Acts of becoming: Autobiography, Frankenstein, and the postmodern body', *Postmodern Culture*, vol. 11, no. 3. doi:10.1353/pmc.2001.0012

Nicholls, DA 2017, *The End of Physiotherapy*. London, Routledge.

Papadimitriou, C 2008, 'Becoming en-wheeled: The situated accomplishment of re-embodiment as a wheelchair user after spinal cord injury', *Disability & Society*, vol. 23, no. 7, pp. 691–704.

Papathomas, A, Williams, TL & Smith, B 2015, 'Understanding physical activity participation in spinal cord injured populations: Three narrative types for consideration', *International Journal of Qualitative Studies on Health and Well-Being*, vol. 10, no. 1, p. 27295.

Phoenix C & Orr, N 2014, 'Pleasure: A forgotten dimension of physical activity in older age', *Social Science & Medicine*, vol. 115, pp. 94–102.

Smith, B & Wightman, L 2021, 'Promoting physical activity to disabled people: Messengers, messages, guidelines and communication formats', *Disability and Rehabilitation*, vol. 43, no. 24, pp. 3427–3431.

Stiker, HJ 2019, *A History of Disability*. Michigan, University of Michigan Press.

Shildrick, M 2015, '"Why should our bodies end at the skin?": Embodiment, boundaries, and somatechnics', *Hypatia*, vol. 30, no. 1, pp. 13–29.

Straus, E 1952, 'The upright posture', *Psychiatric Quarterly*, vol. 26, no. 4, pp. 529–561.

St. Pierre, EA 2020, 'Post qualitative inquiry, the Refusal of method, and the risk of the New', *Qualitative Inquiry*. doi: 1077800419863005

Winance, M 2019, "Don't touch/push me!' From disruption to intimacy in relations with one's wheelchair: An analysis of relational modalities between persons and objects', *The Sociological Review*, vol. 67, no. 2, pp. 428–443.

Chapter 13

Para-Sport Activism in South Korea

Inhyang Choi, Damian Haslett and Brett Smith

As the Paralympic Games is becoming increasingly popular, para-sport activism is gaining attention around the world due to the potential of para-athletes to highlight forms of oppression that disabled people face in society (see Haslett & Smith, 2020). Smith, Bundon and Best (2016) defined para-sport activism as an action taken by para-athletes or para-sport organisations to challenge the oppression of disabled people either *within* para-sport contexts or *in wider* society. Moreover, several recent academic works are now available on para-sport activism (e.g., Bundon & Hurd Clarke, 2014; Braye, 2016; Choi, Haslett & Smith, 2019; Choi, Haslett, Monforte & Smith, 2020; Haslett, Choi and Smith, 2020a; Haslett, Monforte, Choi and Smith, 2020b; Powis, 2018; Smith et al., 2016). These studies have, for example, explored the reframing discourse of para-sports relating to disability identity and activism for broader social change (Powis, 2018), or the influences on performing disability activism from the perspective of Irish Para-athletes (Haslett et al., 2020a). Despite the growth of literature in this field, empirical evidence about para-sport activism has been circumscribed to Western cultures, such as United Kingdom, Ireland and Canada, with little known of the situation of non-Western countries. Given this lack of knowledge, this chapter addresses para-sport activism in what is considered a non-Western country, namely South Korea.

One of the key cultural elements that influence how people approach social interaction in South Korea is Confucianism; a core philosophical system advocating group harmony with hierarchical order for political, social, and family relations (Sleziak, 2014). Confucianism has been dominant in South Korea, reflecting not only what identity people create but also outlining how people should behave in certain contexts (Choi, 2005; Choi et al., 2020; Sleziak, 2014). Against this backdrop, in this chapter we discuss disability activism and the Paralympic movement within a South Korean historical context. Drawing on empirical investigations recently undertaken, we highlight activist propensities between para-athletes and disabled non-athletes and the influence of Confucianism on para-sport activism. Given the importance of cultural milieus that emerged from these findings, next attention turns to how Western (e.g., modern liberalism; individualist approach according to equality and rights) and

DOI: 10.4324/9781003153696-16

East Asian (e.g., Confucianism) culture can both be enabling and constraining para-sport activism. After this, we reflect on how para-sport activism can be promoted by highlighting contemporary approaches from the International Paralympic Committee and the Korea Paralympic Committee. In doing so, we discuss the perspectives of cultural legacy to promote para-sport activism in South Korea. We end by providing directions for further research on para-sport activism as a unique contemporary perspective within wider athlete activism research. Before this however, we feel it is useful to position ourselves as authors.

The three authors of this chapter have diverse experiences in research on disability sport. That said, with regard to cultural position, Inhyang (female, South Korean, non-disabled) has lived in Eastern cultural (e.g., Confucianism) society for over 25 years but has however been educated in the United Kingdom where she has completed her PhD. While Damian (male, Irish, non-disabled) and Brett (male, British, non-disabled but for several years a mental health service user) have lived and been educated in Western culture (e.g., modern liberalism) but have also had mutual experiences in international collaboration with people of diverse cultural backgrounds. These lived experiences are important to recognise as we have shaped this chapter with regard to questions poised, examples provided, areas focused upon, and recommendations given for future research, for instance, we draw attention to each author's native culture. We will now discuss a historical overview of disability activism and the Paralympic movement in South Korea.

Disability Activism and the Paralympic Movement in South Korea

Due partly to Confucian cultural norms (e.g., societal hierarchy) and historical customs (e.g., disability is seen as a punishment inflicted by supernatural demons upon people whose ancestors lived an immoral life), many South Koreans still perceive disability to be undesirable (Kim, Shin, Yu and Kim, 2017). Thus, disabled people have historically experienced unequal treatment in most segments of South Korean society (Ahn and Kim, 2018). Then in 1988, the South Korean government established eligibility criteria for disabled people to access welfare benefits focusing on physical and functional limitations, but this initiative neglected a focus on social barriers, thereby leading to limited support for a range of disability groups.

The disability activism movement in South Korea initially emerged from the unequal treatment of disabled people. The evolution of South Korea's disability rights movement has undergone three broad phases: the quickening phase (1945–mid-1980s—providing care, led by the parents of disabled children), the developing phase (1989–mid-1990s—granting rights, led by people with mild disabilities), and the diversity phase (late 1990s–now—ensuring self-determination, led by people with severe disabilities) (Kim, 2008; You and Hwang, 2018). Although the documented history of the disability rights movement in South Korea is more limited than in Western countries, and discrimination persists

(Kim, 2008), their movements have had some success in terms of improving disability rights. Accordingly, the needs of disabled people have traditionally been addressed by enacting or amending laws regarding their freedom of movement or by improving awareness. For example, in 1991, 'Disabled Persons Day' was introduced to raise public awareness of the difficulties faced by disabled people and to promote their rights. Further, the unfair eligibility criteria for disabled people to access welfare benefits were abolished in 2019.

It has been claimed that one of the strongest catalysts for disability activism in South Korea was the country's hosting of the Seoul 1988 Paralympic Summer Games and the PyeongChang 2018 Paralympic Winter Games. For example, following the Seoul 1988 Paralympic Summer Games, considerable changes occurred in raising awareness of disability and protecting disability rights by enacting new regulations and laws (Son, 2014). More recently, the PyeongChang 2018 Paralympic Winter Games also brought positive attention to disability rights, such as improving disability facilities and promoting para-sport programmes. Thus, hosting the Paralympic games may have created a better awareness about the disability issues by providing a wider visibility of disability and supporting a more inclusive society.

Nevertheless, reactions to the Paralympics games were not all positive in South Korea. In 1987, young disabled activists discovered that the budget for the Seoul 1988 Paralympic Summer Games was over four times the total welfare budget for disabled people who were not elite athletes (Son, 2014). In response to this, they organised a mass public protest encouraging people to boycott the Paralympics games and demanding greater resources and services for disabled people. Further, despite hosting two Paralympic games, the actual events were received less attention than the Olympic Games. Indeed, in terms of media coverage, the PyeongChang 2018 Paralympic Winter Games received greater media attention outside South Korea than inside the country. For instance, while Channel 4 in the United Kingdom dedicated a total of 100 hours to the PyeongChang 2018 Paralympic Winter Games, South Korean television gave a meagre 18 hours of coverage. However, para-sports in South Korea are increasingly becoming a strong platform to highlight disability rights issues (Choi et al., 2019, 2020; Haslett et al., 2020a; Smith et al., 2016). In what follows, we discuss this potential, drawing on two empirical studies of para-sport activism in South Korea (e.g., Choi et al., 2019, 2020).

A Confucian Approach to Para-Sport Activism in South Korea

Choi et al. (2019) used a mixed methodology to explore para-athlete activism in South Korea. In the quantitative phase they hypothesised that disabled non-athletes would be more likely to engage in activist behaviours (e.g., protesting, boycotting) and then measured the extent to which participants would engage in activist behaviours using Corning and Myers' (2002) Activism Orientation Scale. However, they found that para-athletes in their sample scored higher than disabled non-athletes. Thus, the authors suggested that para-athletes were actually more willing to engage in activism than disabled non-athletes in the South Korean disabled community. In the next qualitative phase, their interview data suggested that para-athletes with a 'high activist orientation' were motivated to engage in activism for broader social good by their high social influence with the spotlight of the PyeongChang 2018 Paralympic Winter Games. By contrast, para-athletes with a 'low activist orientation' faced barriers to engaging in activism, such as emotional cost or the fear of a perceived backlash (e.g., being disadvantaged within sport contexts).

In a follow-up study, Choi et al. (2020) interviewed Korea Paralympic Committee (KPC) board members and para-athletes to understand the influence of Confucianism on para-sport activism. The authors indicated five Confucian values, such as positional hierarchy, age hierarchy, factionalism, collectivism and parents' influence. All values have the dual capacity to encourage or discourage para-athletes' engagement in activism. For example, in the context of positional hierarchy, para-athletes are culturally perceived as 'elite athletes' rather than 'disabled people' and, in turn, are given a higher status than disabled non-athletes within the disability community. Thus, athletes with a strong activist identity could use their positional power as a platform for advocacy. However, within the narrower para-sport system than disability society, para-athletes would not engage in activism for fear of disrespecting those who are deemed to occupy a 'higher position' (e.g., board members, non-disabled stakeholders). In other words, given their two-sided identity linked to positional hierarchy, some para-athletes took advantage of their power on diverse social and political issues, but they had difficulty in engaging in sport-based activism because this could be deemed disrespectful by the KPC.

Similarly, age hierarchy implies that younger people are expected to follow and respect older people, even if the age gap is minimal (Yum, 1988). The tacit value of age hierarchy within South Korean para-sport contexts has become a facilitator for older people (e.g., senior athletes, NPC board members) but a barrier for young athletes to participate in activism. For instance, a younger athlete-activist in the study who presented his divergent opinions to senior athletes believed he was ignored and considered to be impertinent and antagonistic (Choi et al., 2020). Also, in this study the Confucian value of factionalism – strong informal personal connection such as similar educational background or hometown – was shown to be closely intertwined with encouraging or discouraging para-sport activism. For example, Choi et al. (2020) highlighted how one elite para-athlete blew the whistle on corruption involving board members of the KPC and, subsequently, this person was ostracised by people who belonged to a rival faction in the KPC and excluded from the national team as a result of activism against them. Another athlete who graduated from the same university as one of the board members was granted a place in the national team instead of him. Thus, some para-athletes avoided becoming embroiled in 'activist' disputes between different factions because they feared repercussions from superior factions, which could stifle social justice efforts.

Collectivism, another core value of Confucianism, can be discussed in terms of two different types. Horizontal collectivism (e.g., the value of seeing oneself as similar to others and highlighting common goals) promotes cooperation among people who have a common activist identity. However, vertical collectivism (e.g., being loyal to one's group and adhering to hierarchical interpersonal relations) discourages athlete activism, as it may result in negative repercussions from high-status board members. According to the results of the study by Choi et al. (2020), one athlete activist spoke out for the development of his sport team against KPC. However, as a result of his behaviour, the KPC board members deemed his entire team to be disrespectful. Consequently, other athletes from the same sport team evaded him because they thought their group was reviled by his dogmatic behaviour. However, they also criticised him for not participating in activism despite being a medallist. This contradictory feedback from peer athletes and KPC board members led him to face an identity crisis, oscillating between an athlete-activist identity and a collectivist identity.

Lastly, parents' attitude has a tremendous influence on identity formation and behaviour of para-athletes, as children should submit to their parents in Confucian value (Yum, 1988). On the one hand, parents' involvement in advocacy could support athletes' activism (Poon-McBrayer and McBrayer, 2014). On the other hand, a drive to overprotect their disabled children and fear of the stigma associated with disability may push parents to bar para-athletes from any outside activities, and any act of rebellion against one's parents is considered immoral. For example, one para-athlete stopped his activism because of his parents' worries that he would be exposed to the media and face social stigma and public shame. Importantly, despite the influences of Confucian ethics on hierarchical social relationships, these two studies indicated how para-sports could be a strong platform for advocacy for the disability rights both within and beyond sport in the unique cultural background of South Korea. Having established the impact of Confucianism on the development of activist identities, we now focus on differentiating cross-cultural understandings of para-sport activism between the inherent value of Western liberalism and Eastern forms of Confucianism.

A Cross-Cultural Understanding of Para-Sport Activism: A Perspective from Western and East Asian Studies

In many Western countries, *modern liberalism* strongly emphasises individualism according to the principle of equality and rights (Tseng, 2016). Thus, modern liberalism considers that the essence of the rule is to negatively set a limit on individual freedom to protect individual rights and freedom (Langlois, 2003). This philosophical frame is also based on a liberal constitutional socio-political system in which individuals become the basic element of social relationships; thus, family morality is retrenched largely to the private sphere in liberalism (Tseng, 2016). By contrast, as highlighted before, the East Asian cultural frame of Confucianism creates a hierarchical social order where the social status of an individual should be dependent on their position in society and the political system; thus, a superior power is absolute (Choi et al., 2020). Confucianism also emphasises cooperation and harmony in a collectivist frame (Choi et al., 2020). These different histories, cultures, and ideologies shape people's behaviour in certain situations, including disability, sports, and activism, resulting in the differences in para-sport activism between Western and East Asian research.

Broadly speaking, a key difference between Western and East Asian research on para-sport activism is how para-athletes perceive public attitudes towards disability equality and inclusion in society. Western-based studies have indicated that disabled elite athletes can perceive that disabled people are treated mostly fairly, equally, and respectfully in society (Smith et al., 2016). By contrast, disabled elite athletes in South Korea believe there is a need to speak out for societal change to improve disability rights from the currently poor and unfair conditions, even though these rights have been legally settled in several documents (Choi et al., 2019).

Furthermore, as Choi et al. (2019) argued, para-athletes perceive their influence has increased with the successful hosting of the PyeongChang 2018 Paralympic Winter Games and have sought to amplify the disability movement through a social, cultural, and inspirational voice. Disabled recreational athletes and non-athletes have also voiced the importance of para-athletes in terms of amplifying disability stories within and beyond sport in South Korea. However, elsewhere, such as in the United Kingdom and Ireland, athletes have said that activism is part of the para-sport story but not a responsibility of all para-athletes; thus, engagement in disability activism for broader social good has been deemed incompatible with para-athletes who choose to reject a disabled first identity (Powis, 2018). Examples included some Irish para-athletes expressing their displeasure towards being contextualised as an inspirational icon for the audience (Haslett et al., 2020b). In this context, non-sport disability activists have considered using para-sports as a vehicle to enhance disability activism can be counterproductive because it can focus on the development of disability sport activism rather than support stories about the day-to-day realities of living with a disability (Braye, Dixon and Gibbons, 2015; Haslett et al., 2020a).

In South Korea, the parents' influence has meant that there is a hierarchy in athlete–parent relationships and disability is performed mainly within the home, whereas parents in the Western rights-based paradigm primarily contribute to supporting disabled children's independence outside the home (Poon-McBrayer & McBrayer, 2014). This has led to para-athletes' voices in South Korea being oppressed and often filtered through the views of their family members. In a similar approach, KPC board members believe para-athletes would follow their vision for disability movement in the hierarchical order of relationship in South Korea. However, in the West, some National Paralympic Committees considered para-athletes as independent individuals and were concerned about them having a disability activist identity that could incur a cost to para-athletes' unforeseen mental health due to public criticism and social pressure (Haslett et al., 2020b).

Lastly, when compared over the limited but growing connection between disability, sport, and activism, Irish and South Koreans value specific and relevant information as a condition for being a political activist (Haslett et al., 2020b). However, Irish para-athletes have more regarded politically informed knowledge as a priority requirement to engage in activism; thus, para-athlete activists are expected to be rewarded proportionately to their capability for disability politics (Haslett et al., 2020b). By contrast, South Korean para-athletes have stressed the importance of factionalism. This cultural difference shows a distinction between outer political action regulated by rules and inner moral conduct governed by autonomy that is blurred through Confucianism (Choi et al., 2020).

Although the West and East Asian culturally based studies seem quite different from, and even opposed to, each other, and notwithstanding their essential chronological difference, some similarities between them can still be drawn for perspectives on para-sport activism. Both appear to suggest that government and administration should guarantee some basic means for individual development (e.g., disability rights) (Choi et al., 2020; Haslett et al., 2020a). In modern Western culture, corresponding to the rule of law, the government should guarantee individual rights, which are expanded to include disability rights for the disabled community. In Confucianism, government, as a high level of social status, should play a predominant role in promoting social prosperity and the welfare of people through their efficient administration. Further, regardless of the Confucian environment in society, the athletes' unique status is exercised in activism in both positive and negative ways. From Western viewpoints from Canadian (Bundon & Hurd Clarke, 2014), British (Smith et al., 2016), and Irish contexts (Haslett et al., 2020a), and from an Eastern perspective in South Korea (Choi et al., 2020), there is positive evidence from empirical studies that para-athletes prefer to advocate for social change to improve para-sport contexts in contrast to activism to improve the lives of disabled people in wider societies. In addition, these studies have also indicated that para-athletes could be reluctant to engage in activism because of public criticism and lack of time due to sport and work commitments.

We have highlighted the importance of the cultural context on para-sport activism. Now that we present how international and national Paralympic committees exercise their influence on promoting disability activism through para-sports at the international and national levels.

Promoting Para-Sport Activism: Approaches from the International Paralympic Committee (IPC) and Korea Paralympic Committee (KPC)

With the growth of research in para-sport activism, Paralympic committees have also contributed to promoting disability activism at an organisational level. In 2019, the IPC produced the 2019–2022 Strategic Plan (IPC, 2019), in which a key aspect is to promote disability activism through para-sports, by stressing the importance of cultivating a generation of para-athletes who can work as advocates for disability rights (Objective 3.6). Moreover, in 2020, the IPC and United Nations Human Rights signed a landmark Co-operation Agreement to deliver a global communications campaign around the coming Tokyo Paralympic Games that aims to change global attitudes towards disability and further the human rights agenda. Cementing this strategy, the IPC used the Tokyo 2020 Paralympic Games as a platform to launch the WeThe15 (www.wethe15.org) campaign that is bringing together the largest ever coalition of international organisations with the aim to end discrimination against disabled people within ten years (i.e., 15% of the whole world).

Historically, in the KPC, the focus has been on developing para-athletes' performance through para-sport sciences and coach support. However, there has been a transition since the new President, Jin-Owan Jung was elected in January 2021. President Jung produced a new strategic plan for 2021–2025 regarding the direction of the KPC to reduce limitations resulting from Confucian values and to promote disability rights. Specifically, to break down factionalism in para-sports, the KPC highlighted the importance of autonomy and independence for each department in the para-sport administration (Objective 1.1). As an example of promoting para-athletes' rights, the KPC aimed to develop guidance for the protection of rights for para-sports and para-athletes (Objective 7.1), called for departments of human rights in all disability sport organisations in South Korea (Objective 7.3), and established mandatory courses on human/disability rights for all key stakeholders, such as coaches, athletes, physiologists, and referees (Objective 7.4).

To promote disability rights in wider society, the KPC specifically outlined the disability rights movement in relation to the para-sport platform. Accordingly, it aimed to establish over 150 Bandabi (disability) sport centres throughout the nation to emphasise the legacy of the Paralympic Games (Objective 8.1) and to support recreational disability sport events (Objective 9.1). The KPC also highlighted its ambition to improve public awareness of disability rights by training para-athletes to become disability rights instructors and placing them at public educational institutions (Objective 13.1) and launching a national Paralympic Day where both disabled and non-disabled people can play sports, enjoy events such as wheelchair dance performances, and meet with elite para-athletes (Objective 13.5).

The KPC's shift in focus emphasises the importance of cultural legacy by showing how Confucian values have led to influence on promoting para-sports at the organisational level in South Korea. In *Outliers: The Story of Success*, Gladwell (2008) described the power of cultural legacy creating an invisible influence on social attitudes and behaviour through intergenerational practices.

> Cultural legacies are powerful forces. They have deep roots and long lives. They persist, generation after generation, virtually intact, even as the economic and social and demographic conditions that spawned them have vanished, and they play such a role in directing attitudes and behaviour that we cannot make sense of our world without them.
>
> (2008, p.125)

While South Koreans no longer learn Confucian theory at school, Confucian philosophy is still the dominant social system and provides the basis for day-to-day life, informing not only the identity people portray but also the words they speak and how they behave in certain contexts (Choi, 2005). The Confucian discourse is noteworthy for being more than a philosophy and for delving into the abundant richness of the tradition to encourage para-sport activism. In this chapter, we offer two perspectives of Confucian cultural legacies on para-sport activism.

First, KPC board members can promote disability activism given their power. Power and culture are continuously being reproduced in the dynamic interactions between individuals and social environments (Kemmelmeier and Kuhnen, 2012). KPC board members have upheld traditional Confucian customs by maintaining a hierarchical structure within the para-sport community; in this structure, they sit in the highest position. Given that the KPC has significant influence and power in the South Korean disability community (Choi et al., 2020), the KPC Strategic Plan 2021–2025 shows that they are well-positioned to lead social change through the disability movement.

Second, the KPC's movement can influence a cultural movement in disability and para-sport society. Before the announcement of the KPC Strategic Plan 2021–2025, the nature of the strong hierarchical culture deteriorated into ostensible bad habits over time. Accordingly one of the Confucian cultural values – the ruler-subject relationship – has degenerated in such a way that only the subject's loyalty to the ruler was emphasised within a hierarchical society rather than the ruler being situated as the subject's ideal role model. However, with the wave of human rights movements in contemporary South Korean society, the strategic plan shows that the KPC aims to be in the vanguard to reduce the shortcomings of Confucian values and produce long-lasting changes in Confucian society. In line with this approach, the KPC emphasises ethical values in the social realm and promotes disability activism through the platform of para-sports. Objective 1.1 demonstrates the relationship between the unique Confucian cultural context and para-sports and underscores the aim to refute factionalism, while Objectives 7.1 and 13.1 show its ambition to create a safe space for para-athletes and those interested in disability activism.

The KPC has tailored the plan to national and cultural needs, as the IPC's strategic plan would be difficult to critically employ at the national level, given the complexity of understanding national cultural intricacy. Nevertheless, the IPC's movement for disability and human rights is crucial as the KPC starts to demonstrate its vision of using its platform to promote para-sports and disability rights by following the IPC's 2019–2022 Strategic Plan. In other words, the disability rights movement at the organisational level (e.g., IPC, KPC) is positioned to foster disability rights at their respective governance levels beyond academia. In line with this movement, scholars could also focus on diverse approaches to para-sport activism with regard to strategy, research, and communication.

Possible Directions for Further Research

One suggestion moving forward lies in developing a quantitative approach to explore para-sport activism. Choi et al. (2019) contributed to providing a meaningful baseline for future quantitative research on para-sport activism in disabled populations by framing the sample of para-athletes within a cultural context that also accounts for the perspectives of disabled people who are not athletes.

Further, researchers should continue to focus on enabling meaningful approaches to para-sport activism, grounded in unique cultural milieus (McGannon & Schinke, 2017; McGannon & Smith, 2015). The route of the disability rights movement in Eastern cultures might not be the same as that of Western cultures, given the different historical and cultural backgrounds. The multiplicity of the lived experience of oppression is also not always reflected in disability activism (Haslett et al., 2020a). When this cultural complexity is overlooked in research, the experiences of minorities may be lost (Ryba & Wright, 2005), and the perpetuation of the stereotyping of these minorities may be reinforced (Ryba, Stambulova, Si and Schinke, 2013). Thus, the intersectional and eclectic perspectives are important to understand the culture of activism within the disability and para-sport society.

In a similar approach, future studies could seek to inform strategic plans for para-sport activist initiatives, such as the IPCs, to be considered not only at the international level but also at the national level. Given the complexity of understanding social attitudes, perceptions, and the unique intricacy of national culture, overlooking cultural subtleties can lead to unintended consequences of international strategic visions in different ways. As Haslett et al. (2020b) suggested, the IPC's 'top-down' strategy can be implemented, resisted, or (re)interpreted at a national level due to different political systems (e.g., democratic or authoritarian), institutionalised cultural values, and political interests. Similarly, future research can examine the ways in which national-level activist discourses influence and shape global activist discourses (Haslett et al., 2020b). This contemporary approach could constitute an important stimulus for the development of disability sport and disability rights, promoting the best contexts to support para-sports and the disabled community.

Future research can also examine how key stakeholders in different positions draw upon different cultural activist discourses over time to argue for or against promoting activism. For instance, Haslett et al. (2020b) indicated that different stakeholders drew on different activist discourses, and this resulted in argumentative tension among stakeholders. Likewise, KPC board members stuck to traditional Confucian customs by maintaining a hierarchical structure within the para-sport society where they sit in the highest position, despite having played an active role as athlete-activists in tackling unfair hierarchical treatment of disability in the past. Thus, future research could consider activist narratives from current and retired elite para-athletes, as well as board members who are retired athletes, working at para-sport organisations at the international (IPC) or national (NPC) level.

There is a need for research to approach para-sport activism through many different perspectives, as the current literature on para-sport activism is limited to the Paralympic Games and the IPC's framework. Researchers could consider expanding the exploration of activism surrounding events such as the Special Olympics (sport organisation for intellectually disabled people), Deaflympics (international game for deaf athletes at an elite level), and Asian Para Games (multi-sport game for Asian athletes with physical disabilities). Such studies could explore the disability sport activism that comes from recreational athlete activism.

Finally, researchers should consider para-athlete activism as a policy factor influencing the development of para-sports and disability politics. Investigations are needed on actions the National Paralympic Committee could take towards athlete activism at the organisational level (e.g., controlling athletes' activism or prompting it with their credible voices). We could also consider how policymakers can amplify their legislative voices for a wider disability landscape by understanding the unique and intrinsic complexity of the disability sport domain (Dowling, Leopkey and Lee, 2018; Patatas, De Bosscher, Derom and De Rycke, 2020).

We would like to finish by encouraging researchers to critically move forward in approaching para-sport activism. We also believe that more disabled people should be encouraged to lead research in this area, in part, because the positive societal impact of para-sports is overemphasised as an "academic discourse on the Paralympics being written predominantly by non-disabled people" (Braye et al., 2015, p. 45). We hope this chapter has helped scholars and practitioners think more critically about para sport activism in South Korea.

References

Ahn, J.C. and Kim, M.C. (2018) Ethical issues related to the disability sports rating classification. *Korea Philosophic Society for Sport and Dance*, 26(4), pp. 31–45.

Braye, S. (2016) 'I'm not an activist': An exploratory investigation into retired British Paralympic athletes' views on the relationship between the Paralympic games and disability equality in the United Kingdom. *Disability & Society*, 31(9), pp. 1288–1300. doi:10.1080/09687599.2016.1251392

Braye, S., Dixon, K. and Gibbons, T. (2015) The 2012 Paralympics and perceptions of disability in the UK, in K. Dixon & T. Gibbons (eds.), *The Impact of the 2012 Olympic and Paralympic Games: Diminishing Contrasts, Increasing Varieties*. London: Palgrave Macmillian, pp. 15–34.

Bundon, A. and Hurd Clarke, L. (2014) Honey or vinegar? Athletes with disabilities discuss strategies for advocacy within the Paralympic movement. *Journal of Sport and Social Issues*, 39(5), pp. 351–370. doi:10.1177/0193723514557823

Choi, B.Y. (2005). 한국 사회의 차별과 억압 [Discrimination and repression of South Korea]. 서울:지식산업사.

Choi, I., Haslett, D., Monforte, J. and Smith, B. (2020) The influence of Confucianism on Para-sport activism. *Sociology of Sport Journal*. 38(2), pp. 140–148.

Choi, I., Haslett, D. and Smith, B. (2021) Disabled athlete activism in South Korea: A mixed-method study. *International Journal of Sport and Exercise Psychology*, 19(4), pp. 473–487. doi:10.1080/1612197X.2019.1674903

Corning, A.F. and Myers, D.J. (2002) Individual orientation toward engagement in social action. *Political Psychology*, 23(4), pp. 703–729.

Dowling, M., Leopkey, B. and Lee, S., (2018) Governance in sport: A scoping review. *Journal of Sport Management*, 32(5), pp. 438–455.

Gladwell, M. (2008). *Outliers: The Story of Success*. New York: Little Brown and Company, p. 125.

Haslett, D., Choi, I. and Smith, B. (2020a). Para athlete activism: A qualitative examination of disability activism through Paralympic sport in Ireland. *Psychology of Sport and Exercise*. doi:10.1016/j.psychsport.2019.101639

Haslett, D., Monforte, J., Choi, I. and Smith, B. (2020b) Promoting Para athlete activism: Critical insights from key stakeholders in Ireland. *Sociology of Sport Journal*, 37(4), pp. 273–282. doi:10.1123/ssj.2019-0174

Haslett, D. and Smith, B. (2020) Disability sports and social activism, in M. Berghs, T. Chataika, Y. El-Lahib, & K. Dube (eds.), *Routledge Handbook of Disability Activism*. New York: Routledge, pp. 197–208.

International Paralympic Committee [IPC]. (2019) International Paralympic Committee Strategic Plan 2019 to 2022. Available at: https://www.paralympic.org/

Kemmelmeier, M. and Kuhnen, U. (2012) Culture as process: The dynamics of cultural stability and change. *Social Psychology*, 43(4), pp. 171–173.

Kim, K.M. (2008) The current status and future of centers for independent living in Korea. *Disability and Society*, 23(1), pp. 67–76.

Kim, K.Y., Shin, Y.R., Yu, D.C. and Kim, D.K. (2017) The meaning of social inclusion for people with disabilities in South Korea. *International Journal of Disability, Development and Education*, 64(1), pp. 19–32.

Langlois, A.J. (2003) Human rights and modern liberalism: a critique. *Political Studies*, 51(10), pp. 509–523.

McGannon, K.R. and Schinke, R.J. (2017) Cross-cultural considerations in exercise promotion. A cultural sport psychology perspective, in M.L. Sachs & S. Razon (eds.), *Applied Exercise Psychology: The Challenging Journey from Motivation to Adherence*. New York: Routledge, pp. 160–174.

McGannon, K.R. and Smith, B. (2015) Centralizing culture in cultural sport psychology research: The potential of narrative inquiry and discursive psychology. *Psychology of Sport and Exercise*, 17, pp. 79–87.

Patatas, J.M., De Bosscher, V., Derom, I. and De Rycke, J. (2020) Managing parasport: An investigation of sport policy factors and stakeholders influencing para-athletes' career pathways. *Sport Management Review*, 23(5), pp, 937–951.

Poon-McBrayer, K.F. and McBrayer, P.A. (2014) Plotting Confucian and disability rights paradigms on the advocacy–activism continuum: Experiences of Chinese parents of children with dyslexia in Hong Kong. *Cambridge Journal of Education*, 44(1), pp. 93–111.

Powis, B. (2018) Transformation, advocacy and voice in disability sport research, in T.F. Carter, D. Burdsey, & M. Doidge (eds.), *Transforming Sport: Knowledges, Practices, Structures*. Abingdon and New York: Routledge, pp. 248–259. doi:10.4324/9781315167909-18

Ryba, T.V., Stambulova, N., Si, G. and Schinke, R.J. (2013) ISSP position stand: Culturally competent research and practice in sport and exercise psychology. *International Journal of Sport and Exercise Psychology*, 11(2), pp. 123–142.

Ryba, T.V. and Wright, H.K. (2005) From mental game to cultural praxis: A cultural studies model's implications for the future of sport psychology. *Quest*, 57(2), pp. 192–212.

Sleziak, T. (2014) The Influence of Confucian values on modern hierarchies and social communication in China and Korea. *A Comparative Outline*, 8(2), pp. 207–232.

Smith, B., Bundon, A. and Best, M. (2016) Disability sport and activist identities: A qualitative study of narratives of activism among elite athletes with impairment. *Psychology of Sport and Exercise*, 26, pp. 139–148.

Son, C.W. (2014) *The Motives of Self-sacrifice in Korean American Culture, Family, and Marriage: From Filial Piety to Familial Integrity*. Eugene: Wipf & Stock.

Tseng, R. (2016) The idea of freedom in comparative perspective: Critical comparisons between the discourses of liberalism and neo-Confucianism. *Philosophy East and West*, 66(2), pp. 539–558.

You, D.C. and Hwang, S.K. (2018) Achievements of and challenges facing the Korean Disabled People's Movement. *Disability & Society*, 33(8), pp. 1259–1279.

Yum, J.O. (1988) The impact of Confucianism on interpersonal relationships and communication patterns in east Asia. *Communication Monographs*, 55(4), pp. 374–388.

Chapter 14

Conclusion
The Future of Disability Sport Research

P. David Howe, Ben Powis and James Brighton

In discussing, organising, and editing this volume *Researching Disability Sport* we established a shared vision regarding what we saw as important for our field moving forward. We in essence have a dream for the future of this field, and we hope that you the reader have bought into our vision. The high-quality scholarship and the scholars that have given their labour to help us produce this volume is not the only excellent scholarship within our field; rather we wanted to bring together scholars who engage with the field in ways that push us all to think differently about disability sport research. It is important that you as a reader of this edited volume, regardless of whether you are an undergraduate student or an over-seasoned academic (like the first author of this conclusion), continually reflect on how your research can be more robust and yet accessible to the widest possible audience.

In other words, we want this volume to stimulate discussions in classrooms, online and in social spaces on the conference circuit of how our field should develop as well as being a pedagogical tool and/or core text that will help students and academic alike embrace high quality scholarship. What we have presented here has been our vision of theoretically engaged and methodologically robust approaches to disability sport research. By looking at the field differently and providing a platform for cutting-edge research, this volume is our attempt to crip (McRuer, 2006, 2018) disability sport studies. Of course, pioneering and innovative practices, by nature, are constantly evolving; how will the field develop over the next decades is in part down to you the academic readers at every stage from students to full professors.

Who Represents the Field?

The politics of representation in the field of disability studies is so often an issue (Goodley et al., 2019). Who has the right to a voice and who is empowered to reproduce it is a constant point of debate. In the process of putting this collection together we were confronted with the desire to include an equal number of authors who have first-hand experience of disability and those who do not and are actively researching in the field. We managed to achieve this aim, but it was

DOI: 10.4324/9781003153696-17

not as easy as we feel it should be. Many authors in the volume nicely articulate all sides of the debate regarding disability representation in both writing and research. It is our hope that this volume will encourage more developing scholars who experience disability to actively engage in chronicling their lifeworld. What is clear to us is that the identity politics that surrounds so many marginalised groups has not had an impact on disability sport research in the same way that it has for studies of gender, sexuality, and race in the context of the social science of sport. There are also fewer social science scholars who experience disability employed in the higher education sector than these other marginalised groups. We believe this should not be the case and in the world of disability sport research (small as it is) equal representation for scholars that experience disability is unfortunately a long way off – in part because traditional disability sport was seen as an apolitical space in which to do research. It is our hope that reading this volume has liberated your mind from this notion!

First-hand experience of disability was not the only issue in relation to representation when putting together this volume. Overall, we feel that disability sport research is far too white and Eurocentric in its construction. The editors of this volume are all white, cisgender, heterosexual, and middle-class men. Of this privilege we are mindful. We as a collective of readers and researchers need to consider ways and means of encouraging a wide variety of people with all sorts of intersecting identities to engage in this type of research. This is generally an issue in other sport studies subdisciplines as well. A diversity of voices that are more global and ethnically diverse is paramount because it will add to the rich tapestry of research that people wish to engage in. There are of course issues regarding the language that is the register of global academe being English. Many non-native English speakers lament that in order to get notice they must publish in this language. Imagine, for example, what wonders we as social thinkers would be missing if the vast majority of work non-English scholarship had not been translated. When we consider the utility and importance of how the English-speaking academy has adopted French social theory – including the work of Michel Foucault, Pierre Bourdieu, Simone de Beauvoir and Maurice Merleau-Ponty among many others. What might we be missing in disability sport research that has not yet been translated? We need to actively encourage academics who are in our field already, who have diverse language skills, to bring innovative ideas that they read about in their first languages to the attention of students and established academics in our field – because we all become potentially theoretically richer as a result.

It is in conducting research that is methodologically and theoretically robust that helps us move our agenda for high quality scholarship forward. This is the essence of why we thought this volume was timely. In recent years there has been a proliferation of research done in the socio-cultural realm of disability sport and much of it has been of poor quality. The production of undertheorised descriptive journal papers that get published is worrying. Scholars who believe they are vanguards because they engage in *critical* disability studies without further justification or demonstration of criticality need to grasp that research is not critical just because they call it that! This is not unique to our field, however. Once the sociology and psychology of sport began to gain momentum in the 1970s and 1980s, we are certain that there were academics who jumped on the bandwagon without the required training to critical engage with these fields. For a playful critique of this time, please see Bourdieu (1978). Of course, this type of development occurred across what can be broadly called sport and exercise sciences that, for the most part, emerged out of programmes that began their lives at universities with the goal of training physical educators. Rather the goal of these new departments was to scientifically research the limits of human potential (Hoberman, 1992) which ultimately impacted upon how societies were organised and structured. The development of sport studies has broadly addressed many social transformations but, as the field expanded, there was a need for more specialisation.

As we know sporting and physical activity opportunities for people who experience disability are more limited than those for the general population. In turn, these inequalities created a critical space for social scientists to examine why this was the case. The development of the socio-culture investigation of disability sport began here and it is relatively less developed within our schools or departments because more mainstream sporting practices traditionally get more attention from our social science colleagues. We also believe this need not be the case if we as a collective are producing more high-quality research.

Ultimately, we want to see this volume as a starting point for a call to action in this field of endeavour and not simply blustery rhetoric. For example, this volume has illuminated numerous methods with which emerging and developing scholars can engage, including autoethnography and creative non-fiction. As discussed in Chapter 4, traditional methods – such as interviews and participant observation – can also sit alongside creative approaches and co-produced research when employed conscientiously. Yet, whatever the methodological approach, the highest quality work in our field is based upon robust engagement with disability theory and should be the starting point of our research designs. We need to be vigilant, however. Regardless of our experience with disability, we must remember that focusing our own research in this area does not make you a good or altruistic person and the simple experience of having an impairment does not allow you to avoid the pitfalls of ableism – we all should continue to grow whether we are at the start of our academic journey or nearing its end.

One thing that is abundantly clear is that if you have gotten this far in our edited collection, we are hopeful that the future of this fascinating and important research area is in good hands. But do not be shy about exploring areas in and around disability sport and physical activity that have yet to be examined. It is all too easy today to focus on high profile parasport as if they are the answer to all the ills that befall people who experience disability. The Paralympic Games are not (and never have been) a virtuous version of the Olympic Games. Additionally, many people who experience disability are ineligible to compete in parasport due to the restrictions of classification systems or have no desire to participate at an elite level. By prioritising the Paralympics, many marginalised individuals are not telling their stories or having them told. So, let's hear those stories and share them in creative and accessible ways. There is a world of untapped possibilities in researching disability sport. Let us begin this new dawn together.

References

Bourdieu, P. (1978). Sport and social class. *Social Science Information*, 17(6), 819–840.

Goodley, D., Lawthom, R., Liddiard, K. & Runswick-Cole, K. (2019) Provocations for critical disability studies. *Disability & Society*, 34(6), 972–997, doi:10.1080/09687599.2019.1566889

Hoberman, J.M. (1992). *Mortal Engines: The Science of Performance and the Dehumanization of Sport*, United States: Free Press.

Howe, P.D. and Silva, C.F. (2021) Cripping the Dis§abled Body: Doing the posthuman tango, in through and around sport. *Somatechnic*, 11(2) 139–156 doi:10.3366/soma.2021.0348

McRuer, R. (2006), *Crip Theory: Cultural Signs of Queerness and Disability*, New York: New York University Press.

McRuer, R. (2018), *Crip Times: Disability, Globalization, and Resistance*, New York: New York University Press.

Index

Page numbers followed by n indicate notes.

able-bodied sport 89, 91–92
ableism 157; within an ableist world 164–166; invisibility of 158; sport as an ableist agent 160–164
Academic Ableism 87
acerbic academic criticism 127
African masculinity 71
Africanness 78
ageing and breaking bodies 134–135
Agitos Foundation 73
Allan, V. 22
Allen-Collinson, J. 154
American neo-liberal politics 15
Anderson, L. 102
Andrews, D. L. 49–50
anti-ableism research 157, 159–160
Apelmo, E. 28, 94–95
Asian Para Games 195
Athens 2004 Paralympic Games 48
Atherton, M. 122
athlete(s) 162; context of IPC athletics 49; disabled experiences of 13–14; with Hollywood 47
athlete–guide partnerships 143; and dyadic relationships 146–147; and intersectionality of disability 150–151; the Olympics 149; VI athletes 148, 152–153; World Championships 148–149
Atkinson, P. 137n1
attitudinal barriers 80
autoethnography 128–129, 137n1

Barcelona 1992 Paralympic 46
Barnes, C. 15, 17–18, 45
Barrett, R. J. 78

basketball 100, 104, 106–107, 109–110, 111n2
Beijing Paralympics 94
Berger, R.J. 57, 60
Berghs, M. 114, 120
Best, M. 185
The Birth of the Clinic (1975) 49
Black like me (1961) 121
Black sport 116, 118–119
Blind athletes 153
Blinde, Elaine M. 90, 93
The Body Silent (1987) 43, 45
Borcherding, B. 94
Boston Marathon 89, 91
Bourdieu, P. 25–26, 199–200
Braidotti, R. 176
Branfield, F. 56, 163
Braun, V. 102
Bredahl, A.M. 160
Breslin, G. 22
Brighton, J. 1–8, 13–33, 57, 61, 64, 126–137, 198–201
Bundon, A. vii, 7, 92, 143–155, 185
Butler 22
Buysse, J.M. 94

Campbell, F. 159, 162–163
Campbell, N. 56, 60–61, 63
Canadian Para-Nordic Ski Team 144
Cape Town 71
Carnevale, F.A. 182
Carrington, B. 123
Cavallerio, F. vii, 7, 114–123
Cerebral Palsy International Sport and Recreation Association (CP-ISRA) 47–48

Index

Chapple, R.L. 114
Charlton, J. 45
Cherney, J.L. 161
Chilimampunga, C. 75
Choi, I. vii, 8, 185–195
Clare, E. 105
Clarke, V. 102
Cockain, A. 23
Cole, C. L. 50
collaborative autoethnography 100–111, 129–130, 137n2
collectivism 188
colonial projects 77–78
The colour of sport 119, 121
Comaroff, J. 79
Comaroff, J. L. 79
Confucianism 185, 189, 191
Confucian theory 192–193
Connor, D. 120
co-production in UK academia 64–66
Corker, M. 22–23
Corning, A.F. 187
Côté, J. 22
COVID-19 on VI runners 61–62, 64
Craven, Philip 51–52
creative nonfiction (CNF) 115–116, 119–122
Crenshaw, K. 150
crip studies 32
critical disability 174, 199
critical disability studies (CDS) 15–17, 42–44
cultural politics 41; contemporary sport and physical activity 42; Foucault's governmentality 48–50; Paralympic movement 46–48
The Cultural Politics of the Paralympic Movement 41
Cushion, C. J. 21

Darcy, S. 92
Davio, K. 158
Deaflympics 195
Dean, N. A. 92, 145
de Beauvoir, Simone 199
Deleuze G. 22
Denzin, N. 102
DePauw, K.P. vii, 6, 85–97, 111, 143, 153
Derridean conceptualisation 22–23
DiFranco, A. 105
disability: and the body *see* disability and the body; category of 44–46; models of *see* disability models; problem of 16, 44; theory 5, 24; Western construction of 43

disability and the body 26; narrative 28–30; phenomenological analyses 27–28; post-humanism 32; reflections 32–33; sensuous scholarship 30–32
disability models: medical model 17–18; models approaches and sport 21–22; social model 18–20; social relational model 20
disability rights in Africa: Alexander Phiri 70–71, 80; involvement in 71; race 71
disability sport: application of Bauman's liquid modernity 33; Black and Deaf 114–122; collaborative autoethnography on 100–111; creative nonfiction 115–116, 119–122; D/deafness 115; intersectionality 114–115, 119–122; Kyra's story 117–119; and physical activity 42–44, 50, 52; researchers in 17; social scientists in 32; spaces 56–57, 60, 62; theorising *see* disability models sociocultural approaches
Disability, Sport and Intersectionality 6
disability sport research 94–96, 198
disability studies 14, 198–201; and critical disability studies 15–17; and feminist perspectives 87–90; movement 14; neo 43; and social sciences *see* sociocultural approaches
disabled identity 18, 25
disabled people 41, 43–45
Disabled People's Organizations (DPOs) 70, 72–73
Disabled Persons Day 187
Disabling Africa: the power of depiction and the benefits of discomfort 78
Discipline and Punish (1977) 49
Donnelly, P. 85
Drake, R.F. 56
Driscoll, Jean 91
Dyson, S. M. 114, 120

Eales, L 3
elite athletes 72, 148
elite competitive sport 85
Erevelles, N. 120
Ethnicity Inc 79
Evans, M. B. 22
exercise 171–182
exercise-based rehabilitation 175

female athletes with disabilities 91–92, 96; participation and experiences 92–94; sporting body 90

Index

Ferri, B. 120
Fine, M. 95
First International Silent Games 91
First Paralympic Winter Games (1976) 92
Fitzpatrick, B. 22
football 58–59, 62, 64
Foucault, M. 23–24, 48–50, 199
Foundations for Disability Sport Scholarship 5
Frank, A.W. 23, 29, 66, 116
Frederick, A. 119–120
From Theory to Practice: Contemporary Issues in Disability Sport 3, 7
Fundamental Principles of Disability 44

Garland-Thomson, R. 76–77, 87, 95–96, 150
Geijer, S. 93
gender and disability 88, 92–96
Get Yourself Active, project 65
Giardina, M. D. 50
Gibson, B.E. vii, 8, 171–182
Gladwell, M. 192
global south 71–73, 79–80
Goffman, E. 43, 45, 85, 120
Goodley, D. viii, 8, 17, 19, 33, 63, 171–182
Gramscian thinking 15, 43
Griffin, J.H. 121
Guatemala 74
Gutkind, L. 116

Hammer, G. 31
Hammett, D. 65
Hammond, A. 93
Hardin, B. 93
Hardin, M. 94
Hargreaves, J.A. 93
Hartel, Liz 91
Harvey, J. 61
Haslett, D. viii, 8, 22, 185–195
Hedrick, Sharon Rahn 91
Hendren, S. 96
Hockey, J. 154
Hoop Dreams on Wheels (2009) 57
Horseman, Bojack 181
Howe, P.D. 1–8, 13–33, 41–52, 79, 86, 92, 145, 160, 162, 198–201
Hughes, B. 27
humanist thinking 173
Hylton, K. 114, 121

impairment 126; ability, masculinity and the (in)visibility 132–133; ageing and breaking bodies 134–135; The Boy with the Brace 130–132; categorisation of 44; Most of Europe has Seen My Penis 136–137; sociology of 27; splitting of 19–20; Three Strikes Not Out 135–136
inclusion of disability 1
individualism 44, 189
ingenuity 76, 80
International Blind Sport Association (IBSA) 47
International Olympic Committee Consensus Group 72
International Paralympic Committee (IPC) 42, 49–51, 72–75, 79, 186, 191–195
International Sport Organisation for the Disabled (ISOD) 47
International Sports Federation for Persons with Intellectual Disability (INAS-FID) 47, 52n3
International Sports Organisation for the disabled (IOSDs) 47, 49, 52n2
International Stoke Mandeville Wheelchair Sports Federation (ISMWSF) 47, 52n2
IPC Athletics Committee 5, 47
IPC's 2019–2022 Strategic Plan 193

Jackson, L. 65
Johnston, L. 137n2

Kalkman, Monique 91
King, G. 182
Kirakosyna, L. 93
Kitchin, R. 62
Korea Paralympic Committee (KPC) 186, 188, 191–194
Kothari, A. 65
KPC Strategic Plan 2021–2025 193
Kuhn, T.S. 86

Latimer-Cheung, A. E. 22, 29
Lausanne 72
LGBTQ+ athlete 89
Liasidou, A. 120–121
lifestyle issues 71, 79–80
liminality 45
Lindemann, K. 30, 137n2
Little Britain 'as the only spaz in the village,' 41
Lock, D. 92
London 2012 Paralympic Games 51
Lord, R. 30
Lowry, A. 137n2
Lucas, Matt 52n1

Lucas, R. H. 78
Lumsdaine, G. 30
Lynn, S. 94

Macbeth, J.L. viii, 6, 55–66
Macdougall, H. 93
MacLachlan, M. 75
Maguire, J. 42
Makope, C. 75
Malawi 73
Mannan, H. 75
Mannella, Staci viii, 7, 143–155
Marchetti-Mercer, M. 78
marginalisation 13
Marx 43
masculinity 88, 90, 94, 96
Mays, N. 65
McCallister, Sarah G. 90, 93
McDonald, K. viii, 7, 114–123
McGannon, K.R. 137n2
McKenzie, J. 75
McMahon, J. 137n2
medicalisation 44–45, 174, 177
medical model 17–18, 87
Meekosha, H. 24–25
mental health 72
Merleau-Ponty, M. 27–28, 199
microaffirmations 109–110
microaggressions 107–109
minimally disabled (MD) 167
minority group model 15–16
Mkabile, S. 74
Monforte, J. viii, 8, 171–182, 188–189, 194
Moola, F.J. 13
Morris, J. 95
Mossman, M. 177
Munthali, A. 75
Musgraves, K. 106
Myers, D.J. 187

Natalie, Abele 92
National Paralympic Committee (NPC) 190, 194–195
neo-colonialism 42
neo disability studies 17
neoliberal-ableism 182
new Africa of CNN 79
1984 Olympics Games 89
1984 Summer Olympics 91
1998 IPC World Athletics Championship 47
non-disabled researchers 55; about impairment 62–64; in disability sport spaces 56–59; giving back 64–66; positionality 59–62
normalisation 50
Norman, M.E. 13
normative rehabilitation system 181

Olenik 92
Oliver, K. 65
Oliver, M. 15, 43–44, 87, 174
Olympic Games 90, 200
The Olympics 90, 144
Outliers: The Story of Success 192

Papathomas, A 172
Para-athletes 185
Paralympians 144
Paralympic/elite sport 1
Paralympic Games 47–48, 51, 90, 143, 151, 160, 200; in Atlanta, USA 46
Paralympic games/Para-sport 2
Paralympic movement 5, 46–48, 90, 92, 154, 161; in South Korea 8, 186–187
Paralympics 72, 77, 143–144, 151, 160, 200; athletes 42, 46, 100; identity 128
Paralympic sport 93; Olympification of 144; para'llel auto-ethnographic accounts 144–145
Paralympic Winter Games in 2018 92
parasport 48–50, 72, 75, 110
para-sport activism 185–186; from IPC and KPC 191–194; in South Korea 187–189; Western and East Asian Studies 189–191
Paterson, K. 27
Peers, D. ix, 3, 6, 24, 32, 66, 100–111, 128, 145, 150, 160, 166
People see disability first 119
Pérez-Samaniego, V. 172
Perrier, M-J. 16, 29
person-first/identity-first debate 3–5
Petrie, K. 137n2
physical activity 42–44, 50, 52, 90, 92, 127
physical education (PE) 161
physicality 88–90, 94, 96–97
political activism 43
The Politics of Disablement (1990) 43
posthuman disability studies (PDS) 8, 171–174, 180–182
post-humanism 32, 176
poverty 70–71
Powis, B. 1–8, 13–33, 55–66, 198–201
practice theory 25–26
Priestley, M. 56

psycho-emotional disablism 20
Purdue, D.E. 86, 162
PyeongChang 2018 Paralympic Winter Games 146, 187, 190

race course 152–153
Rankin-Wright, A. 114
Rayner, C. 137n2
rehabilitation: exercise in 171–176, 180–181; posthuman 178; SCI 178; task 182
Researching Disability Sport manifesto 2
rethinking disability sport 96–97
Rio 2016 Paralympics Games 91
Rugby Union 29
Runyon, Marla 91

Seal, E. 115, 119
sensuous scholarship 30–32
Seoul 1988 Paralympic Summer Games 187
sexuality 88–90, 94–97, 102, 107–109, 114, 150, 199
Shakespeare, T. 15, 19–20, 23, 25, 60
Shifrer, D. 119–120
Shildrick, M. 4, 16
Shogan, D. 163
Shuttleworth, R. 24–25
Silva, C. F. ix, 7–8, 157–168
Sinason, V. 76
Smith, B. ix, 8, 16, 21, 29, 65, 147, 171–182, 185–195
Sochi 2014 Paralympic Games 145
Sochi Paralympics 145–146
social construction 18, 44
social model 18–20, 87
social relational model (SRM) 20, 22
social scientific research 13, 28, 55
sociocultural approaches: poststructural 22–25; practice theory 25–26
South Africa 71–72; childhood disability in 73–74; clever blacks 78; researchers 75
Southern African Federation of the Disabled (SAFOD) 70–71
South Korea's disability rights movement 186–187
space and autonomy 104
Sparkes, A.C. 29, 31–32
Spencer-Cavaliere, N. 3
spinal cord injury (SCI) 29, 172, 178
sport: as an ableist agent 160–164; disability *see* disability sport; and leisure 55; media 93–94; system 151–152

Sport England (2021) 120
sporting body 85–86, 127; disabled female 90–91
Sport is freedom 119, 121
sport of sitting volleyball (SV) community 163, 166
Stienstra, D. 121
Stigma: notes on the management of spoiled identity (1963) 43, 45
Stone, E. 56
Structure of Scientific Revolutions 86
Summer Paralympics 91
Swartz, L. ix, 6, 70–80
swimming 177
Sydney 2000 Paralympic Games 47–48

Tail is Wagging the Dog 47
Tarusarira, W. 75
Taylor, T. 92
Thomas, C. 20
time 75
toilets 74
Tokyo Paralympic Games 192
Townsend, R.C. 21, 137n2
transport 73–74
Tregaskis, C. 63
triumph 78–79
Trump, Donald 78
T's of disability inclusion: time 75; toilets 74; transport 73–74
Turner, V. 45
2000 Olympic Games 91
2004 International Wheelchair and Amputee Sport Association (IWAS) 52n2
2008 Beijing Paralympics 91
2010 Paralympic Games 146
2010 Vancouver Paralympic Games 146
2012 London Paralympic Games 78
2012 London Paralympics 91
2013 IPC's VISTA Sport Science Conference 50–51
2014 Sochi Paralympics 151
2019 North American Society for the Sociology of Sport (NASSS) 2

UK Chief Medical Officer 65
UNICEF 74
Union of the Physically Impaired Against Segregation (UPIAS) 15, 44
United Nations Human Rights 192
Universal Declaration of Human Rights 42
University of British Columbia (UBC) 144
US Paralympic Alpine Ski Team 144

Vannini, P. 31
Vehmas, S. 16
Vergunst, R. 75
Vickers, D. 65
Virginia Beach 2
(in)Visibility of disAbility: female athletes *see* female athletes with disabilities; femininity and disability 87–90; human body 86–87
visibility of sport 85, 90
visually impaired (VI): athletes 60–61, 63, 143, 148, 152–153, 155n2; partners 143; sport 31

Waksul, D.D. 31
Walsdorf, K. 94
WAS physiotherapy 176
Watson, N. 16, 20
Wethe15 51–52, 192
Wheeler, Stephanie ix, 6, 100–111

White racist Afro-pessimism 78
White sports 116, 119
Wightman, L. 65
Williams, T. 50, 57, 61, 64
Williams, T.L. 172
Wiltshire, G.-E. 137n2
Winter Paralympics 92
Wolbring, G. 119
World Championships 148–149
the World Cup 145–147
world of disability: in Africa 72; and decoloniality 77; importance of local activism 76; and poverty 71; sport 71–73, 78–79; T's of disability inclusion 73–75
World Wheelchair Games and Paralympics 89

Zimbabwe 75, 80
Zuma, Jacob 78

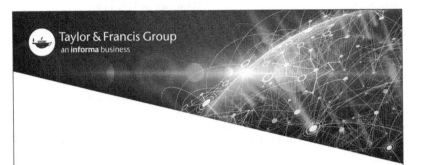

Printed and bound by CPI Group (UK) Ltd, Croydon, CR0 4YY
01/12/2024
01797774-0007